Come Up and Get Me

courtesy: National Geographic Society

Come Up and Get Me

An Autobiography of Colonel Joe Kittinger

* * * * * *

Joe Kittinger and Craig Ryan

with a Foreword by Neil Armstrong

University of New Mexico Press | Albuquerque

Unless otherwise noted, all photos courtesy of Joe and Sherry Kittinger.
Cover illustration by Stuart Brown.
Book design and composition by Karen Mazur.

Library of Congress Cataloging-in-Publication Data

Kittinger, Joe, 1928–
  Come up and get me : an autobiography of Colonel Joe Kittinger / Joe
Kittinger and Craig Ryan.
     p. cm.
  Includes index.
  ISBN 978-0-8263-4803-6 (cloth : alk. paper)
  1. Kittinger, Joe, 1928– 2. United States. Air Force—Officers—Biography.
3. Vietnam War, 1961–1975—Prisoners and prisons, North Vietnamese.
4. Prisoners of war—United States—Biography. 5. Prisoners of war—
Vietnam—Biography. 6. Balloonists—United States—Biography. I. Ryan,
Craig, 1953– II. Title.
  UG626.2.K58A3 2010
  358.40092—dc22
  [B]
                              2010000682

✳   ✳   ✳   ✳   ✳   ✳

For Sherry,
My soul mate and favorite copilot

Also by Joe Kittinger:
The Long, Lonely Leap, with Martin Caidin

Also by Craig Ryan:
The Pre-Astronauts
Magnificent Failure

Contents

Foreword by Neil Armstrong   ix

Prologue   xiii

1 The Gift of Adventure   1

2 Ace of Spades   15

3 Come Up and Get Me   39

4 Escape from Near Space   71

5 Combat   105

6 Hanoi   145

7 Home Skies   183

8 Destination: *Unknown*; Fuel on Board: *Zero*   211

9 Ballooning and Salooning   231

Epilogue   245

Awards and Honors   249

Acknowledgments   251

Index   253

Foreword

Neil Armstrong

* * * * * *

THE 100,000 FOOT CLUB

In 1962, at Century 21, the Seattle World's Fair, nine of the fourteen members of the 100,000 Foot Club, an unofficial organization of flyers who had exceeded 100,000 feet in altitude, gathered to report their experiences. One was a cosmonaut of the Soviet Union, one was an American astronaut, four were pilots of the rocket-powered X-15 research airplanes, and three were balloonists. Few readers will remember that humans have climbed so high in a balloon.

Balloons were the first craft that permitted people to rise above the surface of Earth. History records that Pilâtre de Rozier and Marquis D'Arlandes rose from the grounds of the Palace of Versailles in 1783 in a balloon built by Etienne and Joseph Montgolfier. Again in France the following year, Professor Sébastian Lenormand, suspended below a 14-foot canvas-covered frame, successfully stepped off the top of a tower and landed safely on the ground. He called his invention for escaping the upper floors of burning buildings a "parachute."

In 1793, Jean-Pierre Blanchard became the first person to ascend in a balloon in the United States when he arose from Philadelphia, with President George Washington and four subsequent American presidents observing. Blanchard had jumped from a balloon using a parachute earlier in Europe and did so again in America on a later flight. Blanchard was one of the first to make a canopy of silk that could be folded into a small package.

Balloons became very popular in the nineteenth century, both as exhibitions and as observation posts for military reconnaissance.

Parachuting from balloons was dangerous and could be depended on to draw crowds at county fairs and expositions.

Balloons were also beginning to be used in scientific research. Normal environmental radiation was known to rise from the soil and rocks. Ionizing radiation was even measured above the deep oceans. Where did it come from? scientists wondered.

Measurements were made during balloon ascents but were inconclusive due to measuring instrument problems. In 1912, Austrian Victor Hess designed some instruments that would be unaffected by changing pressure and temperature. He took them aloft in ten balloon flights in 1911, 1912, and 1913, and, lo and behold, they showed that radiation levels increased rapidly. At 15,000 feet, measurements were many times higher than those taken on Earth's surface.

Hess concluded that radiation was indeed beaming down on us from the heavens. He made an ascent during a total eclipse of the sun and noted that the radiation did not decline—so he concluded that the majority of the radiation was not coming from the sun.

This radiation from the sky was called "Hess radiation" but later became better known as "cosmic rays." Hess's contention was questioned for many years, but after the accumulation of much confirming evidence, he was awarded the Nobel Prize in 1936.

During the 1930s, Auguste Piccard in Switzerland made many flights into the stratosphere to study cosmic radiation and the physics of the upper atmosphere. He reached a record altitude of 72,177 feet.

By the middle of the twentieth century, jet engines were taking aircraft to high altitudes, and the high-performance rockets developed for the ballistic missiles of the Cold War suggested human space flight might soon become a reality.

In those days, the unknowns of human high-altitude flight were numerous. Would pilots be able to eject from aircraft in the dangerous conditions at extreme altitudes? What kinds of parachutes would be required? What would be the radiation effects on humans at high altitudes and in space?

In *Come Up and Get Me*, Joe Kittinger tells of the valiant efforts of the people who pursued solutions to these problems and salutes their remarkable achievements. Joe was intimately involved with some of the most challenging and boldest of the projects that were so important to the conquest of space. Some of these activities border on the unimaginable.

The reader will also learn much about the author: his successes, his disappointments, his U.S. Air Force combat experience, his incarceration as a prisoner of war, his wins and losses in ballooning competitions, his world-record achievements.

For those who are fascinated with the history of flight, *Come Up and Get Me* will serve as an introduction to a new and unforgettable chapter. I am confident they will enjoy the adventure as much as I have.

Prologue

*   *   *   *   *   *

E leven minutes. My ground crew informs me that I have exactly eleven minutes.

I let my vision run from the barren blackness of the heavens down through the indigo to the gently curving horizon far below, which for me is not the edge of planet Earth, but the transition from the stratosphere to the familiar robin's egg blue of the troposphere. I try to relax. It is morning, not yet seven o'clock, and my moment of truth is less than eleven minutes away. I glance up once more, and the disc of the sun is sharp and brilliant against the ebony backdrop of deep space. Even shaded by my helmet's tinted faceplate, my eyes burn. Nothing is familiar where I am. Nothing seems real.

I am surrounded by an invisible near vacuum that would kill me in seconds were it not for the constricting protection of my pressure suit. It is murderously cold, and I am wondering if the cameras will function at all in these conditions.

What I'm about to do will strike some as gutsy, others as flat-out crazy. In the years to come, people will ask if I was hesitant, if I was scared. No, I will tell them. There was only one way to get where I wanted to be.

It was the quickest way down.

They will laugh, thinking I'm making a joke.

The voice of my ground crew comes crackling through my headset, asking for my impressions. They want me to say something for posterity.

I find it surprisingly hard to do. *Hostile.* That's the only word I can find at first. Space is neither a comfortable nor a comforting place. Starkly beautiful, yes. Spectacular, definitely. But not in the least reassuring. It is infinite and harsh. I can offer no poetry. I have only one thought: the mission—my survival.

Seven minutes. The psychologists will claim that my words suggest that I've somehow accepted my fate, that I believe I am going to die. They have that wrong. I am a professional fighter pilot, a test pilot. Fighter pilots and test pilots do not accept death. We accept the risk, which is different. All our training is focused on solving the particular problems of survival. I won't say I'm not sobered by where I am and what I am about to attempt, but let me be clear: I do not accept death. I have complete faith in my team. They are among the very best aeronautical engineers and operations people in the world, and no one can doubt their dedication or their collective genius. Their hard work has brought the project to this particular brink, this rarefied place and time. The rest of it will be up to me.

The sun-tipped cloud tops are more than 80,000 feet below me now, the New Mexico desert floor another 20,000 feet beneath the clouds. I can see whole cities in the distance, some of them hundreds of miles away. From this vantage, the world is a map.

As my time approaches, I begin running through the forty-six-item exit checklist in my mind. We've worked toward this moment for more than two years. We've tested everything, second-guessed everything. There is literally nothing left now but the act. Soon I will rise up and fill my lungs with one last deep breath of pure oxygen from the tank.

Three minutes left now. They are giving me a countdown on my radio. I worry about my right hand, which is useless. The pressure glove has failed, and the hand is beginning to swell. I know I won't be able to pull the timer cord on the stabilization chute when I go, not the way we've practiced it in the altitude chamber at Wright-Patterson. I'll have to trust it to pull itself as I fall. I haven't informed my ground crew about the glove, but I decide that I will mention it before I jettison the radio antenna.

Two minutes. Everything else we've done has been preparation for this moment. The planning, the practice, the what-if sessions late at night in which we tried to imagine every possible scenario, every contingency. All the design and redesign. The checklists and protocols. The due diligence.

I am not a daredevil.

I think of my team on the ground, sweating it out. I know the waiting is hard on them. I could see it in their eyes before the launch. None of them has ever cared about anything the way they care about this. I am honored by their commitment, humbled by their total dedication to the mission and the challenge.

With barely a minute left, I read the gauges on my instrument panel one last time. I disconnect my onboard oxygen supply and begin to breathe from the bailout bottle in my seat pack. I take a breath and hold it. This is no fantasy. I am really here. I pull myself up and grab the edges of the doorway. I can feel my heart hammering like a machine.

I activate the cameras.

I release the antenna.

Lord, take care of me now.

I jump from space.

1
The Gift of Adventure

*   *   *   *   *   *

I grew up in paradise on the St. Johns River in the lowlands of central Florida. The river was my lifeline. The slow-moving water as well as the wildlife and the society of men who lived and worked and played on it taught me much of what I was going to need to know about the world. Most and best of all, it gave me the precious gift of adventure.

The St. Johns slides under State Highway 50 at a bridge east of Orlando. About a quarter-mile farther east, a tributary veers off and cuts under another bridge, and right there a haphazard little structure perched on pilings above the water: Lamb Savage's Fish Camp. My father would take me down there nearly every weekend. Dad owned a 34-foot ramshackle houseboat he christened the *John Henry*, and we stayed on the boat whenever we went to Lamb Savage's. It had four bunk beds in back and a little cubbyhole under the front deck where a boy my age could curl up and sleep.

The boat, made mostly of cypress, wasn't much to look at—imagine a steamship on top of a box. There was a crude steering apparatus hooked up to the 10-horsepower Evinrude, and the boat was controlled with a wheel in the front. But since we didn't have a remote-controlled throttle, engine speed was adjusted manually at the captain's command. It was all about teamwork. The kitchen consisted of a Coleman gas stove, and lighting was supplied by a gas lantern. There was an icebox for beer and cold drinks. We had screens on the windows, which could be opened for ventilation, but most of the time passengers rode on the boat's roof, which sat about 15 feet above the water line and provided not only a perfect viewing platform during river trips, but a great spot to sit and cast for black bass. The flat-bottom *John Henry*, in spite of its lack of sophistication, was the perfect vehicle for the lazy, shallow St. Johns, and it gave us just about all the fun we could handle.

My father, Joe, who had his own office equipment business, was the source of everything my younger brother and I knew about hunting, fishing, camping, and the ways of nature. The best times on the river were the spring and the summer, when my mother, Ida Mae, would join us. Over the years, she worked as a nurse's aide, a secretary, an executive assistant, a restaurant owner, a florist, and finally a real-estate broker. She also raised two boys during the Great Depression. She was a true Christian and had an exceedingly generous nature. Whenever hungry people knocked on the door, she was always happy to share food from our table. She was a great southern cook and could whip up a meal at a moment's notice. When she'd join us on the *John Henry*, we'd get biscuits and hush puppies to accompany fried chicken or the meat we'd bring in from our expeditions: frog legs, turtle steak, and a variety of fish. Her meals definitely beat the canned stew we ate when she wasn't along.

I was born in Tampa in 1928, and three months later we moved to Orlando, which was a nice little city of thirty thousand at that time. It was an agricultural area, the heart of America's citrus industry. My brother, Jack, came along a couple years later. We lived in a middle-class neighborhood with a good public school down the street. My mother believed that an education was a necessity. She made sure we had library cards, and if we weren't playing outside, she expected us to be reading a book. She pushed us to join the Boy Scouts, too, but for me there was nothing quite like the river. *My* river.

Lamb Savage's was where it all happened. Lamb himself was a fourth-generation Florida cracker who lived off the land much as his forefathers had. He hunted game with a single-shot .22 rifle, caught alligators, turtles, and fish, and grew his own vegetables on the rich bottomland along the riverbank. Old Lamb didn't own a car or a truck, but once a year he'd convince a friend to haul him over to the Atlantic coast to get his year's supply of sea salt. He dressed in whatever used clothes he could find. You could spot him from a distance in his trademark bandana and ragged old hat.

Lamb's camp offered boat rentals—they always leaked—and a genuine old-time juke joint where a nickel jukebox played scratchy old 78s. We'd tie up near the south side of the road next to the fish camp,

On the St. Johns. My mother, Ida Mae, poses with the inimitable *John Henry* near Lamb Savage's Fish Camp.

and on a Saturday night we could hear the twang of the steel guitars and fiddles and the laughter and the clink of beer bottles into the wee hours. If I'd had a quarter for every time I heard Bob Wills and His Texas Playboys strike up "San Antonio Rose," I could have bought the whole place. There wasn't much of a menu: beer, pepperoni sticks, pickles, and pickled pig's feet, but it was always an adventure at Lamb's. And, of course, every now and then a fight would break out. When that happened, the one guy you didn't want to tangle with was Lamb himself. This was common knowledge. He once bit off a guy's thumb during a disagreement. But there were other dangers. The joint had a back door that opened directly above the river. One winter night a guy not familiar with the place opened that door and stepped outside—and disappeared into space, free-falling 30 feet right into the cold water. It couldn't have been too pleasant. The other thing that opened directly onto the river was the fish camp toilet.

Saturday afternoon was prime drinking time at Lamb's. We usually were several miles away at that time of day, fishing or hunting or scouting places to fish and hunt. But one Saturday we were tied up to the mooring, taking in the festivities, when a notoriously prodigious drinking man from Orlando named Ed Spivey got the notion to try and run his boat through the bridge pilings at full speed. *Try* being the operative word. Spivey got a good running start and hit the bridge head-on at 30 miles per hour, obliterating his boat, which immediately sank in front of an audience of a couple dozen amused bystanders. Ed just bobbed up, swam to shore, and grabbed another beer, laughing and whooping the whole way. One of the onlookers dived into the river and managed to retrieve the only salvageable item, the 22-horsepower engine. It wasn't the sort of performance that much fazed anybody at Lamb's. But *I* paid attention.

Guts and smarts, it was clear, didn't necessarily go hand in hand.

My father, who worked long hours during the week, taught me what he could on our weekends on the St. Johns. I learned the mysteries of the river and became a pretty fair boatman. We had a little 12-foot john boat we'd use for duck hunting. We'd pull the motor off the *John Henry*, stick it on the duck boat, and off we'd go. One day when I was eleven, my father offered me the chance to transport a couple of drunken fishermen a few miles upriver to where they had their boat tied up. I was proud to get the assignment, but I was a bit worried about these particular guys. Three people was the maximum load that poor little boat could handle, and I was worried about it tipping over if the men became unruly. Before I pulled out into the current, I told my passengers that they'd have to stay seated so as not to unbalance things. I was in charge, and I wasn't shy about letting them know it.

We'd gotten only about 30 feet from shore when one of the guys stood up and started swaying back and forth. I guess he thought it was funny. It was just a few seconds before the duck boat flipped us all into the water. We had to take the Evinrude apart and dry out the ignition coil before we could get it started again. I have no idea how the two men finally got to their own boat, but it wouldn't have bothered me if they'd had to swim the whole way.

The St. Johns was like a hundred-headed hydra with tributaries and sloughs running off at every crazy, twisty angle. When the water was high, navigation could be a serious challenge. You really had to know the channel of the river. And, of course, the difficulty was compounded at night. One evening we made our way about 10 miles upriver from Lamb Savage's to a spot called Long Bluff. My father had three of his fishing buddies with him, and at about ten o'clock they ran out of beer. I was asked to take the duck boat back to Lamb's and get them another case—exactly the kind of job I coveted. It was a hot Saturday night, and by the time I got there, the juke joint was packed, and the place was really jumping. I couldn't legally go inside, so I asked the soberest man I could find to help me. He went in, and a few minutes later Lamb Savage himself came out. He looked down to where we usually moored and, failing to see the *John Henry*, asked me where I'd come from. I explained that I'd made my way downriver in our little duck boat to get beer. I don't think he believed me at first. Even an experienced river rat, he said, would have trouble with that stretch of the river at night. He squinted and scratched his chin. Finally, he agreed to sell me the beer but decided he probably ought to escort me back to Long Bluff himself.

I held my ground.

"Listen, Mr. Savage," I told him, "I had no trouble getting here from Long Bluff and don't expect to have any trouble going back." I pointed out that even if I had engine trouble or got confused about where the main channel was, I could always just drift back on down to the juke joint.

"I can take care of myself, sir," I said.

Old Lamb finally agreed to let me go, and for years afterward he told the story of the little red-headed kid and the famous beer-fetching run down one of the trickiest stretches of the St. Johns in the black of night. Even though the beer run was no big deal to me, it became kind of legendary among the men who hung out at Lamb's—and, naturally, I enjoyed the notoriety. I always privately thanked my father for giving me the chance—on that occasion and on many others over the years—to show what I could do. It's the kind of thing that helps a boy grow up.

A little later I made another of those trips with my father and his fishing friends. This time Jack was along, and the two of us slipped away for some gator hunting. We caught a little 2-foot gator, tied some fishing line around its snout, and brought it back to the big boat to show it off. By the time we got there, though, the men were already sleeping off their beer. It was a steamy evening, and they were dozing in their shorts. A man named Frank Morton was stretched out on the upper bunk at one end of the boat, dripping with sweat. I snuck up and plopped the gator down on his bare stomach. It took Frank a few seconds to come to, but when he opened his eyes and saw that gator wiggling on top of him, he bolted upright and jumped right into the river. The other men woke up, found my brother and me howling with laughter, and saw Frank climbing back up onto the deck. By this time, the fishing line had come loose from the gator's jaws, and that's the first thing Frank saw as he climbed aboard—an alligator hissing and snapping right in his face. He jumped right back into the river. Funny thing is, Frank never accompanied us on another one of those fishing trips.

Gator hunting was a favorite past-time for my brother and me. We never saw too many big ones because back then they weren't a protected species. The mature ones had a taste for livestock, so the farmers and ranchers weren't too inclined to let them get very big. They'd usually shoot a big alligator if they saw one. I once saw a gator eat a cattle dog swimming across the St. Johns. The gators could be voracious. My brother and I would usually go at night, using a spotlight to attract them. If we saw one on the bank during daylight hours, one of us would make a commotion with our oars in the water, and the other would sneak up behind the gator and grab its snout to keep the jaws shut, making sure to secure the tail at the same time. We knew what we were doing, and neither of us ever made a serious mistake with an alligator.

These river trips weren't all fishing and gator wrestling and frog gigging, though. Another major source of adventure was the duck hunts, and we usually managed to shoot our limit. I remember one hunt particularly well—not the hunt itself, but the night before. My father had invited a friend of ours, Mr. Starnes, to hunt with us and then asked me to take his place as host when he was called away on business. Mr. Starnes and I left out of Lamb Savage's in the duck boat, and I piloted us downriver to a little piece of land we called Paw Paw Island. The topsoil was rich and deep, and some of the locals grew pumpkins and collard greens out there in the summer. But because it was winter, the little tin shack the farmers used there was empty. The place was right next to the biggest tree on the island, a big sour-orange tree. The shack was only about 10 feet by 10 feet, with a dirt floor, but it was perfect for our duck camp. After dinner, the two of us rolled out our sleeping bags inside the shack—it had turned cold that night—and I set the alarm on my clock.

About two o'clock I woke up to the sound of a rattlesnake rattling away right near my ear. I was terrified and tried not to move a muscle. Pretty soon Starnes started to snore, and every time he'd snore, the snake would start to rattle. This back-and-forth seemed to go on for an eternity. After a while, I decided the only thing to do was to pull myself out of the sleeping bag and kill the snake. Ever so slowly I started to ease out of the bag, but whenever Starnes would start up snoring again, the snake would get agitated and start rattling. My flashlight was up near the snake, so I pulled a pack of matches out of the pocket of my pants and finally got the nerve to strike one. As soon as I lit the match, I heard the snake go sliding off through the rubble along one side of the shack. I didn't hear it anymore after that. I figured it had probably crawled in there for the same reason we had: to find a warm place to sleep.

Since I was supposed to be in charge, I decided not to wake Mr. Starnes. I went outside and built a fire and spent the next hour or so sitting there under the orange tree, staring at the fire and listening to him snoring away inside the shack. By the time the alarm rang and he stumbled outside, I already had coffee and breakfast waiting. I decided not to say anything about the snake. I'd been pretty scared and elected to keep the whole episode to myself.

Rattlers weren't the main snake worry on the St. Johns, though. Cottonmouth water moccasins, easily as deadly as the rattlesnakes, were everywhere, and they didn't advertise their presence. If we saw them around our camps, we'd shoot them. Once, on a frog-gigging expedition, we came across a small pond, maybe 100 feet across, that was full of water moccasins. I mean *full*. Hundreds of them in a big, writhing knot. It's a spooky thing to see. Another time we pulled one of our fish traps full of shiners out of the river, and there was a fat cottonmouth inside. It had already eaten some of the fish and had swollen up to where it could no longer fit through the opening in the neck of the trap to get out.

One of my favorite activities was running a trout line. We'd stretch a long string of fishing line from bank to bank, and every few feet along the line would be another short piece of line with a fish hook. We'd bait the hooks with chicken guts, sink the line into the water, wait a few hours, and then "run" the line—pulling up the hooks to see what we'd caught. It was pretty easy to tell when we had something of any size. I'd take the little duck boat and pull myself along the length of the trout line. On one trip, a schoolmate, a Yankee who wasn't familiar with the ways of southern boyhood, had come along with us, and I took him out to check one of the lines. The sun had set, and it was dark on the water. I had a couple of flashlights in the little boat and a headlamp with a battery pack. I could tell as soon as we got to the line that we had something big—maybe a big catfish or even a gator. I pulled up the middle section of the line, and there was a huge soft-shell turtle, at least a 20-pounder. He had been snagged in the leg, and he was furious. Soft-shells don't look particularly dangerous, but they have powerful jaws and muscular necks, and they can be fierce—especially when you get them out of the water. A big one can take a man's finger off without too much trouble. Lamb Savage told me that once a soft-shell gets a piece of you, it won't let go until you hear thunder. Since I had neglected to grab my .22 rifle before we set out, I decided to try and flip this monster into the boat using one of the paddles. I got him in with us, but in the process the hook came out of his flipper, and he started scrabbling around, snapping away. He was the maddest turtle I'd ever seen. My friend jumped up on the back seat, and I got on the front. I grabbed my paddle and took a swipe at the turtle to see if I could stun it long enough to get it back to the *John Henry*, but the sudden movement caused the boat to tip sideways, and we started taking on water. Moments later I yelled, "Jump!" and my friend and I dived over into the current. Luckily, my headlamp was still working, and I was able to get a good look inside our boat, which was full of water and that turtle, swimming around and still snapping. I managed to maneuver the boat over to the shore and was able to kill the turtle with my paddle. When we got back to the *John Henry*, we showed off our prize catch. I didn't volunteer any details about our unorthodox fishing methods. Sometimes it's better just to let results speak for themselves.

My grandfather Kittinger had been a postmaster in Baltimore. He and my grandmother moved to Florida after he retired, and they lived in a hotel in downtown Orlando when I was young. My mother's parents died before I was born, but they say I got my red hair from my mother's aunt, my great-aunt Agnes. She lived alone with her parrot in a house in downtown Savannah, Georgia, surrounded by a 10-foot-high brick fence. On the back part of the property lived two former slaves who had belonged to Aunt Agnes's father. They were the oldest human beings I had ever seen. After Emancipation, this couple had stayed put, and Agnes's father—and later Aunt Agnes herself—had cared for them. I was fascinated by these exotic people, and one day when my aunt caught me peeking through the bushes, she cautioned me to make sure not to scare or embarrass them in any way. She took me over to meet them, and after that I would carry food over once a day. They had no electricity and lit their little two-room house with a kerosene lantern. They were sweet folks whose lives were a total mystery to me. They were a rare last remnant of the Old South, and I was just barely old enough to get a glimpse of something that would soon be gone with the wind.

My parents sent me and my brother to the Bolles School in Jacksonville for high school. It was a military institution with strict discipline and very high academic standards. If you graduated there, you almost always went on to college. I played the trombone in the school band, and Bolles gave me a scholarship on the basis of that, which helped out quite a bit. My father didn't make a lot of money, and I knew it was a sacrifice to send us away.

I enjoyed school and worked hard, but my heart was always back on the St. Johns. That's really where I learned about responsibility and courage and risk. That's where I figured out how to work with and get along with all kinds of people. In spite of all the dangerous things we did, the worst injury I suffered came when a pressure cooker on the boat blew up and spewed hot stew all over me. I spent a couple of days in the hospital after that one.

I think the course of the rest of my life of adventure was set way back in those days. My brother would eventually decide to follow my father into the office equipment business and spend the rest of his life in Orlando. But as much as I loved Florida and the river, I knew things would be different for me.

My best days may have been on the water, but my dreams were in the sky. Like many kids who dreamed of flying, I built model airplanes and flew them off the roofs of houses and garages. When the models were so beat up they were beyond repair, I conducted my own burial ritual. I'd set them on fire and give them one last launch off of some appropriately lofty perch. I also used to pedal my bicycle out to the Orlando airport and sit and watch the planes come and go. It was my field of dreams. When I turned sixteen, I started asking around about flying lessons, though there was no way I could afford them.

Then in 1946 two very important things happened. The day I graduated from high school I went down to the local United States Army recruiter to find out how you got to be a pilot—specifically a fighter pilot. I couldn't imagine a better job. The recruiter said there was nothing to it.

"Son, just sign up for the Army as a soldier, and once you're in, make an application for flight school."

Something about his suggestion didn't sound entirely right to me, so I started asking about other options. The man reluctantly told me that if I had two years of college under my belt, I could apply directly for the Aviation Cadet Program. That sounded better, so that's what I decided to do. I enrolled at the University of Florida that September.

The second important thing to happen that year was that my father hired a World War II veteran to work in his business as an adding-machine mechanic. The G.I. Bill entitled vets to learn to fly at the government's expense, and Phil Orr took advantage of the opportunity. Our family had a summer cabin on Lake Tibet Butler near Orlando, and Phil would fly up in a Piper Cub with floats and land on the lake. He didn't have his license at that point, but he would still take me up with him and would even let me take a turn at the controls. He eventually allowed me to make takeoffs and landings. That was all it took. If I had any doubts before that summer, I was sure now that I wanted to be a pilot.

While in college, I became serious about racing speedboats and hydroplanes and competed in events all over the state. They called it the Grapefruit League Circuit, and racers from up north would come down for the competition. I had entered my first race just after turning sixteen, taking our duck boat to a race on Lake Harris and managing to win the first prize of twenty-five dollars. Not much later, a former racer and machine-shop owner named Parrish agreed to sponsor me. I raced in two or three different classes. He covered all the expenses and pocketed the prize money, but I kept the trophies I won. I did this for two years, and in spite of a few minor wrecks, I avoided flipping Mr. Parrish's boat and destroying the engine. I think he appreciated that.

I drove my last race in January 1949 in Lakeland. Wind is the big enemy of hydroplane racers, and it was blowing like a storm that day. In these conditions, you really have to concentrate because if a gust catches you the wrong way, over you go. I was leading and coming up fast on a turning buoy at full throttle because the number two boat was right on my tail, maybe 2 feet behind, and just waiting for me to make a mistake. As I dug into the turn, the wind got under the bow and flipped me like a coin. I held onto the wheel with everything I had, knowing that if I were thrown out, I would likely get smacked by one of the boats charging up fast behind me.

That was my last race. I survived, embarrassed but in one piece. Unfortunately, I can't say the same for Mr. Parrish's engine. For the first time in all the events I raced for him, he didn't come over to congratulate me.

The United States Air Force was established as a separate branch of the service on September 18, 1947, and I applied for the Aviation Cadet Program in June 1948. I didn't hear anything for a couple of months. At that point, thousands of World War II aviators were being discharged, and there didn't seem to be much need for new pilots to replace them. Nevertheless, in October I received a notice to report for an aviation flight physical at Orlando Air Force Base (AFB). I was eager to take it, but a little nervous, too. If I failed the physical for some reason, my dream of becoming a fighter pilot would be dead on arrival.

About ten other guys were waiting when I showed up at the clinic. Five of them were there for a repeat test, having failed the first time. I was told that a full 50 percent of applicants were eventually rejected due

In the *Lucky Star*. When I raced Mr. Parrish's speedboats, he got the prize money, but I kept the trophies.

to some physical imperfection—usually related to vision, so I was a little nervous about the eye examination. When the eye test was over, I asked the examiner how I'd done. He refused to tell me anything. I asked the same question after each of the exams and received the same nonreply. I later found out that Air Force policy prohibits giving an applicant any feedback about test performance at the time of the examination. The whole thing took about four hours, and I walked out of that place having absolutely no idea how I'd done. It was frustrating. Nobody seemed to appreciate that my entire future was riding on the results.

About a month later, I found an envelope from the Air Force in the mailbox. This was it, I figured. My hands trembled a little bit as I opened the envelope, but instead of the results of my physical, it simply contained a notice informing me that I would have to meet a selection board for an interview at the base. I showed up on the appointed day, knowing that I would need to make a good impression. I always felt I had an advantage in these situations because my parents had taught me to address my elders as "sir" and "ma'am."

Six officers sat around a table in a boardroom. They told me to have a seat. To my great relief, all the questions seemed like softballs. For instance, "Why do you want to join the Air Force?" I didn't have much trouble with that one. Still, when I was dismissed, I had no idea how I'd come across to my poker-faced interrogators. I waited a few weeks for some response, but nothing came. Finally, I couldn't stand it anymore and called the local recruiter to see if I could get some information, anything. He advised me to be patient.

By the end of December, I was starting to feel a little desperate. I hadn't reenrolled at the University of Florida for my junior year because I had expected to be in the Air Force by then. For me, all this waiting and indecision were agony.

Then, in January 1949, all my prayers were answered. Deliverance came in the form of one very short but very thrilling letter, notifying me that I was to report to pilot training in March. The first phase of my life was done, and the rest of the great adventure was about to begin.

2
Ace of Spades

✳   ✳   ✳   ✳   ✳   ✳

On a March morning in 1949, I walked into the recruiting office in Orlando and was sworn into the United States Air Force. A few days later my family drove me to the Greyhound station, where I caught a bus to Tampa, all my worldly possessions stuffed into a barracks bag. From there, it was a five-day train ride to Goodfellow AFB in San Angelo, Texas. Four other cadets got on board along the way, so at least I had somebody to talk to. This train wasn't a Pullman, so we slept in the seats. We arrived late on a Sunday afternoon. Even though we'd planned to take a quick tour of the town, we were met by a sergeant who chauffeured us straight to Goodfellow. He promised us there'd be plenty of time for sightseeing later, but he lied.

For the next six weeks, we spent every minute on the base.

Because I'd been in the Boy Scouts and had attended military school, where I'd been exposed to some leadership training, I was put in charge of twenty of my fellow cadets. I marched us to the mess hall, where we had to eat like robots and were forbidden to speak. Every second of our day was scheduled and programmed. I studied in the bathroom at night because it had a light. Some of the guys made fun of me. I just told them: "Look, I'm probably not as smart as you. I need more time." At the end of basic training, I would graduate second in my class.

I got lucky at Goodfellow; my flight instructor, 1st Lt. Dan Elliott, was a considerate, easygoing man. He'd flown the P-51 in World War II and really knew his stuff. Unlike the other instructors, who were always screaming and insulting their charges, Dan never once raised his voice. What a break.

My first flight as an aviation cadet was in the T-6 Texan, a single-engine trainer. Just after dawn, Lt. Elliott and I climbed up through a hole in the cumulus, and as I looked down at the feathery cloud tops and up at the great dome of the sky all around us, I realized that I was in love. It was the most beautiful thing I'd ever seen. Nothing compared. "This is going to be my life," I said to myself. "This is it." I felt a companionship with that airplane that was unlike anything I'd ever dreamed of as a kid in Florida.

The earthbound aspects of the training were a whole lot less to my liking. We marched in formation wherever we went and were constantly harassed by upperclassmen, whose job it was to make our lives miserable. We had daily room inspections and received demerits if our shoes weren't lined up perfectly. I hated it, but every time I went back up into the sky with that 600-horsepower engine singing, none of the rest of it made any difference.

After I finished my ninth flight and landed, with a grand total of thirteen hours flight time under my belt, Lt. Elliott asked if I was superstitious. Until that moment, I hadn't realized it was Friday the thirteenth. When I told him no, he said I'd better pull over and let him get out of the airplane. That's when I realized he was about to turn me loose for my first solo. I taxied back out, ran through my checklist, and nudged the throttle forward. I was a little nervous as the T-6 rolled down the runway, picking up speed, but as I lifted off, the anxieties fell away, and it all just felt natural. I made one touch-and-go and came back around for a full-stop landing. No sweat. After the flight, the guys gave me the customary cold shower in my flight suit.

I was a pilot.

Six months later I graduated from Basic Pilot Training with 110 hours in my logbook.

From Goodfellow, I headed farther west, to Las Vegas AFB and fighter-pilot training in the P-51. I was pretty jazzed up about the assignment. The P-51 Mustang was a dream of an airplane and a real thrill to fly. (I would go on to fly ninety-three different airplanes in my career, but the P-51 would always be my favorite. Aviation technology improved in myriad ways over the years, but I never encountered a better combination of airframe, engine, and flight controls.) We started flying formations and then cross-countries. It was pretty heady stuff. My parents drove all the way out to Nevada for my graduation, and my mother pinned my wings on me.

After graduation, most of the guys went into Vegas and bought new cars. I considered it but decided to get mine in Orlando. Bob Heintzleman, who was a pilot himself, had a Ford dealership on Robinson Street right behind my father's office machine business, and I ordered up a light-green, two-door sedan with a radio. In those days, cars in Florida didn't come equipped with heaters, but I asked for one to be installed since my orders had me heading to Germany.

In June 1950, I drove up to Baltimore with my brother to visit our uncle Jack and aunt Mae. I had arranged to have the car shipped overseas and planned to drop it off at the shipping facility at the Brooklyn Naval Yard, but on the drive up we heard an announcement on the radio that South Korea had been invaded. It seemed a foregone conclusion that the United States would be getting involved. Transportation for all U.S. servicemen bound for Europe was handled at Fort Dix Army Base, and

Aviation cadets. That's me on the left, lounging on the wing of a P-51 at Las Vegas AFB. The Mustang is still my favorite airplane of all time. (Courtesy: United States Air Force.)

the next day I went straight to the base and found a captain. I told him that I didn't want to go to Germany—I wanted to volunteer to go to Korea. I said I was a P-51 fighter pilot and explained that P-51s were fighting in Korea. I figured they needed me.

The man looked at me as if I were crazy. A twenty-one-year-old kid who *wanted* to go into combat? He said he had no authority to change my orders. He was Army, and I was Air Force. He advised me to go ahead and report to my squadron in Germany and commented that, unless I came to my senses and changed my mind in the meantime, I could try to get reassigned from there.

The Army captain walked away shaking his head.

I crossed the Atlantic on a U.S. Army troop ship with a small group of pilots. We spent four days in Bremerhaven attending stern lectures on the Status of Forces Agreement between the U.S. military and the German government. As members of the army of occupation, we were briefed on German customs, the local geography, the currency, the language, the rate of venereal disease, and the black market. We spent each night in the officers' club doing our own methodical research into the wondrous qualities of German beer. Next we boarded a train that took us to Munich, where we were sobered by the hundreds of bombed-out buildings and burned vehicles, all depressing evidence of the war. It was as if it had ended only a few days before we arrived. Everyone we saw wore grim expressions.

The Munich train station had been one of the targets of the Allied bombing campaign and had been almost completely destroyed. As our train pulled in, we could see twisted knots of steel rail and massive piles of rubble everywhere. We tried to imagine the suffering the people had endured because of the madness their leaders had perpetuated. None of us said much. There wasn't anything to say. The station was a reminder that war was very real. We weren't in flight school anymore.

From Munich we took a bus to Neubiberg, where the 86th Tactical Fighter Wing was headquartered. The following day I reported to my first Air Force squadron, the 526th Tactical Fighter Squadron. I marched straight into the commander's office and saluted.

"Sir, Lieutenant Joe Kittinger reporting for duty."

Maj. Saunders glanced up at me a little skeptically. He did not return my salute. I was already guessing that we weren't going to hit it off.

"Goddamn second lieutenants," he muttered.

So there was my welcome to the Air Force. It wasn't exactly the reception I'd been expecting. I found out later that the fighter group had lost four lieutenants in aircraft accidents during the previous six weeks. The major apparently figured that all these dead lieutenants were jeopardizing his future as commander. I imagine I really endeared myself to him with what I said next.

"Sir," I said, "I'd like to request a transfer to Korea."

He acted as if he couldn't believe what he'd just heard.

"Goddamn second lieutenants!" he repeated. I thought for a moment that he was going to choke. "Look, Lieutenant, do me two favors, OK? First, try to manage not to get yourself killed. And second, don't *ever* volunteer to leave my squadron again."

There were two fighter bases in Germany, and I had originally asked for assignment to Neubiberg because that's where they flew the F-47 (formerly the P-47 Thunderbolt "Jugs"). We all knew that the entire Air Force would be flying jets before long, which was an exciting prospect, but I wanted a shot at the F-47 before it was gone. This legendary airplane had played a crucial role in World War II. I'd missed the war, but at least I'd have a chance to get a taste of what the pilots before me had experienced. We dropped practice bombs, shot the machine guns, and drilled on formation flight until I was certified as combat ready in that classic aircraft. The situation was quite tense in Europe at that time. The Berlin Airlift had just ended that summer, and the Russians were belligerent. As part of our combat-alert status, we kept four F-47s stationed at Rhein-Main Air Base near Frankfurt, ready to be scrambled to meet any threat.

At one of our morning squadron meetings, we were asked for volunteers to go to Rhein-Main to sit alert for a week. My buddy Milton Byron and I jumped at the chance. We were always eager for anything that would get us more flying time. We flew up to Rhein-Main in two elements, ours led by Capt. Nick Starnick, the other by a black pilot, Capt. Claude Govan, who had enjoyed a distinguished career as one of the Tuskegee Airmen in World War II. Govan's wingman was another second lieutenant named Doak Walker.

Capt. Starnick took special precautions with the three of us second lieutenants assigned to his element. He briefed us extensively on the

procedures we would be using during our week of alert. He wanted
to make sure we didn't join the dead-lieutenant club. The Frankfurt
weather could get downright miserable with low cloud cover and fog
almost every day, so we paid special attention to the procedures we'd
need to follow if one of us was separated from the leader in that soup.

Starnick, Milt, and I would sit on alert status from sunup until noon;
Govan and Doak would take the shift from noon until sunset. They
wanted us to get some flying time while we were there, and the weather
fortunately cleared up nicely for us. They'd send us up every other day,
and we'd fly straight for the Russian border, turning back just before
entering the forbidden zone. We knew we were on the Russian radar,
and we made these flights just to keep them alert. They never knew our
intentions, of course, and they frequently scrambled MiGs, their own
Soviet-designed fighter aircraft (the abbreviation is short for "Mikoyan-
i-Gurevich"), in response. We had a ball tweaking the Russian bear's
nose. On the way back to base, we would usually drop down and fly low
over the countryside, working on our formation technique. After each
of these "tweaking" missions, Capt. Starnick would debrief Milt and
me, giving us critiques of our flights. Starnick was an extraordinarily
conscientious flight leader.

After our week at Rhein-Main, we were set to return to Neubiberg.
The weather that day was dreadful: heavy fog, with a 300-foot ceiling and
a half-mile visibility. We sat around the operations building checking
the weather every half-hour. Finally, things began to break up a little,
and by noon the ceiling was up to 500 feet with a mile visibility. That
was all we needed. Capt. Starnick briefed us again on what were known
as the "lost wingman procedures." He was clearly a little apprehensive
about taking us up into the thick clouds. Govan was going to delay his
takeoff for thirty seconds and then try to join up with us before we
entered the cloud base so that we could go up as a five-ship flight. If he
couldn't catch us, his plan was to turn 15 degrees off of our heading and
continue on up through the top of the clouds, which were reported to
be at 8,000 feet.

I was on Starnick's left wing, and Milton was on his right. We
managed to stay in tight formation. Shortly after takeoff, we heard
Govan on the radio saying that he had us in sight and was going to join
up on Milt's right side. I should have been able to see him, but for some
reason I couldn't. We hit the clouds, and Govan announced that he'd be

deviating 15 degrees as we'd been briefed. This was the first time that I had ever been on the wing in actual instrument flight conditions—no visibility—and I'm sure it was the same for Milt. Doak, however, had four formation instrument climb-outs under his belt.

Shortly after Capt. Starnick entered the clouds, it felt to me as if he did a left barrel roll into me. I knew that I was experiencing some vertigo. (By the way, I've been told that every fighter pilot who ever flew on a wing in instrument or night conditions has known vertigo, and I'd wager that any fighter pilot who says different is a liar.) Anyway, I decided that if he wanted to roll, I'd roll with him. I wasn't feeling too comfortable, but I held my position. It was charcoal-smoke dark in those clouds, and at times I'd lose sight of Milt on Starnick's right wing. The last thing I wanted to do was fall off the leader's wing. I wasn't going to be branded a wimp. Loop, roll, spin—whatever—I'd still be right there on his left wing when he hit the ground.

About that time, I heard Capt. Govan call on the radio, asking Doak to check in. That was bad news. Govan called again, but received no response. At 8,000 feet, we broke through the clouds—to my considerable relief. When Govan came through, Doak wasn't with him. We circled to the left, expecting to see Doak climb out of the clouds. He didn't. Numerous calls tried to raise Doak, but nothing came back. Starnick called back to Rhein-Main to see if they had the missing aircraft on their radar, but they didn't. We finally headed back to Neubiberg with sick hearts. One of our wingmen was missing.

When we landed, the tower directed us to report immediately to the group commander's office. A weapons carrier picked us up and gave us a solemn ride. The administrative officer instructed Capt. Starnick to enter the commander's office. The rest of us—Govan, Milt, and I—were to wait outside. We were silent. Capt. Govan was summoned into the office next. Milt and I waited for another half-hour. Finally, we were told to go in. The colonel informed us that Lt. Walker had crashed and been killed. He then looked at both of us and asked, "Were you men briefed on the lost wingman procedures?" I replied that we had indeed been briefed several times on the procedure. He nodded and dismissed us.

The group commander was very young for a full colonel, and Doak Walker had been a close friend and drinking buddy. The colonel took the loss hard and very personally. He blamed Capt. Govan for Walker's death, which, as far as Milt and I were concerned, was very unfair.

Govan had had a distinguished career as a fighter pilot and a leader. All of us second lieutenants appreciated him because he would always take the time to answer patiently any flying question we came up with—and we had *lots* of questions.

The word got out pretty quickly that Capt. Govan was the designated sacrificial lamb for the loss of Lt. Walker. The entire group felt that it was an injustice, but this was the Air Force, and there was absolutely nothing we could do about it.

Govan had served in Italy during the war and had learned to speak Italian. Because the U.S. Air Force was getting ready to transfer our F-47s to the Italian Air Force, that's where they sent Govan: Vicenza Italian Air Base.

Some of us would see Capt. Govan again.

In September 1950, we flew twenty Jugs in formation for five hours nonstop to Wheelus Air Base outside of Tripoli, Libya. The Italians had built the air field in 1923, the German Luftwaffe had used it as a base during the Battle of North Africa, and the British Army had captured it in 1943. The trip was a new thrill for me. The aircraft were fitted with belly tanks to supply the extra fuel we'd need for such a long flight, and the pilots sat on dinghies and wore life preservers in case of a forced landing in the Mediterranean. We flew across the water at wave-top level all the way to Tripoli. My flight leader had warned us never to fly lower than he was, and I listened. A few weeks before our trip, a lieutenant had lost concentration and flown right into the sea.

We spent the next two weeks housed in a little tent city on one side of the remote desert airfield, twenty men to a tent. Our purpose in being there was aerial gunnery practice, which was a new experience for me. All our flight commanders were World War II combat veterans.

After a lengthy briefing the following morning, we taxied out and climbed up to 8,000 feet for our first gunnery run. The aerial target was a banner about 30 feet long and 10 feet high, towed about 3,000 feet behind a B-26 medium bomber. A flight consisted of four fighters, each with eight .50-caliber machine guns, although we used only two when shooting gunnery. The bullets had been painted four different colors, with each aircraft having its own color in order to facilitate identification of target hits. The flight commander always had the red bullets, with the other three aircraft using green, yellow, and blue.

The gunnery range was about 30 miles long and 10 miles wide, just offshore over the Mediterranean. We positioned ourselves about 5 miles adjacent to and about 1,000 feet above the tow-target B-26. The flight leader called out, "Arm 'em up and take spacing." I activated the gun switches, pushed the arming circuit breaker in, set the gun sight on the proper mil setting, and moved out into position. When the leader was positioned properly, he made a sharp 90-degree turn toward the target and then swung back in the opposite direction in a "curve of pursuit" flight path toward the target. The idea was to end up about 1,200 feet from the target banner in a 20-degree angle of bank when it came time to shoot. I touched the trigger and fired my guns as I was closing in on the target at 200 miles per hour. The firing opportunity was there and gone in a flash. We had to be sharp, and we had to be quick.

After firing, I immediately leveled the wings to keep from striking the target. When I reached the end of the range, I reversed direction and came around for another pass. We flew patterns from both directions until the ammunition was gone. Then the B-26 towed the target back to the field, where the banner would be released, examined, and scored. We always placed bets on who would score the most hits on the target. The flight commander made the ruling on what color of bullet had made a particular hole in the banner. Sometimes it was hard to tell. A bullet that hit the target at a high angle would burn a little hole that looked like a red bullet, and we quickly learned why the flight leader always won the bets. But I shot the best of all the new pilots, and that was enough for me.

On a dull, overcast Saturday in November, with a low ceiling and reduced visibility, several hundred of us congregated on the flight line at Neubiberg. We were awaiting the arrival of seventy-five brand new Republic F-84E fighter jets from the United States. They were the aircraft we'd soon be flying. We'd been talking and dreaming about little else since we'd been informed about them five months earlier. All the pilots had completed the familiarization course, and the maintenance guys had been through their training, but none of us had ever seen a real F-84E Thunderjet.

I had made my orientation flight in a jet aircraft in a Lockheed T-33 Shooting Star trainer back in September. There were no two-seat trainers for the F-84, so each pilot's first flight would be solo. They had us take up the T-33 to get us familiar with what it took to fly a jet, which was very different from flying a prop fighter.

We were waiting on the flight line, listening, when several F-84s suddenly appeared on the initial approach to Neubiberg. Man, were they gorgeous machines! Directly over the approach end of the airfield, the first jet in formation broke smartly, executed a 360-degree turn, and made a perfect landing. Seventy-four more F-84s followed suit. There were three fighter squadrons in the 86th Tactical Fighter Wing, and each had its own parking ramp. Each of the F-84s taxied to its designated ramp and shut down. It was hard to believe that in a few days I would be flying one of these beauties and that in just a few months I would be combat ready.

We'd been instructed to entertain the ferry pilots, take them where they wanted to go, and drink with them as long as they wanted to drink. In addition to helping them out of the aircraft and assisting them with their baggage, we also handed them cold beers as they stepped onto German soil and then escorted them to the officers' club, where our welcome party lasted for two days. The ferry pilots eventually went back home, and those of us stationed at Neubiberg got serious about the business of getting to know our new jet fighters.

Of course, the old hands got the first flights, while all of us lieutenants drooled and waited our turn. We attended all the debriefings, hanging on every word. We all wanted to make sure our initial flights were good ones. This would not be the time to screw up. Finally, on November 9, I got my first solo. Wow!

I'd been assigned my very own F-84, number 209, along with my own crew chief, Tech. Sgt. Cheita, who immediately inscribed our names on the canopy of our aircraft. We polished that thing until it glistened. In future weeks and months, whenever the fighter group wanted one of our jets for static display, they used mine because it was always the shiniest. When Gen. Eisenhower assumed command of the North Atlantic Treaty Organization (NATO) and made an inspection tour of Neubiberg, Sgt. Cheita and I stood at attention beside our F-84 as Ike walked by. We were really proud because the general stopped and spoke with us for a moment.

I would be a captain the next time Eisenhower and I would meet. He'd have a better job as well and a pretty nice residence on Pennsylvania Avenue in Washington, D.C.

Our squadron commander decided to take the entire squadron back down to Wheelus in Libya for more training. The winter weather was usually great down there, we were told, and we'd be able to get plenty of hours in. Table-flat desert stretched for hundreds of barren miles around Wheelus so it was a perfect place for low-level flight training. We buzzed the occasional camel, which was about all there was to see in that expanse of sand. Between December 12 and 19, I flew seventeen missions in the new jet fighter, sometimes getting in three flights in a single day. The F-84 turned out to be a fairly straightforward aircraft, and we grew familiar with it in pretty short order. We dropped practice bombs and shot our .50-caliber machine guns on a range near the airfield. Every evening we debriefed in the officers' club.

On December 13, I had just flown an early-morning mission and was shutting down the engine when I noticed our squadron's first sergeant waiting for me, which was unusual, and I noticed he wasn't

Republic F-84E Thunderjet in Neubiberg, Number 209. By the time my crew chief and I got through with this plane, it was quite possibly the shiniest aircraft in the United States Air Force. (Courtesy: United States Air Force.)

smiling—also unusual. As I climbed down, the sergeant informed me that the squadron commander wanted to see me immediately. I asked what it was about but received no reply. Now I was worried.

After dropping off my parachute and survival equipment at the operations tent, I walked into the squadron commander's tent and saluted. He normally would invite me to take a seat, but this time he left me standing at attention. He wore a stern expression, convincing me that for some reason he was upset with me, but I couldn't figure out why.

"Lieutenant," he said, "why haven't you written your mother?"

I was stunned and a little embarrassed. I'd been so busy for the previous two weeks that I had neglected to write home. I suddenly imagined her getting worried and calling Neubiberg, and I knew that they would not have told her where I was. But it was worse than that. She had in fact called a U.S. senator from Florida and asked for help finding out what had happened to me. The senator had contacted the Air Force chief of staff, who had sent a terse message to my squadron commander inquiring about my welfare.

"Major," I said, "I'm sorry as hell, but I've gotten a little behind the power curve with my family correspondence. I'll write my mother tonight."

The commander looked at me.

"No, you won't, Lieutenant," he said. "You're going to sit down and write a letter right now. Then you're going to address the envelope, put a stamp on it, and hand it to me."

I nodded. This major was upset.

"In addition," he said, "I'm removing you from the flying schedule tomorrow so that you will have some time to contemplate the fact that you will never again neglect to write your mother while you are a member of this squadron."

Well, that hurt. I sat down and wrote the letter. In it, I pleaded with my mother not to call anybody about me again. I reminded her that if something were to happen to me, the Air Force would notify her immediately. If she hadn't heard anything, I explained, that was good news. From that day forward, though, I wrote to my mother once a week—no matter how busy I was or where I happened to be. I didn't ever want to lose my place in the flight schedule again. Of course, when word got out about my "problem," the rest of the pilots teased me about it for weeks. I learned my lesson.

With Christmas approaching, the decision was made to move the squadron back to Munich. That sounded like a very good idea to all of us. It was snowing back in Germany, and with light holiday work schedules there would be skiing and beer and plenty of cheer. We'd had our fill of the desert. One matter needed to be attended to, though. The squadron commander announced that he would need two bachelor lieutenants to volunteer to stay behind at Wheelus to command a group of enlisted men assigned to care for several of our jets that were to be left behind, along with a cache of supplies for the squadron that would replace us. Nobody volunteered. Who wanted to spend Christmas in the desert in godforsaken North Africa?

"All right," the squadron commander said. "Then we'll draw cards. The two losers will stay behind."

I piped up with the bright idea that the two high cards should be designated the losers. Everybody nodded. Why couldn't I have kept my mouth shut? I proceeded to draw the ace of spades, and my buddy Milton Byron pulled the king of hearts. It was what poker players call a cold deck. We were going to spend the next three weeks in the land of camels and blowing sand. Ho ho ho!

Before the rest of the squadron left, the supply officer, a captain, asked me to sign for all the equipment being left behind, for which I would now be responsible. He showed me a foot-high stack of papers detailing every item. I sighed.

"OK, Captain," I said, "let's go through this list of stuff."

"Lieutenant, it would take a week to review all this, and I have to depart in one hour." He glared at me. "It's all here. You're going to have to trust me."

I balked at signing for things I couldn't verify.

"Sign, Lieutenant!" he told me. "I now have exactly fifty minutes before departure."

I signed his papers, but I had a sick feeling in my stomach as I did it. I was in new territory here. I didn't know anything about administrative matters. I was a fighter pilot, not a bureaucrat.

Milt and I stood a little forlornly as we watched the twenty F-84s and five C-119s take off for Germany and Christmas. Those of us left behind, including the enlisted men, were a little depressed. Hellhole duty for the holidays. As the formation rumbled off and the desert silence returned,

Milt and I gathered the men together and told them what we expected of them over the next three weeks. There wasn't a smile in the bunch.

The base was set up with the aircraft on the west side of the compound and all the tents where we lived on the sandy eastern edge that ran down to the Mediterranean. The tents were outfitted with Army-issue cots and pot-bellied stoves that had chimneys that poked out through the roofs. We needed those stoves. The desert nights were frigid. Milt and I immediately set up a guard detail to protect all the spare parts and stacks of equipment stored in the tent area. We had to watch out for bands of natives who on occasion would sneak up from the sea and infiltrate the area. I was responsible for the whole shebang; I'd signed for it, and I was determined to make sure nothing walked off during those three weeks.

At midnight on our first day, I decided to check on the oncoming guard detail to make sure the tent area was covered. It was a good thing I did because the sergeant assigned to that duty hadn't shown up. I put the next highest-ranking man in charge of the detail and went off in search of the sergeant. I finally found him at the enlisted men's club on the west side of the base, hanging over the bar and regaling a small crowd with a tale of woe about how he was being forced to spend Christmas in such a wretched place. When he saw me, it dawned on him that he'd missed his assignment.

"Sergeant," I said, "get your hat and come with me."

He didn't say a word at first. On the way back to the other end of the base, he asked if he could begin his detail as soon as we arrived. "Hell no," I told him. "You missed the formation, and you're drunk." I informed him that he was restricted to the tent area until further notice.

The next morning I paid a visit to the base provost marshal, a crusty old major who'd seen it all. I explained the situation with the sergeant and the missed guard detail.

"Sir," I said, "I'm a fighter pilot. I don't know anything about being a commander or how to handle disciplinary action. What should the penalty be? I need some help on this."

He smiled. He was old enough to be my father.

"Well, son," he said, "I appreciate the fact that you know you're just a dumb lieutenant, that you admitted it, and that you came to me for assistance. I like your attitude."

He sat back and thought for a minute.

"First of all," he said, "you have an opportunity to get things off on the right foot with these men. Everybody on your detail knows that the sergeant of the guard missed the military formation and that he was drunk. If you don't act swiftly and harshly, you will lose control of this detail. They're all waiting to see what you're going to do. But, Lieutenant, you can't be *too* harsh. That's important. The punishment must fit the crime."

The major suggested that we initiate an Article 15 on the sergeant, fine him one hundred dollars, and give him a suspended bust—which meant he would lose a stripe if there were any more violations during a certain period of time. This punishment would hurt, but it would give the guy a chance to redeem himself. The major also suggested that he personally read the charges to the sergeant to make sure we got his attention. I liked all of these ideas. I liked this major.

I went back to the tent area and ordered the sergeant to put on his Class A uniform and accompany me to the provost marshal's office. In the office, the sergeant stood at attention, pale and scared, and listened to the major read him the riot act. When we returned to the tents, I assembled all of the available men and told them what had happened. If the sergeant screwed up again, I announced, he would not only lose a stripe, but go to jail. I think this announcement got their attention. We certainly had no more issues with guard detail for the remainder of our time at Wheelus.

Which is not to say my problems were over. One night a bunch of natives snuck into our camp and stole one of the tents—the entire 200-pound structure along with tent poles, stakes, the wood stove, and the chimney! Our guards were positioned just a few feet away and never heard a thing. Those guys could have slipped in and slit all our throats.

After that, we were much more vigilant.

One day, to kill the boredom, Milt and I headed out on a day trip across the desert to see some spectacular Roman ruins known as Leptis Magna that dated back to 1100 BC. Later, we found some natives with a big herd of camels and rented one for a few hours. It cost us a pack of cigarettes. The one thing I recall: that camel had one speed, and it wasn't overdrive.

We ate most of our meals in the officers' club. On occasion, we'd pay a visit to the British officers' club in downtown Tripoli. It wasn't much, but we weren't especially picky about our entertainment at that point.

The base was slammed by a major dust storm the day before Christmas. The wind howled at 40 miles per hour, and these great tornados of sand rolled across the desert from the south as if they were alive. Sand was everywhere. It penetrated the tents and covered everything in a matter of minutes. Our mouths were full of grit. It was the closest thing we were going to get to a white Christmas.

As New Year's Eve approached, everyone at the officers' club agreed to pitch in to hire an Italian band and fly them in to help us ring in 1951. Each of us contributed one hundred dollars, but at the last minute the C-47 that we'd arranged to pick up the band broke down. We got our money back and sat around drinking champagne and making New Year's resolutions that the next year we'd make sure to be someplace a whole lot more agreeable. We were sick and tired of sand and camels.

As we assembled on the morning of our scheduled departure for Neubiberg, a C-54 bringing the replacement guards and new detachment commander to Wheelus touched down. Imagine my surprise when I saw a certain supply captain walk off the plane—the same guy who'd forced me to sign for everything blind three weeks earlier. I grabbed the big stack of paperwork listing all the supplies and carried it right over to him.

"Is everything accounted for, Lieutenant?" he asked.

"Sir," I said—and really enjoyed saying it—"you're just gonna have to trust me."

In March 1951, Milt and I volunteered to fly in a large formation of our old F-47s from Neubiberg down to Vicenza, Italy, where a contingent of Italian Air Force pilots and mechanics was anxiously awaiting them. We buzzed the Italian airfield in a twelve-ship formation, broke up into flights of four planes each, and buzzed the field again. When we pulled into the parking area, we were greeted by a full contingent of Italian fighter pilots and mechanics. These planes made up the first group of seventy F-47s they'd be receiving, and they were as thrilled as we had been to get our jets a few months earlier. A pilot climbed up to each cockpit and greeted us with a cold Italian beer. The colonel who was brought out to greet me addressed me as "sir." We second lieutenants didn't hear much "sir" up at Neubiberg, so I didn't correct the colonel. We were then loaded into a bus and driven to the officers' club, where a day-long party commenced. I guess fighter-pilot DNA is the same everywhere.

Shortly after arriving, we were reunited with our old friend Capt. Govan, who was responsible for getting the Italian pilots combat ready in their new aircraft. He had some pretty entertaining stories for us. Italy had one of the world's most venerable aviation traditions, and Govan told us that since 1923, when Mussolini established the Regia Aeronautica (Royal Air Force), the pilots had been treated like royalty. He described a typical day on the flight line as the Italian pilots learned to fly the F-47.

The crew chief would do the entire preflight inspection of the aircraft and prepare it for flight. The pilot would show up at 10:00 a.m., and the crew chief would help him up into the cockpit and make sure he was comfortable in his seat. The pilot would then raise his arms straight up, and the crew chief would snap on the parachute and attach the shoulder harness and lap belt. With the pilot sitting immobile, the crew chief would prime the engine and start it up. He would remain bent over into the cockpit so he could make sure everything was in order as the engine warmed up. He would switch on the radio, present the pilot with his helmet, help him fit it on his head, and attach all the wires from the helmet to the aircraft systems. When the engine was warmed up, the pilot would give a dismissive little wave of his hand, at which time the crew chief would salute the pilot and jump down off the wing. After the chief was given the signal to remove the chocks and he had done so, he saluted the pilot one last time as the aircraft taxied away.

The pilot would then take off and do about fifteen minutes of aerobatics before returning for a landing. After the aircraft was parked and the chocks were in place, the crew chief would again jump up on the wing, hit the magneto switch to shut down all the systems, remove the pilot's helmet, undo his safety belt, unstrap his parachute, and help him out of the cockpit. This guy did everything but fly the damn plane, Govan told us. The pilot just sat in the cockpit like a king on a throne. One time, when one of the pilots had let the engine quit at the end of the runway, they had to run a crew chief out there because the pilot literally did not know how to start the airplane back up. He'd never done it!

Once the pilot completed his fifteen minutes of aerobatics—the Italian pilots were very good at aerobatics, by the way, because that's basically all they did—he would proceed to the officers' club for lunch and a big jug of Chianti. He would spend the rest of the afternoon playing cards or napping. These guys led a charmed life.

Govan did what he could to help the Italians get serious about flying combat missions. At least, he told us, he'd insisted that they all learn how to start their own engines.

If the Italian pilots were treated like kings, we were treated like gods during our visit. During the day, each of the American pilots had an escort officer assigned to him, and those fellows stayed with us like glue. If I went to the bathroom, my escort stuck just as close to me as I'd allow. At night, we partied and drank until we couldn't stand it. As we left the officers' club for the final time prior to our return to Neubiberg, they handed each of us four bottles of wine. It was as if we'd known these men all our lives.

The Italians escorted us out to the C-82 that would take us back to Germany, and as we climbed onboard clutching our bottles of wine, we made the sorts of uncomplimentary comments fighter pilots will make to transport crews. After takeoff, I noticed a few of our pilots huddled up, and I could tell they were cooking up some sort of mischief. Sure enough, thirty minutes into the flight, eight of these guys locked arms and ran together toward the rear of the aircraft. The weight of eight men suddenly lunging to the rear caused the plane's center of gravity to shift and sent the whole thing into a sudden climb. At this point, the eight ran toward the front, forcing the C-82 into a dive. They ran back and forth a couple of times, giving us all one hell of a roller coaster ride. Our pilots, of course, were howling with laughter. Then the transport pilots decided to strike back. When the eight rowdy pilots reached the rear of the plane on one of their runs, the C-82 pilot put the aircraft into a much steeper accelerating climb, forcing our band of slightly drunken lieutenants uncomfortably to their knees. The C-82 pilot then countered with a punishing dive, this time sending our group flailing about for a moment of near weightlessness as in a suddenly descending elevator. Now these guys were clawing at each other and trying to catch themselves. The fun was clearly over. One of them finally shouted, "No more!"

We had broken wine bottles all over the place, but the rest of the ride was fairly uneventful. I had belted myself in pretty tightly and didn't suffer much. I was still lost in the whole Italian adventure. I volunteered several times over the coming weeks to fly some more of the old Jugs down to Vicenza but was never selected.

Volunteering became habit forming for me. I was game for anything that would give me more flight hours in the F-84, and I put in for every mission I could. So in June 1951, when our operations officer Maj. Virgil Noriega asked for volunteers for a mission to an anonymous location—he wouldn't tell us anything about it—I raised my hand. Noriega picked six of us, then informed us that we'd be flying to Brussels. I was pretty happy because I hadn't yet had a chance to see that city and understood that it was considered a very hospitable place for a bachelor second lieutenant.

We left Neubiberg with Noriega flying lead and me in the number two position on his left wing. When we landed at Brussels, a Belgian Air Force lieutenant colonel briefed us. The following morning we were scheduled to make a series of ceremonial flights over the cities of Brussels and Antwerp as part of the birthday celebration for the king of Belgium. He told us he wanted us to come in low and fast and mentioned that there would be no minimum altitude in effect. That news was pretty exciting for all of us because we didn't often get permission to buzz a major city.

We checked into a local hotel and went out for a little walking tour. Brussels is a spectacular town, full of historic buildings and picturesque squares. We tempered our fun that night because Noriega made it clear he wanted us sharp for the following day's formations.

Next morning, after double-checking and determining that the Belgian Air Force really was encouraging us to fly as low as possible over Brussels, we took off. Noriega had made it clear, however, that he wanted us always to fly slightly above him. I was on the leader's left wing, and the other two aircraft in the element were on his right. We flew our first pass at about 300 feet. On the second pass, we dropped down to about 100 feet. Let me tell you, when you're flying just above the rooftops at 450 miles per hour, stuff comes flying by at a breathtaking clip. For most of that pass, I was absolutely convinced I was going to hit something—a steeple or a tall tree. In true fighter-pilot fashion, however, I held my

position tight on the leader's wing. If Noriega ran me into something—
well, then shame on him.

On our next run, we split up and made solo passes over the city. I
was even a bit lower this time, but, flying solo and able to pick my own
course, I felt much more comfortable. I couldn't stop grinning. For a
fighter pilot, this exercise was just about as much fun as you could have
with your clothes on.

After finishing at Brussels, we headed to the coastal city of Antwerp
to repeat the whole show. Again, on the formation flight I was sure I was
going to clip something. It didn't seem possible to sneak through there
cleanly. But again I stayed in formation.

Then I felt a tremendous shock rock my aircraft. It scared the hell out
of me. I knew I'd hit something and informed Noriega of the situation.
I pulled up above him and checked my engine instruments. Everything
looked fine. Noriega followed me back to the air base, where I made a
safe landing.

After parking and shutting down the engine, I jumped out to look
for damage. The tip tanks were still in place, and we didn't see any
obvious evidence of impact. Then we peered into the air intake. On the
F-84, air for the engine entered through a large opening in the nose,
and when we looked inside, we could see a knot constructed of four
different layers of aluminum that had once been the air divider. Then we
noticed a large gash and feathers and blood everywhere. I'd hit a large
bird at 450 miles per hour. This discovery was actually a great relief to
me. I didn't want the embarrassment of having pulled out of formation
for nothing, so all those bird guts were my vindication.

That night we donned our full-dress uniforms and attended an
official function at the Brussels Opera House. King Leopold III and his
queen arrived to great fanfare, and the festivities cranked up. At one
point, the announcer informed the audience that the U.S. Air Force
pilots who had flown right down the main street of town that morning
were in attendance, and we received a rousing round of applause. We
were celebrities. None of us knew it at the time, but we were participating
in the end of an era. Belgium was on the brink of civil war, and the king
would abdicate the throne just a few weeks later in order to preserve the
monarchy.

After the ceremony, we visited a local bistro to sample the famed
Belgium ale and debrief. I was happy to hear that all of our pilots had

felt just like me and were convinced they were going to hit something as we came in low.

The next morning I was informed that because I'd flown back to the base following the bird strike, my aircraft could be safely flown back to Neubiberg for repair. I was a little nervous following takeoff but made it back without incident.

The squadron was given the F-86 in 1952. This aircraft wasn't quite the thrill the F-84 had been, but for most of us it was better than any package on Christmas morning. As soon as I was assigned a plane, my sergeant gave me a funny look.

"Lieutenant," he asked a little reluctantly, "we're not going to polish this one, are we?"

What we'd discovered with our F-84 was that once you put polish on the aluminum skin, you had to keep polishing it regularly—*very* regularly—or it looked like hell. We wore our fingers to the bone keeping it shined up.

"No, Sergeant," I said. "We're going au naturel this time."

I'd been in the U.S. Air Force three years by this point, and I was learning the ropes. You had to pick your battles. I wanted to spend my hours in the sky, not polishing and buffing a fuselage.

In March 1952, the squadron commander announced that he needed a volunteer for a one-month assignment, but he wouldn't say any more. Many of the guys were wary of volunteering blind that way, but of course I threw my name in the hat. Only five of us were willing to take a chance.

"OK, here's the deal," the commander told us. "I need a test pilot in Copenhagen for thirty days. You'll be flying F-84Gs. Everyone still interested?"

We all stayed. It sounded intriguing—at least it would be a change of scenery for a month. I had fallen in love with Germany, but I knew it would still be here when I finished this assignment.

"All right," he said. He grabbed a deck of cards. "You're going to cut for it. Highest card wins."

He offered me the deck first. I cut the cards and showed the rest of the group the ace of spades. This time—unlike the ace I'd drawn in Libya—I'd picked a winner.

"Thank you, gentlemen," I said, enjoying the chorus of groans. "I'll send you all postcards from Denmark." I think if you believe you're lucky, luck comes your way. I don't know how else to explain it.

I caught a flight to Copenhagen that same day. The following morning I reported to the American Embassy. I met the chief of the Military Aid and Assistance Group section. He was a one-star general named Snavely, and his mission was to provide the F-84G aircraft to our NATO allies.

"Lieutenant Kittinger," he said, "we're behind schedule. The truth is that I don't really need your pilot skills for another month. We've had terrible delays in delivery of the airplanes. But now that you're here, I want you to stay and get everything organized for me."

I went out to Kastrup Airport (today it's Copenhagen International) and met all the guys working on this project—an American captain who was a maintenance officer, a couple of American supply sergeants, a representative from the Republic Aircraft Company, a representative from the Allison Engine Company, and military reps from all the NATO countries. They were there to process the aircraft that came in: accept the shipments, set up the planes, test-fly them, and prep them for delivery to the various militaries. A full month went by, though, before we had any aircraft to work with. I had to contact my base and get a one-month extension to my assignment.

The brand-new F-84Gs finally arrived by ship. They were covered in a plastic coating to protect them from the salt spray. Officials closed down the highway from the port at two in the morning, and the planes were towed through the streets of Copenhagen to the airport.

It took the crews another two weeks to get the planes ready to fly. I was the only test pilot, so they had to get orders for each of the individual countries processed. On my first flight, I had trouble starting the engine and had to use the emergency fuel system just to get it going—nobody was very happy about that. Once I got the engine started, it ran fine, but none of the tech reps could troubleshoot the problem with the fuel system.

I decided to fly it anyway, and at first everything seemed just fine. Then, at an altitude of about 30,000 feet, I hit the throttle to test the engine response, and the engine flamed out. I had to glide down to a lower altitude to get it going again, and, once more, I had to use the emergency fuel system to start it.

I made an appointment with Gen. Snavely the next morning. I told him the story, and he asked if I had a recommendation.

"Well, sir," I said, "the engine tech rep told me that when they process the planes, they put solvent in the fuel regulator. He thinks the solvent might be screwing up some aneroids and bellows in the regulator. If that's right, I'd bet that it'll all come out after we've run enough fuel through there."

Snavely looked at me a moment.

"I'd like to hear your specific recommendation, Lieutenant."

"Sir," I said, "I think we should just keep flying 'em. If we report this situation to Systems Command, they'll spend six months investigating, and there's no telling how long it'll take us to complete the tests. I think we can solve it right here."

"Lieutenant," Snavely said, narrowing his eyes, "if you crash one of my airplanes, there's going to be hell to pay."

"Sir, I don't crash airplanes."

After a minute or two, he nodded.

"Go ahead," he said. I gave him credit for not covering his butt and doing the no-risk thing, but I could tell he wasn't going to sleep very well that night.

For the next few days, I ran the airplanes through a precise series of tests. I'd go up, flame out the engine, and glide it down. I determined that if I didn't get the engine started before the tailpipe temperature came down to less than 200 degrees, I'd have to use the emergency regulator to get it started. But once I did get it going again, I could switch back to the main system. I did about a hundred of these flame-outs and restarts to establish the criteria. Then I sat down and composed a detailed operational program. I briefed all the NATO ferry pilots on the procedure and made sure they understood it. I made each of them read it and sign it. In the end, everything worked out pretty much as I'd told the general I thought it would: after ten to twelve hours of flight time, the solvents were flushed out of the regulator, and the fuel systems operated normally.

I was a little surprised to find out how much I enjoyed this work. It seemed to suit me. I went at it seven days a week. I liked the problem solving that was required of a test pilot. Nothing was routine. I kept myself busy in Copenhagen. I flew more than three hundred airplanes during my time there. I let the general know that I wanted to stick around as long as he had a use for me, but after I had been in Denmark for five months, my squadron commander sent me an ultimatum.

"Kittinger," he said, "if you're not back in Germany by the end of this month, don't bother to come back. You are through with this squadron."

Snavely offered to get me a transfer if I wanted to stay. I thought seriously about it. Copenhagen wasn't bad duty, but in the end I told him no.

"Sir," I said, "I'm a fighter pilot. I'm ready to return to my squadron."

Test pilot. Posing with one of the brand-new NATO F-84Gs in Copenhagen. I flew more than three hundred of them in the span of just a few months. (Courtesy: United States Air Force.)

Now that I'd had a taste of the test pilot's life, though, I decided that when it came time for my next assignment, I was going to look for something in research and development.

The ace of spades turned out to be a fateful card.

3

Come Up and Get Me

*   *   *   *   *   *

The war in Korea was over, and I'd missed the whole thing. That was the ballgame for fighter pilots, and, in spite of my repeated attempts to get transferred, I'd spent the duration in the minor leagues in the skies of Cold War Europe. Now, after my experience flying the NATO jets in Copenhagen, I had decided to try the test-pilot game. The only other real option was flying the F-84G with the Strategic Air Command, comparatively boring duty that was considered a fate worse than death for fighter pilots, so I requested an assignment flying experimental aircraft. I was hoping for Edwards AFB in California, but instead received orders to report to the Fighter Test Section at Holloman AFB in Alamogordo, New Mexico.

It was June 1953, and I found myself living an aviator's dream in the high desert alongside the White Sands Proving Grounds. It was a fantastic place to live and raise a family—I was now a twenty-five-year-old captain with a wife whom I'd met in Germany and a two-year-old son, and I could fly whatever and whenever I wanted. I flew all day, every day, including Saturdays and Sundays. I flew the P-51, the B-25, and B-26; the L-19 and L-20; the C-45 and C-47; the F-80, F-86, F-89, F-94, F-100, and F-104. Fighters, jets—you name it, they had it at Holloman, and if they had it, I flew it.

As soon as I began to settle into life at Holloman, I began hearing about some of the experimental work going on at the Aerospace Medical Laboratory north of the main base. If the stories were accurate, those guys were involved in some highly unusual stuff out there. The chief of the Aero Med Lab was a renegade colonel and medical doctor named

John Paul Stapp. I'd seen Stapp a few times, and he certainly didn't look very remarkable.

In time, I would come to the conclusion that Col. Stapp was not only one of the smartest, but also quite possibly the bravest man in the United States Air Force.

One day my commander, Lt. Col. Oakley Baron, called all of his test pilots together and briefed us on a request he'd received from the Aero Med Lab.

"Colonel Stapp needs a pilot for a project on zero gravity," he said. "Honestly, I don't know what the hell this is all about, but I'm looking for a volunteer."

That, of course, was the magic word for me. Everything good that had happened to me in life had come from volunteering. I had no idea what zero-gravity research would entail, but I had my hand up before Baron had even stopped talking. Then I looked around and saw that I was the only man volunteering. Was I making a big mistake here?

"OK, Kittinger," he said. "You're Stapp's project pilot."

I figured I'd better do a little digging. Stapp, it turned out, had the reputation of something like a mad genius. He was an evangelist for the notion of space travel. He'd grown up in primitive fashion as the son of missionary parents in the jungles of Brazil, but he believed that human beings could *and should* go into outer space. It was still an uncommon idea in those days. But could we really survive out there? I knew there wasn't much data on human performance in a zero-gravity environment. We needed to determine whether weightlessness would be a limiting factor for an astronaut. Stapp had found a researcher in Argentina who was already working on zero G. Dr. Harald von Beckh was a former German flight surgeon who'd published papers on response to weightlessness in turtles, so Stapp arranged to bring him to Alamogordo and made him project officer for the Air Force's zero-G studies.

I went out to the Aero Med Lab to meet with Stapp and von Beckh. Dispensing with preliminaries, Stapp immediately sat me down and explained what he wanted. I'd be flying medical research personnel, and I'd be using a T-33 because it was the only jet airplane we had access to that carried two people. He described how a zero-gravity flight worked. I would put the plane into a steep dive, then pull up sharply. The flight path was a huge parabolic arc. At the top of this trajectory, I'd push hard on the stick, and as we completed the top of the arc, we'd get ten, fifteen, maybe even twenty seconds of weightlessness. It sounded pretty simple.

In the beginning, our instrumentation consisted of a golf ball and a string. I tied the golf ball to the string and hung it from the rearview mirror. When the golf ball floated, we had zero gravity (or close to it). Cameras were installed in the cockpit to record everything. In one experiment, the medical technician in the rear cockpit held a cat in his lap. We knew that cats are able to orient themselves in a fall and land on their feet, but we didn't know if the cat was reacting to G forces or to visual cues, so the backseater would roll the cat over on its back as we hit zero gravity to see what would happen: our weightless cats oriented themselves right side up. On one flight, the cat floated up into the front cockpit; I gently shoved it back toward the rear, where my partner caught it in midair.

I flew hundreds of these flights, and over time the instrumentation and the experiments became more sophisticated, and we were given better airplanes. We went from the T-33 to an F-89B to an F-94C to an F-100F to an F-104B. By the time we were using the F-104, I was able—after some practice—to achieve a full minute of weightlessness on each arc. You can collect quite a bit of data with a sixty-second duration. This was groundbreaking stuff, and I was proud to be involved—even if the common wisdom at Holloman held that space research was disastrous for a pilot's career. Hell, I didn't care. I loved this kind of flying! It was different, it was exhilarating, and it was cutting-edge. I was aware that not everybody shared my passion. About half the people I took up with me got sick in zero gravity. One scientist who had a bad reaction to weightlessness—all you had to do was say "Airplane!" and this guy would throw up—wrote a paper predicting that human beings would never go into space because they would be incapacitated by nausea. I later asked this scientist why his paper failed to mention that the project pilot never got sick—that, in fact, he enjoyed the sensation. "Pilots are different," he told me. "Well, hell yes, they're different!" I said. "Which is why pilots are going to be the first space travelers." There was a lot of academic B.S. around during the infancy of space research.

Zero gravity wasn't the only thing Stapp was working on at Holloman. Far from it. He must have had thirty projects going at the same time— all kinds of things that would teach us about human adaptability to life in space. The more I was around the man, the more impressed I became by the quality of his mind and the extent of his vision. He could see the future of space travel, and he understood that addressing the biomedical and human factors, along with the development of adequate survival and protection systems, would be a challenge every bit as significant as the rocket technology. I decided he was a guy I could learn from, and I had a hunch the days ahead at the Aero Med Lab were going to become very interesting.

I continued to fly every day for the Fighter Test Section, but I was on loan to the Aero Med Lab for the zero-gravity work. One day I received word that Col. Stapp wanted to see me. I assumed it had something to do with the zero-G flights. Instead, it turned out to involve another of Stapp's programs that I knew almost nothing about.

"Sit down, Captain," Col. Stapp said when I showed up in his office. "I've got a deceleration study going on I want to talk to you about. Next month we're going to fire off nine rockets attached to an aluminum sled and send it down a 3,500-foot track. At the end of the track, we'll go from a top speed in the vicinity of Mach 1 to a full stop in about one second." He paused for a moment to let that sink in. It was hard to believe such a thing was possible. "I need photographic documentation—aerial photos—and I want you to fly the photographer. Are you interested?"

I didn't have to think very long. "Yes, sir. I'd like to volunteer for the job."

"OK, then." As usual, he got right down to business. Stapp didn't like to waste time. He flipped open one of his notebooks. "Now, my calculations show that you'll need to be 3,825 feet from the track at a velocity of 522 feet per second, accelerating at a rate of 35 feet per second for twelve seconds. That'll get you to the takeoff point at the correct speed."

"Colonel Stapp," I said, "there's no way I can work with those numbers, but let me go out there and practice it a few times. I'll come up with a procedure and make it work."

"Well," he said, "once the countdown starts, you're committed. I need you to be right there at 350 miles per hour when the rockets fire."

"Just let me practice it, sir. I'll figure it out."

I got a T-33, put the photographer in back, and flew a dry run. I had mission control give me a countdown. *Minus five, four, three, two, one—fire!* I missed it a little bit early. We tried it again, and this time I was a little bit late. We made twenty practice runs that day. I never missed it by much, but I never hit it exactly right, either. I made five more series of practice flights over the next few weeks, trying to get the timing down so I would hit the launch end of the track at just the right speed at just the right moment.

It wasn't until the day of the sled run that somebody informed me that Stapp himself would be aboard the sled when all those rockets fired. He'd somehow neglected to mention that part to me. I was incredulous. He was going to strap himself in and ride 40,000 pounds of thrust at the speed of sound and slam to a stop. The purpose was to determine whether pilot bailout at supersonic speeds was survivable. The data would also be

The fastest man in the world aboard the *Sonic Wind*. In my opinion, Col. John Paul Stapp was not only the fastest and smartest, but also the bravest man in the United States Air Force. Here he prepares for one of his near-supersonic rocket-sled runs at Holloman AFB in New Mexico. (Courtesy: United States Air Force.)

To JOE KITTINGER,
you can be outnumbered.
You can be outranked.
But you can never be outclassed.
To the finest pilot and gentleman
I ever met, from,
John Paul Stapp

useful years later when deceleration during atmospheric reentry from orbit became an issue. I couldn't quite fathom the punishment Stapp's body was going to take if this rocket-sled thing went off as planned—or, worse, if it didn't. I was told there was an honest difference of opinion among the medical staff at Holloman about whether it would kill him or not. To be safe, they were going to park an ambulance with the motor running at the end of the track.

On the appointed morning, with Stapp's support crew ensconced in a concrete blockhouse 100 feet from the track, I came in hot in the T-bird, right on the deck, hoping like hell we'd hit the launch close enough to get the pictures. I was going to get only one shot at this. The track was oriented toward the north, and I remember thinking that if the brakes on that sled failed, Stapp would be going so damn fast he'd probably only bounce once or twice before coming to ground in Albuquerque 200 miles away. I heard the countdown as we approached the track, and things felt good to me. This time I hit the launch site perfectly at precisely 350 miles per hour just as the white smoke boiled out of the rockets and the sled Stapp had named *Sonic Wind* shot past us in a blur. It reached a top speed well in excess of 600 miles per hour. The photographer got some tremendous shots. It was the only time our timing was dead on—but when it mattered, we nailed it.

The brakes on the sled held, and Stapp survived 41 negative Gs as he slammed to a stop. (One G equals the acceleration due to the force of gravity at Earth's surface.) The Air Force had always insisted that 18 Gs was the limit of human tolerance to G forces. Stapp had proved that a pilot could in fact eject at supersonic speed and live to tell about it. It was hard to believe that he'd be willing to put himself through something like that, but he explained later that he would never ask someone else to do something he wasn't willing to do himself. I thought that was a pretty good motto for a colonel. They rushed him to the hospital afterward. He was bruised up pretty badly. It turned out that he'd been making these sled runs for a while, although few people had known anything about it, and he'd sustained concussions, lost teeth, broken bones, hernias, and God knows what else. Following the run I witnessed, all the blood vessels in his eyes had burst, and he was a frightful sight for a few days, but in typical fashion he never stopped laughing about it. All the rest of us could do was shake our heads in awe. Stapp made the cover of *Time* magazine, which dubbed him "the Fastest Man in the World."

Not much later Stapp requested permission to try the sled run again—he wanted to add yet another rocket and get a little more speed—but the brass turned him down. Too dangerous, they said. The official explanation was that they feared he'd hit a bird and kill himself. The truth was, I kind of wanted to try one of those rocket-sled rides myself, but I never said anything to anybody about it. There's such a thing as pushing your luck. (I did get a chance to make a run on what the Aero Med Lab called its "gravity sled." After the abrupt stop, all I could see were stars. I decided to leave that type of fun to Stapp and the medical guys.)

The original name for the high-altitude research program Stapp dreamed up was Project Daedalus, but when it turned out that a classified atomic-powered airplane development effort was already using that designation, the project officer came up with "Man High" (later streamlined as Manhigh). The objective was to raise a human being into a space-equivalent environment, above 99 percent of Earth's atmosphere, and leave him there for a twenty-four-hour period. We didn't really know what might happen to the body in the near vacuum of the upper stratosphere. The list of unknowns was long. This effort marked the start of the investigation into life-support systems, communications, physiological monitoring, human tolerance to cosmic radiation, and the astronaut-selection process that would usher in the space age.

The aircraft to be used for Manhigh was one wholly unfamiliar to me: a pressurized capsule suspended beneath a giant helium balloon. The project was an extension of the cosmic radiation research Maj. David Simons had been conducting at Holloman using, at first, V-2 rockets captured from the Germans following World War II and, later, balloons to fly small animals. In preparation for Air Force approval and funding, however, Col. Stapp recast the project as a contribution to the design and test of a proposed manned space vehicle, which is how Project Manhigh became the world's first manned space program, an unheralded predecessor of NASA's Project Mercury.

When I volunteered for Manhigh in August 1956, Stapp wrote to Col. Baron requesting that I be assigned to the Aero Med Lab for the duration of the project. Baron approved the assignment, even if he didn't understand it. "Joe," he wrote me, "here's your approval. More guts than brains." There would be times in the months ahead when I wondered whether he might have been right.

I was designated the alternate pilot on the project. Stapp had already given me a list of prerequisites. To qualify, I needed to get a parachute rating, the latest pressure suit, a balloon pilot's license, and a twenty-four-hour claustrophobia test and to pass an entire battery of physiological and psychological exams. I got busy right away.

First, I went out to the Naval Air Station in El Centro, California, where a small group of U.S. Air Force and Navy parachute experts tested new chute designs. I got my jump, and it was so much fun that I hung around and jumped nine more times, all of them involving free falls, which earned me my Navy parachute wings.

Parachute wings. With jumpers in El Centro, California, after making my first parachute jump and my first free fall. The only thing more fun than flying an airplane is jumping out of one.

To this point in my career, my colleagues had mostly been pilots. They were the men I understood. At the Aero Med Lab, I found myself surrounded by doctors and academics and engineers. Dr. David Simons was Stapp's project officer for Manhigh, and as far as I was concerned, he was a pretty weird character. We were like oil and water right from the start. Simons made the day-to-day decisions, and he assigned himself to make the Manhigh research flight. Because part of the objective was to monitor physiological response, it was appropriate that the pilot be a medical researcher familiar with high-altitude physics. Simons was a doctor, though, not a pilot, so Stapp announced that he wanted me to make a test flight with the Manhigh system first. That decision was also appropriate. This highly experimental aircraft would be entering an extremely hostile environment, and because there were no plans to test the complete system in a decompression chamber—a mistake, in my mind—a test flight conducted by a trained test pilot was a no-brainer. Stapp wanted me to take the system up to somewhere around 100,000 feet and descend immediately. A shake-down run. If something went wrong, I'd be in the best position to evaluate it and deal with it. As Stapp explained to us, "To put the Manhigh system up now for a full-scale flight without at least one manned test flight would be like trying to send a new fighter plane into combat without wringing the bugs out of it first."

Maj. Simons opposed the test flight. In fact, he hated the idea. I think it galled him that I would be the first one to go up with his gondola and his balloon. He was sensitive about it. He tried to talk Stapp into canceling the test flight, but he lost the argument.

Winzen Research in Minneapolis was awarded the contract to build the capsule and the balloon. This company had done some pioneering work with the U.S. Navy and was already associated with the Holloman Aero Med Lab. Otto Winzen was a courtly German immigrant who had experience working with the latest plastic films. He wasn't really an engineer; he was more of a promoter and entrepreneur—and a dreamer. His whip-smart young wife, Vera—whose family had provided the capital to start the company and sustain the operation—actually ran Winzen Research and solved the problems of how to construct a delicate polyethylene balloon envelope capable of holding millions of cubic feet of helium.

In the meantime, both Simons and I needed to learn to fly gas balloons. Stapp had required both of us to obtain a free-balloon pilot's certificate. The Civil Aeronautics Administration required six instructional flights of at least two hours each, one controlled flight to an altitude of 10,000 feet and a one-hour solo flight. We practiced with an open-gondola system Winzen had built called the *Sky Car*. It had seats for two people. We made most of our training flights over the farms and fields of rural Minnesota. It was certainly nothing like flying a jet, but I found out quickly that it was a tremendous amount of fun. The biggest surprises were the silence and the calm. Because I was moving with the wind, my relative airspeed was always zero. Inside the gondola, it was perfectly still, and I could hear every word of a conversation on the ground hundreds of feet below. It was almost as if I was momentarily immune to the laws of physics or as if I had dropped in from another dimension to spy and eavesdrop on mankind.

We learned how to manage ballast and how to valve helium from the balloon in order to initiate a landing. It was a tricky business because the sun would be heating the gas and creating lift while we were releasing gas in order to descend. We learned through trial and error, and we had a few near-crash landings, but it didn't take long to get me hooked on lighter-than-air flight or to get me thinking about what might be possible with the right balloon design. I didn't see why you couldn't fly one all the way across the country. And if you could do that, why not around the world?

I would go up to Minneapolis for weeks at a time and help out in the Winzen factory. I wanted to learn everything I could about the capsule. If I was going to ride that contraption deep into the stratosphere, higher by far than any balloon pilot had ever been, 19 miles above the surface of Earth, I didn't want to leave anything to chance. I approached it the same way I would approach any experimental aircraft. I'd sit in the Winzen gondola for hours, familiarizing myself with the controls, the hardware, and the procedures, visualizing how I would fly the system. It was a very tight space, about the dimensions of a telephone booth. I tried to imagine every potential problem and review every contingency. There was so much we didn't know about this kind of mission. I asked thousands of questions and made almost that many suggestions. I was putting my life in the hands of the Winzen engineers; I wanted to know them and make damn sure they knew me.

One of the things we talked about was temperature. When a man gets overheated, his efficiency goes, and he makes mistakes. Part of my job was to eliminate mistakes. Sitting in the capsule and dressed in the

In the Manhigh capsule. I spent hours in the Winzen gondola trying to visualize the flight I was going to make. I wanted to know everything about the vehicle, the team, and the mission. (Courtesy: United States Air Force.)

pressure suit, which is by design an uncomfortably tight-fitting garment, I got hot. There was no ventilation in that suit. They had devised an air-cooling system for the capsule, but it worked only in the low-pressure environment of the stratosphere. I was worried about the early stage of the ascent and the final stage of the descent.

Maj. David Simons inspects my survival system. The MC-3 partial-pressure suit was—for its time—a sophisticated piece of equipment, but it was not a comfortable garment. It felt as if I was wearing an octopus. (Courtesy: United States Air Force.)

On the unmanned, instrumented test flights of the system, I noticed that even at ceiling altitudes the interior temperature was always quite high. I had expressed my concern, but the engineers had assured me that I would be comfortable during the actual flight. Nevertheless, on one of the ground tests in which I'd worn the pressure suit, the temperature had climbed above 80 degrees, and I knew firsthand how miserable that was. I was adamant that I did *not* want to be hot at any point during my flight, so I told Maj. Simons and the lead engineer, Don Foster, to fix it.

"I don't care what you do," I said, "but you've got to make sure I don't overheat."

They didn't always care for my ideas, but I was determined to get my way on this one. After some discussion, they came up with the simple notion of attaching a 30-pound cap of dry ice to the exterior of the gondola. Simple solutions are often best, and this one worked like a charm.

While the hardware for the Manhigh flights was being designed and constructed in Minneapolis, we conducted a series of test balloon flights with animals on board. Our standard payload consisted of twelve guinea pigs and three hundred black mice that we'd fly up to 100,000 feet to test the life-support system. (We used black mice because a primary cosmic ray strike would turn the black hairs white and help the biologists pinpoint the particle's path through the body.) This load of critters represented the equivalent of a man in terms of oxygen requirements, carbon dioxide output, and heat generation, and it allowed us to fine-tune our cabin atmosphere and air-regeneration systems. We also flew monkeys on occasion, but they turned out to be more trouble than they were worth. Primates required all kinds of special care, and they weren't always friendly—kind of like some human beings, come to think of it.

To support the project, I had my own C-47 Skytrain (the military version of the DC-3), my own crew, and lots of spare parts. We flew out of a little airport in Brainerd, Minnesota, which was near Crosby, where we launched the balloons from a 300-foot-deep iron ore mine pit. The balloon team would launch the payloads, and I'd chase 'em. We'd land, pick up the equipment and the animals, and return everything to the scientists and engineers for evaluation.

Shortly before one of these chase-and-recovery missions, some sort of plague wiped out our black mouse population. The mice were kept in incubators in a gymnasium at the Army Armory in Crosby, and the whole lot of them dropped dead. I had to make an emergency run to Providence, Rhode Island—a lab at Brown University was our source—to pick up new mice. I returned just in time for the launch. In the meantime, the researchers had fitted all of the guinea pigs with little frame helmets equipped with emulsion plates to record cosmic ray impacts on their brains. To say they looked bizarre is an understatement.

We had a full-scale prototype of the Manhigh capsule, and we launched our menagerie into a gorgeous summer sky. The balloon rose without incident up to 103,000 feet as I circled below in my C-47, ready to retrieve the capsule when it came back to Earth. I had two veterinarians on board and a couple of veterinary assistants, along with some Air Force technicians and Winzen engineers. On a warm day, it was critical to get to the capsule shortly after it came down before too much heat built up and killed off our test subjects. At lower altitudes, the cooling system was incapable of off-setting the heat generated by the animals and instruments on board.

At the appointed moment toward the end of the second day of the flight, a technician sent a signal to cut the balloon away, which would drop the capsule beneath a cargo-recovery parachute. We were about 50 miles out of Saginaw, Michigan, at that time, so I called the Saginaw airport to inform them that we were going to drop this unusual load somewhere west of their town. Our radio-controlled cutaway failed, however, and the balloon continued to drift, carrying the capsule with it. I notified the airport that we were going to be dropping our capsule closer to them than we had first thought. Again, though, the technician couldn't get the damn balloon released.

Fortunately, the cutaway system had a backup. At 4:30 p.m., if the balloon was still attached, an onboard timer would fire a small explosive charge and drop the capsule on the cargo chute. We were getting close to 4:30, and I was a little concerned because we were coming right up on Saginaw. Moments later: BAM! The balloon cut loose, and here came the Manhigh capsule on a course that would set it down right smack in the middle of residential Saginaw. I radioed the airport for the third time and told them our situation. I knew it was going to be a mess. It was a Sunday afternoon, and all kinds of people were out and about. As the package descended, I circled the cargo parachute until it touched down, hoping to attract attention so that nobody would get hit by this thing. Luckily, it just barely missed a house and tipped over on its side. I made a very low pass over the landing spot and scribbled a quick note: "Please set the capsule upright and stand back. We'll be there soon. Signed, United States Air Force." We tossed the note out in a message bag trailing a streamer. I watched as the spectators read the note and stood the gondola up. Then I headed for the Saginaw airport. I called the tower and requested that my aircraft be met by either state, county, or city police who could take us to our capsule.

As soon as we were on the ground, we hustled out and piled into three police vehicles that sped us toward the landing site with lights flashing and sirens wailing. The capsule had come to rest in a backyard, and by the time we arrived, a crowd of several hundred had gathered and clogged the streets. I think everybody in Saginaw had come out for the show. We had to park about 400 yards away and run. We could see that the capsule was surrounded by curious onlookers. When the citizens of Saginaw peered into the glass portholes, what did they see? Swarms of black rodents running around like crazy and creatures with strange-looking emulsion-plate helmets on their heads, their beady eyes staring back. The gathering throng put out word that their town had become host to an honest-to-God extraterrestrial visitation, and I'm sure that a bunch of cops and doctors and Air Force personnel rushing to the scene didn't do much to dispel that notion.

We had a serious problem. The afternoon sun was turning the capsule into an oven, and about half the guinea pigs and some of the mice were already dead. The vets and their assistants took charge of the survivors, and we rushed them back to the airport. We needed to get the guinea pigs and their emulsion plates to the Armed Forces Institute of Pathology in Washington, D.C., where the analysis would be done. By the time we were fueled up and ready to go, only four of the guinea pigs were still alive. It was a race to get our test subjects to the lab before they expired.

We had to refuel in Dayton, Ohio, and by the time we left on our final leg, only two live guinea pigs remained. I pushed the C-47 as hard as I could, while the vets ministered to the two laboring rodents. We touched down at Bolling Field, now with only a solitary live guinea pig, and traveled with another high-speed police escort to the Institute of

Pathology on the grounds of the Walter Reed Army Medical Center. We jumped out and sprinted up the steps of the building. Just as we stepped inside, the final guinea pig gave up the ghost. We'd lost the race. Even though we laughed about it over late-night beers, this result was a bitter disappointment for the project. It was the kind of thing we dealt with in working for the Aero Med Lab in the pre-NASA days. We made it up as we went along; we worked with the materials at hand, and things didn't always go the way we planned.

One lesson I learned from the Saginaw experience was that if a real UFO ever *does* land in an American city, the authorities won't be able to get anywhere near it. Curious human beings will travel from far and wide to witness the phenomenon, and they'll tie up the roads. It'll be like a rock festival. People aren't afraid of this stuff. They want to see it and touch it. Man is drawn to the unknown. My advice to the aliens: expect an audience, learn to work a crowd, and avoid Saginaw, Michigan, on Sundays.

Balloons were always being mistaken for UFOs in those days—especially at twilight when a balloon at altitude was still catching the sun and glowing even after darkness had fallen for observers on the ground. One particular incident caused more than its fair share of controversy. It started with a routine balloon training flight from Holloman in May 1959. I was the only qualified balloon pilot at the Aero Med Lab at the time, and Col. Stapp suggested that I check out a couple more pilots in the event that I was not available for a flight. I put out a notice that I was looking for volunteers, and two captains assigned to the lab, Dan Fulgham and Bill Kaufman, got in touch with me. I set up a series of training sessions at Holloman. We made a short flight, and both pilots shot a few landings. Two days later, after waiting out some bad weather, we took off at eight at night for a longer flight. A 10,000-foot mountain range looms just to the east of Alamogordo, so we had to climb quickly in order to clear the peaks. I'd been busy on another project and hadn't had much sleep, so I really needed to catch a few winks. I took the balloon up to 11,000 feet and leveled off.

"OK," I told the two guys with me, "I'm going to lie down and take a little nap. I want you to keep the balloon right here—at 11,000. If the altimeter shows us dipping below that, drop some ballast, and get back up right away. Wake me up if you have any problems."

I made myself comfortable and took a nap. Some people are surprised that I can sleep during a balloon flight, but lighter-than-air travel is usually very peaceful, and I've never had any trouble falling asleep. When I woke up, the sun was shining. I took a look at the altimeter and saw that we were only 500 feet above the ground.

"Damn it, guys," I said. "I told you to keep us at 11,000."

"Well," Capt. Kaufman said, "we cleared the mountains, and we didn't want to wake you up. We just brought her down gradually."

Our meteorologist at Holloman had told us to expect weather on the east side of the mountains, and, sure enough, about 5 miles up ahead I could see the ground winds whipping up. My plan had been to stay high, pick a good landing spot, and come right down on top of it. These guys had put us in a bad position. We were coming up on the little town of Roswell, and I couldn't see a great place to put down.

We were traveling at about 20 miles per hour over the ground—a pretty good clip. I turned to Capt. Fulgham and told him I was going to let him make the landing.

"It's all yours, Captain," I said. "As you come down, pick a spot and aim for it."

I didn't have much experience as a balloon pilot instructor. I should have given him more direction. Just as the balloon hit the ground, Dan hit the button to cut the balloon away. A better tactic in that situation would have been to open the gas valve and let the basket drag a little bit as the gas escaped, but he had cut the balloon away before I could stop him. We hit at maybe 15 miles per hour, and the gondola flipped. The centrifugal force kept us all inside, but when the thing came to rest—upside down—the lip of the gondola was planted right on Dan's head. He was lucky: he was the only one of us wearing a helmet. Nevertheless, his head was smacked awfully hard, and the impact ruptured all the blood vessels in his scalp. I managed to push the basket up enough that we were able to crawl out. All three of us were peppered with the steel filings our system was using for ballast, but Dan definitely got the worst of it.

We managed to get his helmet off, and we watched his head literally expand as the vessels filled with blood. We laid him down. As I leaned over him, I saw a little pool of blood on the ground. I couldn't find where the blood was coming out of him. I wiped the blood off his head, and in a few seconds it was back again. I was starting to panic. A minute or so went by before I realized what was happening. It was my own blood. I had a cut above my eye, and I was dripping all over Dan. There was a moment of relief.

But Dan seemed to be getting worse. I was afraid we were going to watch a man die. We had a chase helicopter following us, and just a few minutes after we were down, the chopper landed in a field nearby, and we were able to get Dan onboard. It was about 5:30 in the morning at this point. We called Walker AFB, which is about three miles south of Roswell and told them that we needed an ambulance to meet us on the flight line when we landed. We had an Air Force medic with us in the chopper, and he instructed the base hospital commander to be ready to receive a case of massive head trauma. We landed, and they rushed us all inside. While the doctors examined Dan and tried to reduce the swelling in his head, I washed the steel filings out of my eyes. I had a nasty gash right above one eyebrow, and the eye was closing fast. They stitched me up and then took me in to see Dan.

I wasn't quite prepared for what I saw. The poor guy's head looked like a basketball. It was grotesque. You could barely see his nose. All the blood vessels in his face and scalp had hemorrhaged. It was one of the spookiest things I'd ever seen.

"Is he gonna be all right?" I asked.

"We think so," one of the doctors said. "If we can get the swelling to subside, he should be OK."

Now I started considering our situation. We'd just had an aircraft accident, and I had been in charge. I definitely didn't want any publicity if we could avoid it. About that time, somebody on the hospital staff informed me that the aircraft accident investigation officer would be there shortly. Well, I did *not* want to talk to that guy. I didn't want to set eyes on that guy.

I grabbed the doctor and pointed at Fulgham. "Can this man travel?"

He looked at me as if I were crazy.

"Sir, we need to transport our man back to the base hospital in Alamogordo."

"If you're going to move him," the doctor said, "we'll prep one of the ambulances."

"No, sir," I said, "we'll use the helicopter."

"Absolutely not," he said. "His head might swell with a sudden altitude gain."

"Listen, sir," I told him, "we'll go around the southern edge of the mountains, and we'll fly 10 feet above the ground. No altitude gain."

I kept after him. Finally, the doctor relented and gave us permission to move Dan. They had bandaged his head, and it looked like a giant egg. We managed to get him in the helicopter, while I was pushing the staff away and doing everything within my power to get us out of there.

"Wait a minute," somebody yelled. "What about the accident investigation officer?"

I turned to the pilot.

"Let's get the hell out of here," I said. "Now!"

We took off for Holloman, flying right on the deck the whole way. We got Dan safely to the base hospital and made sure they went to work on him right away.

The thing was, I had arranged for the Federal Aviation Administration (FAA) to show up the next day for our new balloon pilots' check rides. Dan, under observation with his head wrapped up like a mummy, was obviously out of the picture, but Capt. Kaufman needed two more landings, and I would have to fly with him before the FAA arrived. My eye was rapidly puffing up from the swelling, and I was worried about it closing completely. I could still see out of it, but just barely.

When the flight surgeon on the base saw me, he shook his head and told me I was going to have to pass a vision test, or he'd ground me, so I hurried back to my room, got an ice pack, and kept it pressed to my eye for the next two hours. I held the ice pack in place as I drove back to the flight surgeon's office. I ran up there and took the vision test. I passed it, and moments later the eye closed up for good. It didn't open up again for five days. The next morning, wearing a pair of dark sunglasses, I flew with Capt. Kaufman, who needed the additional landings. When we were done, Bill went up for his flight test with the FAA examiner and passed with flying colors.

Dan, meanwhile, needed to get back to Wright-Patterson AFB, where we all were stationed, but I didn't see any way we could let him get on an airliner looking the way he did. I called Col. Stapp, and he offered to get us transportation. Dan was really worried that his wife might find out about his accident and overreact. He asked me to have

Mrs. Fulgham meet him at the airport but begged me not to mention anything about his head, so I called her and gave her the arrival time for our flight the following day.

We flew into Wright-Patterson on a C-131 that Col. Stapp had arranged for us. As we taxied in, I saw Dan's wife awaiting our arrival. I took Dan's arm—the poor guy couldn't see anything through the bandages—and escorted him slowly down the ramp at the front of the airplane. He looked like a creature from another planet.

I introduced myself to his wife.

"It's nice to meet you," she said, looking around. "But . . . where's Dan?" She was practically standing next to him.

"Mrs. Fulgham," I said, "I'm very sorry to tell you this, but . . . *this is Dan.*"

She wailed like a banshee. "What have you done to my Dan?!" I thought she was going to pass out. "*What have you done?*"

It didn't take me long to figure out why he hadn't wanted me to tell her about the accident. She was an excitable woman. I guess the whole scene is kind of funny in retrospect, but at the time we honestly didn't know how well he was going to recover. It turned out that Dan was fine once the swelling went down and his head returned to normal size.

The whole incident became part of the ongoing Roswell legend that had its genesis in the summer of 1947 when a rancher reported evidence of an alien landing in the desert. The alien debris turned out to be part of a classified Air Force high-altitude balloon program called Project Mogul. Somebody in Roswell—maybe somebody who worked at the hospital—got a look at Dan as we helped him out to the chopper that morning and formed the idea that he was some kind of space alien. He was described in the literature as a "creature with a huge, grotesque head." I was described as the "abusive, red-haired captain" who was frantically trying to cover up the whole incident and get the creature back to some secret Air Force location in the desert. The legend grew from there. The simple truth was that a guy's head was bashed on a balloon landing, and I was worried about getting written up by an accident investigator.

People desperately want to believe this stuff, though. One survey indicated that 65 percent of Americans believe that extraterrestrial beings visited Roswell, New Mexico, in the 1940s and 1950s. There's nothing I can do to change their minds—not even when I tell them that *I* was the abusive, red-haired captain.

Many years later one of the TV networks asked me to participate in a story they were doing for the fiftieth anniversary of the original Roswell incident. I guess I was asked because my name had become associated with the whole affair through various reports published over the years. I went down to the local network affiliate in Orlando for a remote interview. I had no idea what they were going to ask me. It was July 5, 1997, and it just so happened that on the previous day the NASA lander had touched down on Mars and was already sending back pictures from the Red Planet. To me, this event was just phenomenal. Actual pictures from the surface of Mars!

When the national news anchor, who was broadcasting live from New Mexico, came on, he said: "Here we are in beautiful Roswell, New Mexico, on the fiftieth anniversary of the UFO landing here." You could hear a band tootling away in the background. It was a party atmosphere. The guy went on: "We have with us from Orlando, Florida, Colonel Joe Kittinger. We'd like to ask him some questions. Hello, Colonel."

"Hello," I said. "Good morning."

"Well, what's your opinion, Colonel Kittinger, about the incidents so many years ago here in Roswell that we're celebrating today?"

"Well," I said, "do you know that right now there's a *real* scientific incident happening on the planet Mars? It's sending back *real* pictures. To tell you the truth, I'm afraid what you're celebrating there is more like a nonevent."

There was a long pause, and the anchor cleared his throat.

"Thank you very much, Colonel," he said.

And I was off the air. Just that quick. They had their story line and didn't have much use for mine. The funny thing was that no one had bothered to ask me in advance what I thought about the Roswell mythology. I just said what occurred to me at that moment. I never did get another invitation from that particular network.

We'd had trouble with the guinea pigs on what we came to call "the Saginaw Incident," but as a pilot on Project Manhigh, I was something of a guinea pig myself. One of the project's goals was to investigate human response to the stresses of space flight. I underwent a battery of physical exams. *Thorough* exams. In the week leading up to the test flight, I was required to collect all of my urine output. The medical monitors assigned to the project wanted a chemical analysis of the steroids in the urine, which could be used as a control and compared against the urine collected during and immediately following my trip into the stratosphere. So each day during the final week of May 1957, I collected my output. I had one bottle for 12:00 a.m. to 12:00 p.m., and another bottle for 12:00 p.m. to 12:00 a.m. Wherever I went, I had to carry around a paper sack containing one or both of the bottles.

A few nights before the flight, a bunch of us decided to venture into downtown Minneapolis for dinner. After a leisurely meal, we stopped into a bar near the restaurant and had a few beers. At one point, I went to the men's room to relieve myself. I had my paper sack with me, of course. When I pushed through the door, I found a line waiting for the facility. Well, I figured I had everything I needed right there with me. I stepped aside, took the correct bottle out of the sack, and made my donation. One of the guys standing in line took a look at me and commented: "My, ain't we fancy?" I thought it was pretty funny, but I didn't offer any explanation. I went back in, stuck the paper sack under the booth we were sitting in, and finished my beer.

Later, a few of us took a cab back to the Curtis Hotel, where we were staying, and as I walked into the lobby, I suddenly realized I'd left my sack at the bar. I found the number of the bar and called. I was in a little bit of a panic. The phone rang for a while before a man's voice answered.

"Sir, what time does the bar close?" I asked.

"We're already closed," he said. "Only reason I picked up the phone is that I thought you were my girlfriend."

"Sir," I said, "I was with the party that sat in the first booth."

"Yeah, I remember."

"Well, sir," I went on, "I inadvertently left a paper sack under the booth. It's extremely important. Can you check and see if it's still there?"

After a minute, he came back on the line.

"Yep, still here," he said. "But listen, buddy, there's a couple of bottles in there that look like piss."

"Well, that's amazing," I said. "Can I come get it?"

"Naw," he said, "I'm gonna be leaving in about five minutes. I've gotta pick up my girlfriend."

"Listen, sir," I said, "I'm at the Curtis. I can catch a cab and be there in ten minutes. I've got twenty dollars for you if you'll wait for me."

"Twenty?"

"Yes, sir."

"Hell," he said, "for twenty bucks I'll wait an hour."

When I got to the bar and knocked on the door, the bartender met me with my precious paper sack. Under the circumstances, I was pretty happy to see it. I gave him a twenty. He took the bill and laughed.

"That sure looks an awful lot like piss in those bottles," he said. He narrowed his eyes and shook his head as if now he'd seen everything.

"That sure is funny, sir," I said.

I decided not to mention this little adventure to Maj. Simons when I turned in my samples the following morning. I just smiled and handed over my twenty dollars worth of urine. It was the only time in my life I've had to pay for the beer on the way in *and* on the way out.

The Manhigh gondola had gotten most of my attention as we neared the date for the manned test flight, for obvious reasons, but while we were flying all over the countryside chasing mice and monkeys, development of the balloon had been in full swing at the Winzen plant. Nobody had ever built a balloon this big. In order to get me and the one-ton payload up to the edge of outer space, we needed a balloon measuring 200 feet high and 172 feet in diameter at full inflation at peak altitude, big enough to hold 2 million cubic feet of helium. (Later flights would use even larger envelopes and more helium.) This size of balloon required acres of an extremely thin polyethylene film. The 2-mil plastic was strong but would become dangerously brittle in the frigid regions we wanted to visit. Building such a monster required the utmost care, patience, and ingenuity.

A few weeks before our test flight was scheduled to launch, Teamsters Union employees at the Winzen plant announced plans to go on strike. The extrusions for the balloon were made at a plant in Indiana, and I was worried that the strike would prevent the plastic from being delivered and delay the construction of the balloon, so I jumped in my C-47 and flew to Terre Haute. We loaded the crates with the balloon material into the airplane, and I snuck it into the Minneapolis airport under the cover of night. We unloaded everything onto a truck and drove it into the plant about four hours before the strike was scheduled to commence. If I had been caught, it might have been a real embarrassment for me and for the Air Force, but I just didn't feel that I could allow a strike to jeopardize everything we'd worked for. Luckily, we got away with it.

Vera Winzen supervised the construction of a mammoth table system upon which the sixty long gores of polyethylene were heat-sealed together and the 120 load bands were applied. Armies of Vera's "balloon girls," who worked in stocking feet and submitted to fingernail checks each morning, bent for hours over their creation, searching for pinholes and imperfections. The quality control at Winzen was rigorous, and the final product reflected the attention to detail.

Mrs. Winzen built great balloons.

The weather for June 2, 1957, looked promising. Our forecasts were provided by one of the best meteorologists in the Air Force: Bernard "Duke" Gildenberg. If Duke said go, you went, or you'd wonder why you hadn't. So, at about eleven on the night of June 1, I completed my preparations at the Winzen plant, wriggled into my pressure suit, and stuffed myself into the Manhigh capsule. They sealed me inside, flushed the air out, and pumped in a precise mixture of oxygen, helium, and a very small portion of nitrogen. We didn't want to use pure oxygen under pressure because of its fire-accelerating properties. One spark, and it would all be over. After numerous tests, we'd come to the conclusion that the three-gas environment would be the safest for our purposes. Finally, they installed the dry-ice cap on top to keep me cool.

By the time everything was stabilized, and we'd worked through our checklists, it was 4:00 a.m. The weather still looked good, so they rolled the gondola into the bed of a pickup and trucked me some 18 miles in the dark to our launch site at the South St. Paul airport. They unspooled the balloon, laid it out alongside the runway, attached the mouth of the balloon to a big cargo parachute, and then attached the parachute to the top of the capsule. I was able to watch the preparations through my window. A thick ground fog swirling in the floodlights gave the scene an eerie theatrical quality. By the time the sun came up, we were ready for launch. The whole team was there: Maj. Simons, the engineers, the balloon girls, and even Col. Stapp. We all had a great deal riding on this flight, and I was determined to do a good job. My goal was an altitude 35,000 feet higher than a human had ever ventured in a balloon.

We'd never had much money; the entire project operated on a shoestring. Space research just didn't attract the big bucks in those days. In fact, if it hadn't been for Col. Stapp's willingness to divert funds from his other equally strapped Aero Med projects, and Vera Winzen's willing-ness to put up substantial sums of her own money, we probably couldn't have gotten off the ground. We never, for example, had a budget that allowed for adequate altitude chamber testing. Nevertheless, the team was creative, and it was a testament to them that we were ready to go on June 2.

Unfortunately, shortly after I was launched in what we were calling *Manhigh I*, an annoying problem cropped up. We'd never done a full communications check, and I discovered almost immediately that I was unable to transmit on the VHF radio. I could hear my ground crew loud and clear, but they couldn't hear me. It was a little maddening. This glitch wasn't a show-stopper because I could still use the CW switch and send messages using Morse code, but it was definitely a pain in the rear. Morse code is extremely slow and laborious, especially if you don't use it often. It put me at a real disadvantage, but I wanted to let them know that I could adapt. In my first communication, I carefully tapped out: NO SWEAT. That was a trademark line of mine, and I knew they'd know I was OK.

Then, at about 40,000 feet, less than an hour into the flight, another problem bit us. I glanced down at my oxygen supply gauge and saw that I'd already expended about half of my supply. I had left the ground with 5 liters of liquid oxygen, which provides about 15,000 liters of oxygen gas. We used this supply to pressurize the gondola. At this point in the flight, I should still have had most of my oxygen left. I knew right away I was in a world of hurt. I turned everything off and started bleeding oxygen into the capsule from the supply in my pressure suit. I was fly-ing with the suit and helmet faceplate open because of the pressurized environment. If I lost pressure, I'd need to seal the faceplate and pres-surize the suit quickly.

I probably should have aborted the flight at this point, but I didn't. Not only did I want to keep going for my own sake and for the project's sake, but I was fairly certain that I could make it to peak altitude and get back down safely if I was judicious with my use of oxygen. After all, I was a test pilot, and I was there to test the system.

So up I went, toward the tropopause and, eventually, the stratosphere. Duke had warned us about the potential for 100-mile-per-hour jet stream winds, and at 45,000 feet I prepared myself. I knew this was the point where most balloon failures occurred. Sure enough, the

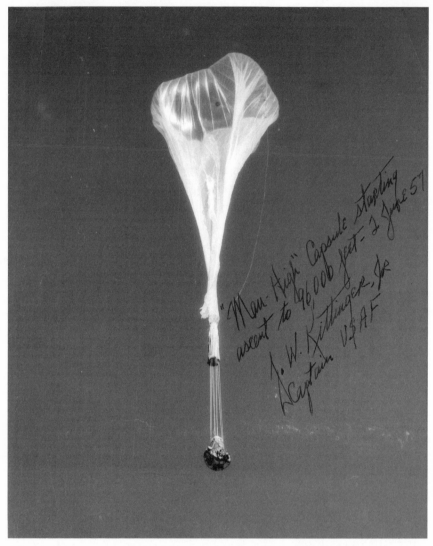

Manhigh I aloft. At launch, the plastic balloon resembled a jellyfish. As the balloon ascended, the air pressure dropped, and the helium inside expanded. At equilibrium, near 100,000 feet for this balloon, the envelope would swell into an onion-shaped ball 200 feet across. (Courtesy: United States Air Force.)

instant I hit the jet stream, I was hammered. The effect was not subtle. The capsule went over almost 90 degrees, and when I took a look at the balloon envelope using a mirror rigged for that purpose, I saw a deformed, concave bulge of plastic hauling me rapidly to the east. There wasn't much I could do but sit tight and wait it out. Luckily, *Manhigh I* passed right on through the jet stream, the balloon resumed its natural shape, and the capsule righted itself. Vera and her balloon girls had done themselves proud.

As I passed 72,400 feet, I saluted Army Air Service captains Orville Anderson and Albert Stevens, who held the altitude record. Their *Explorer II* flight in November 1935 had established a balloon altitude mark that had stood for twenty-two years. They were true pioneers, but there was a crucial difference between their flight and mine. The Explorer project's two-man crew had been engaged in general scientific observation and measurement; we were preparing for space flight with a lone astronaut.

At about this point, the world outside my windows began to change. The pale blue of the sky that we're used to seeing from Earth was still visible in a thick band along the horizon, but if I let my eyes drift up, I could see the sky gradually darken from dark blue to indigo to an almost indescribable black. It was the blackest black I'd ever seen. Blacker than ink. And it was morning! The sun was shining, but the sky surrounding it was the color of midnight.

It was an awesome thing to behold, and I felt privileged to be able to take it all in. I knew then that I was in a very different realm.

Space.

One unnecessary source of tension on the project was Maj. Simons's fear that I would try to find an excuse to bail out of the Manhigh capsule. I had talked openly about how much I'd enjoyed my parachute training at El Centro and had speculated about my belief that it might be possible to survive an emergency jump from the stratosphere, but I had told Simons flat out that I had no intention of trying such a thing. Why would I? I was a captain in the United States Air Force and an experienced test pilot. I understood full well that such a move would be extremely dangerous. I would never be so irresponsible as to jeopardize a project by introducing unnecessary risk. That would be just ludicrous. At the same time, bailout remained a last-resort emergency option in the event of disaster—for example, if I had a fire on board—and I was prepared for that if circumstances required it. But Simons never stopped worrying that I would jump out, and he would lose his capsule.

At 8:54, I heard Maj. Simons on the radio. He told me their calculations showed that I had just enough oxygen left to make it back down, but no more—a fact I had already determined. He ordered me to descend. At that point, *Manhigh I* was at 96,000 feet, and I had a view that no living creature had ever enjoyed. A handful of rocket-plane pilots had arced up this high, but only for an instant. I was able to sit there, run my eyes along the horizon, and see the curvature of Earth. I could see hundreds of miles in all directions. I marveled at the strange coloration of the sky, and it occurred to me that I was the first man to leave Earth's atmosphere for any significant duration. I had become the first astronaut: the first man in space. The thought was sobering, but I had no time to savor it.

Well before I'd received Simons's order to descend, I had already begun the process of valving helium from the balloon. With the amount of ballast I had, I couldn't valve too much too fast, or my rate of descent would overcome my ability to slow to landing speed as I neared the ground. I needed to respond to Maj. Simons now, but I thought I'd have a little fun with him.

I pondered for a while, then tapped my reply in Morse code:

C-O-M-E U-P A-N-D G-E-T M-E

Simons went nuts. Kittinger was going to try and bail out! He'd been seduced by the rapture of space! Psychologists had theorized about a syndrome they called the "breakaway phenomenon." To me, it was all pretty silly. Fighter pilots don't suffer "breakaway." Flight surgeons, maybe, but not fighter pilots. A few moments later I received another message, this one from Col. Stapp himself, ordering me to descend. No more messing around. I tapped back: VALVING GAS. In fact, I was already on my way down.

I finally got a good descent rate going and by 11:30 was back down to 53,000 feet. Some clouds had moved into the area by this point, obscuring the ground. An hour later, with my oxygen supply completely depleted, I punched through the overcast, and my crew could pick me up visually. They put a helicopter in the air to track me from that point. Both Simons and Stapp were on board. When I reached a height of 400 feet above the ground, I dropped some batteries for ballast to slow me down. I made a perfect landing just a couple of minutes before 1:00 p.m. on the bank of a little creek. I hit a switch that released the balloon, and the capsule eased over into mud. I'd traveled 80 lateral miles from the launch site, landing just a bit to the north of Weaver, Minnesota.

Maj. Simons made it to the capsule first and helped me out. Col. Stapp took a bunch of pictures, all of which show me grinning. I couldn't hide my elation. What a ride! They did a quick medical evaluation and found out what I already knew: I was fine.

They hauled the capsule back to the Winzen plant for a postmortem. An engineer named Ed Lewis was able to troubleshoot the oxygen problem almost immediately. Somebody had mixed up the oxygen and vent hoses and reversed their connections to the pressure controller. My oxygen supply had been vented *to the outside*. Learning about this error was a little disturbing, but these things happen with experimental vehicles. They also figured out the radio problem. It was nothing more than a loose switch. These mechanical failures proved the wisdom of Col. Stapp's insistence on a shake-down flight with a qualified test pilot. If Simons had gone up for the longer-duration mission with the system I'd flown, Project Manhigh might have ended in disaster. As it was, we could consider the test flight a success. With the mechanical fixes, the team was now ready to begin planning for the twenty-four-hour-plus research mission scheduled for Maj. Simons. I encouraged them to find a way to do the altitude chamber testing they'd skipped prior to my flight, and I reiterated my support for the dry-ice cap prior to launch because it had given me comfortable temperatures throughout my flight.

Project Manhigh went on to make more history and to fulfill all of the program's objectives. On August 19, 1957, Maj. Simons stayed aloft in *Manhigh II* for thirty-two hours, reaching a peak altitude of 101,500 feet. It was a great achievement. Then, fourteen months later, a third Manhigh flight went up. Lt. Clifton "Demi" McClure, a prototype astronaut if there ever was one, got to within a football field of the 100,000-foot mark. Unfortunately, McClure's flight nearly killed him. The dry-ice cap that was supposed to have been replenished just prior to launch was somehow neglected. McClure left the ground without any external cooling. During the ascent, the capsule overheated.

Manhigh III launched from Holloman just before 7:00 a.m. on October 8, 1958. By noon, Demi McClure's body temperature had already climbed above 100 degrees. Less than an hour later it was 103 and rising.

Not much later, with McClure's head throbbing and his throat burning due to a problem with his drinking-water apparatus, his personal thermometer read 105.6. It was a gritty exhibition of toughness and will that he continued to function at all. He managed to bring the system back to Earth despite muscle cramps, vivid hallucinations, and radio failure that precluded communication with his crew. McClure brought *Manhigh III* in for an emergency landing in the rugged San Andres Mountains at night. His pulse rate as he touched down was 180 beats per minute, and his temperature registered 108.5 degrees. That he was still conscious astounded the project's medical team. And then, to everyone's complete amazement, McClure climbed out of the capsule and walked unassisted to the rescue helicopter. I doubt anybody else could have survived it. The omission of the dry-ice cap really bothered me. How could something like that have happened?

There has been a lot of speculation about this error in the years since Manhigh. McClure believed, and both Col. Stapp and I came to believe, that someone simply forgot the dry ice. I've also heard it suggested that a last-minute executive decision was made to dispense with it. We'll probably never know.

One thing I'm sure of: if I had been there for the launch of *Manhigh III*, McClure would never have left the ground sans external cooling. Shortly after my test flight in *Manhigh I*, though, Simons had me removed from the project. I guess he never got over the COME UP AND GET ME line or, perhaps, the fact that I'd been the one to become the first man in space.

The legacy of our efforts on Manhigh can be seen in the successes of NASA's Project Mercury. We pioneered the systems and processes that would be needed to put a man into orbit, and we demonstrated that human beings can survive and work efficiently in a space environment. One of the project's most important contributions was the multigas cabin atmosphere. We did lots of testing on that. Mixing helium with the oxygen gave us a breathable atmosphere inside the capsule and alleviated concerns about fire aloft. NASA initially chose to ignore this lesson, though. In 1962, when I presented a paper at the School of Aerospace Medicine at Brooks AFB, a NASA engineer sitting right in front asked, "Are you certain you need the multigas mixture?" I told him that the Air Force had studied the problem extensively and that a fire in an overpressure 100 percent oxygen environment would be catastrophic. Nevertheless, he said that NASA intended to use 100 percent oxygen in its Apollo space capsules. "Sir," I said, "I highly recommend that you reconsider." I offered to share our Air Force and Project Manhigh research with him, but by that point NASA was going too fast to slow down and refused to consider that somebody might have already solved the problem. It was the old NIH—Not Invented Here—syndrome. The launchpad fire on *Apollo 1* broke all of our hearts. It killed three fine men. Gus Grissom was a colleague and a friend, and I'd personally helped Ed White get into the astronaut program. At least NASA changed course and went to a multigas atmosphere after the tragedy. It was pretty hard to take at the time, though.

Col. Stapp deserves the lion's share of the credit for Project Manhigh. We had a great team, but without Stapp's vision and persistence and oversight at crucial moments, none of it would have happened. America would still have gone to the moon if there hadn't been a John Paul Stapp, but we might not have gotten there so quickly or so safely.

One morning after I'd left Project Manhigh—it was September 1957—I headed out from Holloman on a routine test flight in an F-100 Super Sabre. Seconds after takeoff, the hydraulic pressure went to zero, and my airplane caught fire. It was a worst-case scenario. I turned downwind and was in the process of lining up for an emergency landing when, at an altitude of 800 feet, the airplane pitched up and stalled, forcing me to eject. If I'd had time to think about it, I would have come to the conclusion that I was a dead man. I was simply too low. But, once again, I drew a very lucky card. I came out of the airplane cleanly, took one quick swing on the parachute, and hit the ground. I was alive. It was as close to a miracle as you can get. Everything had needed to go exactly right, and somehow it did. (Not many people know that Col. Stapp, among his many accomplishments, coined what became known as Murphy's Law: that if something can go wrong, it will. Well, I'd just put the lie to Murphy's Law.) The ejection seat and that chute saved my life. There had been zero margin for error. I had to tip my hat to the men who'd designed and built the system.

About a month later, I got a call from Stapp.

"Joe," he said, "I'm going to Wright-Patterson to assume command of the Aero Med Lab there, and I'm looking for somebody to help me work on emergency escape systems. Are you interested?"

I'd just had my butt saved by an emergency escape system, and, of course, this was Col. Stapp asking. If he wanted *me*, I wanted in.

All I said was, "When do we leave?"

That's how the two of us ended up in Dayton, Ohio, on a project that would turn out to involve a supersonic parachute jump from the edge of outer space. "Fate is the hunter," wrote Ernest K. Gann, a great American pilot. I'd always liked that line.

4
Escape from Near Space

✳   ✳   ✳   ✳   ✳   ✳

B ack in the mid-1950s, the Air Force had run an extensive series of high-altitude ejection tests at Eglin AFB in Florida. Using a B-47 at altitudes up to 40,000 feet, these studies demonstrated that a falling body doesn't just fall, but instead has a devilish tendency to spin and tumble—making it difficult to deploy a parachute effectively in emergency situations. Barnstorming parachute jumpers had observed the same phenomenon as early as the 1920s. Later, during tests at Holloman, Air Force researchers attached a variety of monitoring devices to their test dummies and were able to get a better understanding of the problems faced by a pilot leaving a disabled aircraft. Unfortunately, they didn't make much progress toward a solution.

In 1954, the Escape Section of the Aero Med Lab at Wright-Patterson in Dayton initiated a project called High Dive. The Wright Biophysics Branch was where the Air Force did most of its research on pressure suits, gravity suits, parachute systems, ejection seats, water-flotation devices, life rafts, and anything associated with aircrews involved in emergency escape. Project High Dive focused on solving the riddle of "flat spin"— the accelerating, whirling spin that can render a jumper unconscious. Using sophisticated test dummies, the team recorded flat-spin rates as high as two hundred revolutions per minute—enough centrifugal force to kill a man. The High Dive team was heavy on experienced jumpers, and they naturally looked at the problem from a skydiver's perspective. They assumed that flat spin could best be defeated by proper training in skydiving techniques. But what if the falling airman wasn't a skydiver or was incapacitated in some way or was unconscious?

By the time I arrived at Wright Field in 1958, High Dive had already been canceled. Col. Stapp had seen immediately the fundamental flaw in High Dive's approach: it had failed to see the problem of high-altitude escape from the *pilot's* point of view. Not every airman in distress was— or ever would be—an experienced skydiver. We needed an approach that would get *all* of our pilots down safely.

This kind of work was right up my alley, and as a fighter pilot and test jumper I had my own ideas about how it should be approached. Stapp called me in and asked for my thoughts. I told him I wanted to start the program back up but come at the mission from a completely different angle.

"OK, Captain," he said. He sat back in his chair the way I'd seen him do at Holloman. "I'm listening. Tell me what you'd do differently."

So I laid it out for him. That was the great thing about Stapp; it was what set him apart from other senior officers. He didn't care where an idea came from or how many feathers it might ruffle. He was interested in one thing: results.

"All right," he said when he'd heard me through. "It's your project, Kittinger."

This approval was what I'd been waiting for: a chance to do it my own way. High-altitude escape was just one of a number of challenges facing me, though. My oldest son, Joe, was growing up fast, and my second son, Mark, had been born while we were in New Mexico. They were bright boys, and I tried to spend as much time with them as I could, but the truth was that I worked tremendously long hours and was gone for long stretches of time, and my kids had no way of knowing what my job was all about or why I was so dedicated to it. It was no surprise that the situation put some stress on my marriage, a not uncommon dilemma for military officers with families.

So while I was puzzling over a solution to the problem of stratospheric bailout, I was also trying to figure out how to manage my family life and keep everything balanced. Both my job and my family were important to me, but it was pretty clear even then that one of them was going to suffer from neglect.

At Wright-Patterson, the first thing I did was grab the three guys from the High Dive team who I thought could help me. Lt. Ray Madsen was a razor-sharp young engineer and parachutist, and I knew he had the kind of mind we needed. Master Sgt. George Post was one of the most experienced test jumpers in the entire Air Force. But perhaps the most important of them all was Francis Beaupre, a former Navy parachute rigger and engineer who'd come to work at the parachute branch at Wright as a civilian. I loved the guy's conscientiousness—he was a first-rate parachute engineer—but also his sense of humor and his style. He smoked a big cigar all the time and had a great way with people. I had big plans for Beau.

I put the rest of the team together by asking for volunteers. I had Air Force officers, enlisted men, civil service personnel, and civilian contractors, but I didn't want anybody who didn't want to be with us. I'd learned some important lessons on Project Manhigh. I didn't want to hear about overtime or union dues. We were going to work long hours—that included Sundays and holidays—and I needed everybody pulling in the same direction. If I heard someone complain, he would be off the project. I had two pressure-suit technicians led by Tech. Sgt. Robert Daniels; they were responsible for assembling and testing that vital piece of our survival system. They'd check a fitting ten, fifteen, twenty times. I had great parachute riggers led by Sgt. Frank Hale. I had Ken Arnold for the camera equipment, one of the best in the business. By the time we had the whole group assembled, it wasn't just a good team—it was a *great* team.

I explained to these guys that we wouldn't be able to operate the program I envisioned using powered aircraft, much as I would've preferred it. I wanted to go to extreme altitudes, and we simply didn't have access to a plane that could get us that high. That meant we were going to have to use balloons—just as in High Dive. I knew that the balloon was going to complicate everything. We were going to have to find a way to simulate the speed of a jet or a spacecraft when we tested emergency escape, and it was going to make our lives miserable. I came to hate the very idea of the balloon. We were studying high-altitude egress from jets and spacecraft, not balloons, but there was just no choice with the mission we'd been given.

I picked 100,000 feet as our target altitude. This figure was arbitrary, but it was a nice round number, and Project Manhigh had already shown us we could get up there. I knew Stapp would like it because our project would have a chance to prove that we could survive escape from a high-altitude jet or a disabled spacecraft in the early phase of ascent. Stapp—who in many ways had the soul of a poet—gave us our name: Project Excelsior, from a Latin word that means "ever higher."

As we got under way, I did my best to keep a low profile at Wright. I told very few people what I was up to. I wasn't allowed to classify the program, but at least I could instruct my guys to keep it quiet. The High Dive team had done far too much gratuitous public relations, and it had come back to haunt them. Every time they screwed up, they were the subject of reams of negative press. They even managed to get a grade-C Hollywood movie made about their exploits, called *On the Threshold of Space*, and, if anything, it served to undercut the serious work with which High Dive was involved. My style was to keep things under wraps and demonstrate progress by accomplishment. Besides, I knew there would be some resentment from some of the former High Dive crew when they found out a lowly captain from the Aero Med Lab was now leading the charge.

One flaw in the High Dive approach was that when the crew dropped their dummies from balloons, they deployed the parachutes immediately—like a static-line pull on a paratrooper drop. That technique simply didn't work because a balloon has no airspeed. A body falling from a balloon platform must accelerate to achieve enough airflow to open a chute cleanly. Ideally, you'd like to reach terminal velocity before opening. None of this would have been an issue if we could have run our tests with jets. Eject at high speed, and you've got terminal velocity instantly. Using balloons, however, we were going to have to develop a delayed-opening procedure for our jumps. We couldn't delay too long and risk exposure to flat spin, but we also couldn't open too fast, or we'd encounter inadequate airflow and a tangled parachute. It was a damned tricky timing problem, and we had to get it just right. After some experimentation, we determined that for a balloon jump from the stratosphere—higher than, say, 50,000 feet—the ideal delay would be about sixteen seconds. But we had another complication to deal with: even after a sixteen-second delay, we would still be far too high to open a standard parachute. We had the unfortunate example of Col. W. Randolph Lovelace to consider.

Randy Lovelace was chief of the Aero Med Lab in the early 1940s. Like Stapp, he was a doctor interested in the biomedical problems faced by aviators. In 1943, Lovelace—who had never made a single parachute jump—leaped from a B-17 at 40,200 feet to simulate a high-altitude emergency escape. Lovelace's chute deployed immediately, as planned. It was a long, nightmarish descent. The opening shock knocked him unconscious, and the minus 46-degree temperatures nearly froze him. A brave pioneer who came very near to losing his life, Lovelace taught us that a stratospheric opening of a standard parachute simply wasn't practical.

I put Francis Beaupre on the problem. His solution was an ingenious variation of a multistage parachute system. It worked like this: Approximately sixteen seconds after a jumper leaves the balloon platform, a spring device propels an 18-inch-diameter pilot chute from a backpack. As that pilot chute deploys and fills, it pulls a 5-foot-diameter stabilization chute from the pack. The stabilization chute deploys, stabilizing the jumper without appreciably slowing his fall, thus allowing him to descend in a feet-to-earth attitude and counteracting the forces responsible for flat spin. The stabilization chute also pulls about three-quarters of the main chute out of the pack. A nylon web attached to the pack keeps the main chute from opening at this point. At a predetermined altitude, an aneroid device releases the web and allows the main chute to open. We called it the BMSP: the Beaupre Multi-Stage Parachute. In a sense, the BMSP became the secret ingredient of Project Excelsior.

The Beaupre system was a little complicated, but we tested it until we had complete confidence in it. One of my requirements was that the new chute work equally well at all altitudes. It had to be functional in a real-world environment. I didn't want a hothouse-flower design that would work only on a balloon jump from 100,000 feet. Our goal was survival during emergency escape, so this parachute system had to be useful for any airman leaving an aircraft regardless of the conditions. We did plenty of low-altitude tests tossing dummies out of C-47s and C-54s. The BMSP opened as fast as the Air Force's standard-issue parachute, and it proved itself time and again. We knew it would work for all applications at all altitudes that required a parachute for survival.

Like all of the projects under Stapp's control, we had a tight budget. We couldn't overwhelm problems by throwing money at them, which is why I made the decision early on to go with an open-gondola design for Excelsior. Project Manhigh, of course, had used a pressurized gondola,

Francis Beaupre checks out the parachute system. Project Excelsior's secret ingredient was Beau's multistage chute. It was a brilliant piece of engineering. (Courtesy: United States Air Force.)

and Project Strato-Lab—the U.S. Navy's high-altitude balloon-borne research program—had done the same. High Dive had planned all along to send two men aloft and depressurize their capsule at altitude. One man would jump, and the other would bring the system back down. But I couldn't see the point. If you were going to jump, you had to depressurize somewhere. If there was any problem with the pressure suit, I wanted to discover it on the ascent while there was still a chance to get out and get back down into the atmosphere alive—not at 100,000 feet, where there was no margin of error. It's true that nobody had ever been up there with only a pressure suit for protection, but we'd save a great deal of weight and complexity and money by doing away with a pressurized gondola. We would essentially make the trip to the edge of space in an open basket.

Another thing we did differently from Manhigh: we tested the hell out of our system in the altitude chamber at Wright. I insisted on it. What you worry about on projects like this are the unanticipated things, the unknowns. Beaupre and I would sit around for hours asking, "What if *this* happens? What if *that* happens?" I'd gather the whole team—the balloon guys, the pressure-suit guys, the life-support guys, the parachute guys, the communications guys—and I'd ask them over and over: "What if?" We found problems with timers and the helmet faceplate, and we solved them through relentless testing and retesting. We revised our checklists almost daily.

I had known from the moment Stapp handed me the program that I would be the test subject on Project Excelsior. Just as Stapp had done on his rocket-sled rides in the desert, I was going to put my own hide on the line. It wasn't that I didn't trust anyone else—I named George Post, an experienced parachutist in whom I had complete confidence, as my alternate—it was simply that I wanted to demonstrate my faith in our approach and planning by showing that I was willing to take the system up myself. Having been up there once before, I had a pretty good idea of what to expect. Stapp never mentioned it, but I think he would have been disappointed if I'd done it any other way.

Before we could schedule a test of the system with a pilot onboard, Beaupre's boss—the long-time chief of the parachute branch at Wright— gave us the requirement of completing thirty-five consecutive dummy drops with the Beaupre system without a failure. That's a pretty tall order for an experimental chute. We made thirty-two good drops in a row before we had a minor malfunction, and this guy let it be known that we would need to start all over. I thought this requirement was a little ridiculous, and I was worried about our schedule—it had taken us nearly a year to complete the thirty-two drops. So I did something I did only in extraordinary circumstances. I went to see Col. Stapp.

Stapp never messed around. He called a meeting right away. He brought me in and called in the parachute branch chief. He listened while we made our cases. When we were through, he asked one question, and it was directed at me.

"Captain," he said. He always spoke quietly. There was no unnecessary drama with Stapp. "Will this thing work?"

"Yes, sir," I said.

He stood up and announced that Project Excelsior had immediate approval to continue with the Beaupre parachute. No more test drops would be required. Without Stapp's intervention, we might have been dead in the water. Now that we had a qualified chute, we could turn our attention to the rest of the equipment needed for survival.

Once we'd completed our final altitude chamber tests and were ready to proceed with a human test flight, we sent word through channels that we intended to move to the next phase of the project. The following day, both Stapp and I were summoned to a meeting with Gen. Bernard Schriever, commander of the Air Research and Development Command in Baltimore, Maryland. When we arrived there, we found five other generals in the room. It was a little intimidating. There was some real concern about what we were doing. We didn't have a big fan club among the brass. They saw the project as being too risky, and they feared a repeat of High Dive's bad publicity if we failed. I think they also wanted to take my measure and determine Stapp's level of confidence.

First, I gave a briefing that explained what we intended to do, how we were going to do it, and what we had done to prepare. Stapp remained silent. The generals seemed nervous and a little cranky. They had a few technical and procedural questions, which I answered as best I could. Finally, Schriever directed himself at Col. Stapp.

"Stapp," he asked, "are you willing to approve this thing?"

Stapp didn't hesitate. "Yes, sir."

I was flattered because Stapp hadn't actually observed a single one of our tests. He hadn't been through our data or interviewed any of my team. He was proceeding completely on my assurances.

"Do you understand the ramifications of a failure here?" the general asked. Schriever was a formidable guy, a German immigrant who'd served as a bomber pilot in the Pacific during World War II and who was a brilliant engineer and leader.

"I do," Stapp said.

"Very well," Schriever said, with a little sigh. "You're both excused."

Stapp and I waited in the hall for about ten minutes. Then they called us back in and told us we had the go-ahead, but it was pretty clear to me what had happened. The brass had let Stapp know that it was his butt if anything went wrong. He was basically staking his career on my judgment. I left the meeting grateful for Stapp's support but with a renewed sense of personal responsibility. There was just no chance I was going to let Project Excelsior fail.

With autumn advancing on the upper Midwest and the forecasts deteriorating, we decided to move the launch operations down to Holloman. The weather in southern New Mexico looked good for November 15, 1959. Duke Gildenberg had advised us to initiate our test flight somewhere to the west of Holloman so that the westerly winds aloft would blow us over White Sands Missile Range. That afternoon we trucked the equipment and the helium tanker across the Jornada del Muerto desert to the little town of Truth or Consequences and checked the crew into a motel. The others woke me up at 2:00 the next morning, and I drove with photographic systems specialist Ken Arnold and Francis Beaupre out to the launch site about 20 miles east of town. As the balloon inflation began, I put on my gear. I was wearing the Air Force standard-issue MC-3 partial-pressure suit made by the David Clark Company and the XMA-1 helmet that had been developed at Wright-Patterson, but underneath the suit I had on heavy long underwear, three pairs of socks, and two pairs of gloves. It was chilly in the desert, but it would be brutally cold in the stratosphere. Once I was decked out, they spread a tarpaulin out on the ground, and I lay down on my back to wait.

While I stared up into the black sky, picking out constellations, watching for shooting stars the way I'd done as a kid on the *John Henry*, my helmet and faceplate were sealed, and I began breathing pure oxygen. Aero Med Lab doctors had worked on studies years earlier that had shown the wisdom of flushing nitrogen from the bloodstream prior to a high-altitude flight. If there was an accidental exposure to the near vacuum in the stratosphere, the nitrogen would quickly bubble out of solution. It's a myth that an unpressurized human body will actually

Gear layout. All this equipment was what it took to keep me alive in the stratosphere. (Courtesy: United States Air Force.)

explode, but the reality is none too pleasant. You would get a massive case of the bends, just like a deep-sea diver rising to the surface too quickly. At our altitude, decompression would be catastrophic. Plus, I wasn't going to have the security of a sealed cabin as on Manhigh; my pressure suit would be my only protection, so I breathed the oxygen for two hours to be on the safe side.

At dawn, with the inflated balloon attached to the open gondola, I climbed in, made myself comfortable, and—just as dawn broke beyond the mountains—away I went. The plan was to rise up to about 60,000 feet, which would give us a chance to check out the system and run through the jump procedure. The balloon performed beautifully, and I ascended at a steady 1,000 feet per minute. I did have a couple of annoying issues to deal with, however. First, the glare of the sun was much more intense than I'd expected. Even with the tinted faceplate on my helmet, it was hard to read my gauges. Even worse, the faceplate itself was fogging up. A layer of electrically charged gold film imbedded in the clear plastic was supposed to take care of any condensation, but it wasn't working very well at all. The bottom line was that for parts of the ascent, I was basically flying blind.

In projects like this, you test all the equipment to death, and you still discover problems. We learned on Project Manhigh that a shake-down flight was likely to reveal things we'd never considered. In spite of all the "what if" sessions we held, these balloon flights were nevertheless highly experimental, and it was not too surprising when things went wrong.

The next challenge involved the helmet itself. The damn thing kept creeping upward. It was tugging on the nylon bladder that formed the pressure seal around my neck, as if it wanted to pop off. I had no idea what to do about it. I tried to push it back down, but it wouldn't stay in place. Luckily, one of my engineers had thought to attach some nylon cord from clasps on the helmet to my parachute harness so I wouldn't lose the helmet during the jump. I tried not to think about what would happen if the helmet came far enough up to break the pressure seal.

The good news was that by this point in the flight, the faceplate was clearing up, and I could see once more. The bad news was that by the time I could read the gauges again I'd already passed right through my planned jump altitude. My altimeter read 65,000 feet. I went through my checklist. As a test pilot, you learn never to rush anything. I radioed the ground that I was initiating the prejump procedure. I cut free my antenna, which ended any communication with my team. I disconnected myself from the electrical system on the gondola and switched over from onboard oxygen to the oxygen supply in my instrument kit. The kit, essentially a box strapped to my rear end (I was sitting on it during the ascent), contained oxygen bottles and a regulator, an eight-channel tape recorder, a 16-millimeter movie camera, and batteries to run them. It even had its own parachute so that I could detach it near the end of the jump. The thing weighed about 60 pounds, and I sure didn't want to land with it still attached. I weighed more than 320 pounds with all the gear I had on.

By the time I was ready to go, I was already beyond 70,000 feet. I grabbed the handles positioned on either side of the gondola's open door to pull myself up. That's when I discovered yet another problem. I was stuck in my seat. No matter how hard I pulled, I couldn't get up. The seat was basically a Styrofoam box with a cutout in the middle where my instrument kit fit. We wanted to keep the kit as warm as we could during the climb, so we'd inserted fifteen 1-pint water bottles in holes around the perimeter. Because the water would freeze as I ascended, and because water must release its heat as it freezes, we had the thermal equivalent of fifteen 100-watt light bulbs surrounding the kit. This rig is the kind of stuff engineers come up with when they don't have any budget. It was ingenious. We'd tried it out several times in the altitude chamber, and it had kept the kit from freezing.

But the Styrofoam box had gotten pretty banged up during all that testing. A couple of days before the test flight, one of my sergeants had decided the thing was just too ratty looking for the project's maiden flight. He knew we'd have some photographers around. So, without telling anybody, he made a new box for us. The problem was that he'd cut the new slot for my instrument kit just a shade smaller than the original box, and as the water bottles froze, they expanded. By the time I'd finished my checklist and tried to stand, I was trapped—squeezed into my seat.

I eventually was able to wrench myself free, but it was awkward, and it took a while. By this point, I was at 76,000 feet and still rising. I hit the button to start the onboard movie camera, unstrapped myself, and jumped.

I'd made the first test jump with the BMSP from a C-130 at 30,000 feet with a twenty-second free fall, so I had a pretty good idea of what the system felt like in operation. As I left the Excelsior gondola that morning, I knew right away that something was wrong. It was a very strange thing to be falling through the stratosphere. With the near absence of an atmosphere, there was no wind and no sensation of speed. I knew that the stabilization chute had not deployed properly and that I was free-falling just like the unstabilized dummies spinning violently in the films from Project High Dive.

Then, all at once, I began turning to the left. I was able to stop the turn by maneuvering my body position. Then I started a turn to the right and got that stopped, too. But then I started going left again, this time with a very rapid rate of onset. I couldn't govern my momentum. I was spinning out of control. This wasn't supposed to be happening. I had an altimeter on my wrist, but with the centrifugal force I couldn't pull my arm in close enough to get a look at it. A tremendously powerful beast had hold of me. I couldn't fight it. I was spinning at about 120 revolutions per minute at that moment.

I passed out.

The next thing I knew, I was dropping beneath my reserve chute about 3,000 feet above the desert floor. I didn't know what had happened. I was still in something of a daze when I hit the ground. It seemed almost miraculous that I was alive. We finally pieced the event together later that day when we looked at the data on the recorders in my instrument kit.

In my wiggling around to try and free myself from the Styrofoam seat, I had inadvertently activated the jump timer on the first stage of the parachute. The timer ran for thirteen and a half seconds before I left the gondola, which meant that the stabilization chute had popped free only two and a half seconds into the jump, before I'd acquired enough velocity to fill the canopy. The 5-foot chute flopped around for a few moments before curling around my neck. Not much later, I went into the flat spin that caused me to lose consciousness. The aneroid device triggered the release of the main chute at 17,000 feet, as designed. Unfortunately, because the stabilization chute was still wrapped around me, the main canopy fouled. I was still in free fall and still spinning.

If the jump had gone as scripted, after my main chute opened, I would have secured a strap on the reserve chute on my chest to keep it from opening automatically. The automatic reserve deployment was a precaution in case the jumper lost consciousness and the main chute had failed. Because I was unable to pull the override strap up and snap it, my reserve parachute opened at 10,000 feet. Now things became even messier. The little pilot chute popped out of the reserve pack, but instead of filling with air and pulling the reserve out cleanly, it tangled with the other chutes. This is where Francis Beaupre's true genius saved my life. We had actually discussed this precise situation in one of our what-if sessions, and Beau had cleverly substituted 100-pound lines (in place of the normal 1,000-pound variety) between the reserve pilot chute and the reserve canopy. When the reserve pilot chute fouled, the force of the drag snapped the lighter-weight line and allowed the reserve to deploy—which is how I survived a jump that had been governed from start to finish by Murphy's Law.

Our first live jump test from altitude had been a disaster, but I saw a silver lining. Even though we hadn't intended it, Excelsior had proved exactly why we needed a stabilization chute system. Without it, a pilot is likely to enter a flat spin and never come out of it. We had proved the need for precisely the kind of system we had designed. All we had to do now was make sure nothing interfered with the system's proper operation. We had some work to do.

We tried to tamp down publicity about the jump. The Air Force issued a press release claiming a new record for the highest manned parachute jump, but none of us on the team was very interested in that. We were especially concerned that word about the malfunction be kept quiet. We needed approval and continued funding if we were going to achieve our goals for Project Excelsior, and we knew some people out there were rooting for us to fail.

When I gave Col. Stapp my report, I told him that we knew exactly what had gone wrong and exactly what to do to fix it.

"Sir," I said, "I'd like to try the test flight again. Right away."

Of course, we had to go back in front of Gen. Schriever and the others in Baltimore in order to get approval.

"This test only justifies the research we're doing," I told them. "And by God, we just showed you what happens when a body falls from these altitudes without the proper parachute system."

Schriever looked at me as if he doubted my sanity.

"You really want to do it again, Captain?" he asked.

"Yes, sir," I said.

They made us wait in the hall for a little longer this time, but they eventually called us back in and gave us the green light. Once again they let Stapp know that he was on thin ice, and Stapp didn't have to tell me that I was out there on that ice with him. We could afford no more missteps.

I took the team back out to Truth or Consequences a month later, and we repeated the test flight. We had redesigned the timer-arming mechanism on the BMSP, and we'd done some work on the Styrofoam seat. We modified the heating mechanism on the helmet faceplate, made sure the helmet was firmly secured to my suit and parachute pack, and put in some cardboard visors and intensified the faceplate filter to cut down on the solar glare. This is what test flights were all about: discovering all the things you can't imagine during the "what if" sessions on the ground. I had absolutely no doubt that everything would work this time.

I was right. *Excelsior II* rose up to 74,400 feet without incident. I stood up, ran through the final items on my checklist, and jumped out. The multistage parachute system was flawless: pilot chute, stabilization chute, main chute—just as we'd designed it in the lab. I cut the instrument kit away and landed gently in the desert sand. No drama, no worries. We were ready to set our sights on the big jump from 100,000 feet. Although we were confident, we never underestimated the profound difference between 75,000 and 100,000 feet. I'd felt all along that if we'd had a major malfunction in our pressure suit, I could jump from 75,000 and have a fighting chance to get back into the atmosphere in time to avoid disaster. But from 100,000—literally on the edge of space—well, there was no room for error at that height. If any of our systems were to fail, I'd be dead. It was that simple. We had no choice but to get it right.

Over the following months, we conducted a new series of altitude chamber tests. If we'd had the budget, I would have scheduled even more. The National Geographic Society had been with us during the entire project, and after the second jump, the photographer, Kurt Wenzel, asked if I'd allow him to put one of his cameras in the gondola. The Leitz Company had recently built a 35-millimeter lubrication-free Leica camera for use in the Arctic that would operate at 100 degrees below zero. Once activated, it would run for thirty-six frames and stop. I was pretty impressed. I decided the project should buy one of the cameras for our own documentation purposes, so I made the request to the Air Force procurement people. They asked how much it would cost, and when I told them eight thousand dollars, of course they said hell no. So I gave Kurt permission to put his camera in our gondola. I wanted a high-quality photographic record.

We went through the approval process one final time. I briefed Stapp, and he made our case with Gen. Schriever at headquarters. Everything was right on schedule. The third Excelsior flight was planned for the summer of 1960. At that time of year, the winds would be blowing east to west rather than west to east, so we selected a spot outside the little ranch town of Tularosa, due north of Alamogordo, as our launch site. The balloon would drift out over the White Sands Proving Grounds and give us a nice fat landing target. The site even had a name on the Air Force maps: "50-Mile Impact Area."

I played a little tennis the afternoon before Excelsior's big day. I had a simple meal early in the evening and went to bed about eight that night. I didn't really sleep too well. Somebody always offered me sleeping pills in these situations, but I never took them. It seemed to me that you'd be bound to pay for it later. The great thing was that I didn't have to worry about any of the preparations. I knew my team was on top of everything and that all I had to do was be ready to go when the time came to launch.

Very early on the morning of August 16, 1960, hours before sunrise, with the crew and the equipment already on site, I drove out to the launch location with Ken Arnold and Francis Beaupre as we had done on the previous flights. Everybody in Tularosa was busy, the setting floodlit by banks of bright lights. Each member of the launch crew worked through his individual checklist, making sure nothing was neglected. It gave me tremendous confidence to see the men so focused and everything proceeding so smoothly. I had a veteran team by this point, and I knew they were going to give me a great flight.

One of the issues with a summer launch—a not inconsiderable concern in my mind—was the heat. Even at the early hour, it was hot in the desert. I suited up in all my gear—the long underwear and the socks and the gloves—in an air-conditioned trailer because it was critical that I avoid sweating: any perspiration trapped in my garments could turn to ice in the stratosphere. The whole time I was getting decked out, one of our survival system specialists stood there with a hose blowing cool air on me.

Once I was ready and I'd had my two hours of pure oxygen, the team sealed the helmet and helped me up into the gondola on the bed of the launch truck. Counting the Manhigh flight, this test would be my fourth high-altitude balloon launch, and I knew that it would be the most challenging mission by far. There was a tension in the air. We all felt it. Down at the base of the gondola, somebody had attached a little sign:

THIS IS THE HIGHEST STEP IN THE WORLD

What I was going to try to do was unprecedented. We'd prepared thoroughly; we knew our roles and our procedures. We had a professional operation. Still, this launch was different. All of us would be put to the test.

Ready for the highest step in the world. With all my gear, I weighed nearly 320 pounds. (Courtesy: United States Air Force.)

Balloon inflation begins. I watch and wait inside the Excelsior gondola. At this point in the mission, I'm the only member of the team who gets to sit down. (Courtesy: United States Air Force.)

What I didn't know as I sat there waiting for the launch signal was that Duke Gildenberg's weather forecast had started falling apart. Duke didn't miss very often, but this particular morning . . . he missed. Unexpected clouds had already begun to move in, which was a problem because we had several long-range cameras that were prepared to film me all the way to peak altitude and back down again. Because the polyethylene balloon had already been inflated and could not be reused, canceling the launch would have been a real blow to the project. Nevertheless, Duke raced up from Alamogordo with the intention of grounding us.

He arrived too late. We launched one minute early. I was gone before he could get to us.

The initial ascent went according to plan, *Excelsior III* rising 1,000 feet each minute. When I reached about 40,000 feet, and the partial-pressure suit had fully inflated, I ran through my checklist to make sure everything was working properly. My suit was my lifeline, and I checked every part of it: the neck seal, the pressure socks. I checked my hands and the pressure gloves. I flexed my fingers. That's when I discovered that the right pressure glove had not inflated. We'd tested it a hundred times on the ground—in fact, we'd inspected it just prior to launch—but it definitely was not working.

This was a very big deal. I was concerned and furious. If I radioed the ground that the glove had failed, the flight would be over. It was an easy call. They would order me to descend, and I would have no choice but to comply. To go to 100,000 feet with an unpressurized hand was usually not considered an option. We'd never tried it in the altitude chamber—for obvious reasons—but we knew enough to understand the consequences. Without pressure, the hand would balloon up. Best case: the hand would simply be useless for the rest of the flight and the jump. Worst case: Who knew? All I could think of was going back to Gen. Schriever, explaining this failure, and then arguing for the funding and approval to try it again. I could imagine the generals glaring at Col. Stapp. I believed that this shot might be our last.

I thought for a couple of minutes. I knew that my medical team was monitoring my respiration and my pulse. I wondered if they'd noticed any change. It was important to remain calm. I did have a very tight silk glove on the hand beneath the pressure glove. I thought there was a reasonable possibility that the silk would constrict the hand enough to hold the swelling in check. I just didn't see how I could give up on this flight. The whole team shared the sense that we were fighting the good fight, from Col. Stapp down to the guys running around below me in Tularosa. I was almost halfway up by this point. I decided to keep the pressure glove problem to myself. I knew I could function adequately with one hand. I could still make the jump. I wouldn't be jeopardizing the project. It was a calculated risk, and I judged it to be an acceptable one. Having made the call, I resolved not to give it another thought until I was back on the ground.

The voice of the project's chief medical officer, Dr. Marvin Feldstein, came over the radio. "Everybody's with you, Joe."

It was just before 7:00 a.m. when I reached the balloon's equilibrium at 102,800 feet. In order for me to exit directly over my landing target, Duke's calculations required that I float at peak altitude for eleven minutes before jumping. I saw that requirement as a blessing. It gave me some time to do what I hadn't gotten to do much of on any of my previous high-altitude flights: indulge in some sight-seeing, some reflection. Just a handful of human beings had ever been privileged to witness anything like this. I welcomed the chance to savor these few minutes.

I could see way down below the layer of clouds that had rolled in shortly after my launch. It was disappointing to know that my ground team with all their optical gear and multiple camera angles wouldn't be able to witness the jump and frustrating not to be able to get a visual on where I'd be landing. But the spectacle was breathtaking. I could see a thunderhead boiling up above Flagstaff, Arizona, 350 miles to the west. I could make out Guadalupe Pass in Texas to the east. It was almost like a painting. I can't really describe the feeling I had hanging there in that tiny gondola and seeing this magnificent planet set against the utter black backdrop of outer space. I suddenly had a powerful and unfamiliar sense of my own remoteness from everything I cherished in life.

I was never able to forget, even for a moment, even surrounded by the fantastic panorama, that the environment outside my pressure suit was a death zone. More than 99 percent of the atmosphere was below me. Stapp once told me to think of it as being enveloped in cyanide. You were essentially swimming in an invisible poison that would kill you in seconds. If the suit were cut open, there would be no contingency. You'd have less than ten seconds of useful consciousness. It didn't matter how smart you were, how well prepared you were, how tough you were. You were simply dead.

My ground crew asked me for some words. It took a few moments to figure out what I wanted to say, but here's what I told them: "Looking out over a very beautiful, beautiful world . . . a hostile sky. As you sit here, you realize that man will never conquer space. He will learn to live with it, but never conquer it." In spite of the confidence I felt in our program and in my own ability to execute the mission, I had a powerful sense of humility and solemn vulnerability as I looked out at a universe that seemed too vast, almost out of scale. I'm sure that every one of the NASA astronauts who saw such sights in the years to come felt the same way. You can't prepare yourself for it.

I tried to describe it all to my team.

"Looking up, the sky is absolutely *black*. Void of anything . . . I can see the beautiful blue of the sky, and above that it goes into a deep, deep, dark, indescribable blue, which no artist can ever duplicate." And then, running out of adjectives, I added, "It's fantastic."

As I neared the big moment, there was one sight that I found most incredible of all: the altimeter dial on my control panel. Almost 103,000 feet! Nothing gave me a greater sense of awe and humility than that six-digit number. Then something else caught my eye. A week earlier, back in Dayton, I'd been eating breakfast with my family, and my boy Mark—he was five years old at the time—had cut something off the back of a cereal box. It was an Oregon license plate, part of some promotion. He handed me this little piece of cardboard.

"Daddy, you need a license plate for your balloon."

I'd taped it to the inside of the gondola, and as I looked at it now, hovering 19 miles above the surface of planet Earth, I thought about my boys and wished I could talk to them and share the whole thing with them: what I was seeing, what I was about to do, why it was important. I missed them terribly in that moment.

The gondola rotated slowly, and each time it brought me face to face with the sun, I had to close my eyes to keep from being blinded by the intense solar glare.

My hand felt like a chunk of ice inside my glove. It had swollen to about twice its normal size, but there wasn't a thing I could do about it. I was glad when I finally received the OK to begin the prejump sequence.

I settled myself and got focused.

I ran through my checklist.

I unplugged the various monitoring systems connected to my suit and helmet and stood up—easily this time. I was eager to get on with it. Where I wanted to be was on the ground, and there was only one way to get there.

Dr. Feldstein was giving us a countdown over the radio. When he reached ninety seconds, I interrupted him.

"For your information, Marv, my right hand is not pressurized."

I didn't want to cause any unnecessary anxiety or stress, but I wanted the team to have the information in case something went wrong. Marv immediately started asking me questions, but I barely heard them. I wasn't interested in talking about my hand.

"I'm OK," I told Marv. "No sweat."

I cut loose the 200-foot antenna—we didn't want it dangling below the gondola as I jumped—and severed my final connection with the ground. I was very much a man alone now. Telemetry would show that my pulse was up to 136 beats per minute. I took my last breath at Jump Minus eighteen seconds.

I was supposed to pull a lanyard just before leaving the gondola to trip the timer mechanism on the BMSP, but my right hand was useless, and I couldn't reach it with my left. This really wasn't a problem because the lanyard was attached to the gondola, and I knew it would pull itself as I fell. I grabbed the sides of the door, inched the toes of my boots over the edge, and glanced up at the black heavens.

"Lord, take care of me now," I said.

I hit the switch to start Kurt Wenzel's Leica and Ken Arnold's five downward-angled 16-millimeter cameras . . . and plunged forward.

Accelerating, I gained 22 miles per hour of speed each second. I managed to roll myself into position to look back up at the balloon, brilliant white as it caught the sun against the blackness, and see it speeding away from me, the circle of light closing like a lens. I wanted to view the stars, but all I could see were the blackness and the emptiness. I realized in a flash that the sunlight reflecting off the huge ball of plastic had blinded me.

I free-fell for sixteen seconds before I felt a soft shudder on my back and the pilot chute popped out, followed by the 5-foot stabilization chute, right on cue.

I began to breathe again.

"*Chute opened*," I said for the benefit of the tape recorder in my instrument kit. I wanted a record—real time, first person.

Every time I started to turn a bit one way or the other, I was able to arrest the spin immediately by extending my foot as a rudder. The stabilization chute was doing its job. It was the ride of a lifetime. I had absolutely perfect control.

"*Multistage working perfectly!*"

At 90,000 feet, I was traveling well in excess of 600 miles per hour—about the speed of Stapp's final rocket-sled run—approaching the speed of sound. At terminal velocity—this is something that's often misunderstood—whether you're in the low-density environment of the stratosphere and falling at the speed of a bullet or in thick, near-Earth atmosphere at 186 feet per second (about 120 miles per hour), the dynamic force on your body is equivalent. It's known as the Q force. From my perspective, the force against my body felt about like a routine free fall even though for all intents and purposes I was supersonic.

I couldn't relax. I was continually reading off my altitude and trying to document the behavior of the parachute and the pressure suit. I wished Beau could be alongside me to see his system working with his own eyes. It was a beautiful thing.

Then something unexpected happened. It came on without warning. I began to experience a tightening against my throat, almost as if I were being choked. The pressure wasn't bad at first, but it intensified rapidly.

"Can't get my breath . . ."

I tried to wait it out, but it just got worse. I was starting to get lightheaded. It was a maddeningly helpless feeling. I had to bear down and concentrate to keep from passing out.

"Can't get my . . . breath."

What was happening? *Why* was it happening?

I fought it for as long as I could. I imagined fingers digging into my windpipe. I had no idea how to fight it.

Then, as suddenly as the pressure had begun, it relaxed, and I could breathe almost normally. I tried to put the incident out of my mind and focus on the mission. I still had a very long way to go.

"Seventy thousand."

I'd been falling for more than a minute.

"Perfect stability."

I was starting to feel in control once again.

The moment of truth at 102,800 feet. As I pitch forward and leap from *Excelsior III*, a cord pulls the timer on my stabilization chute. Kurt Wenzel's Leica, designed to operate in Arctic conditions, captures the scene for *National Geographic*. In just a few seconds, I will be flirting with the speed of sound. (Courtesy: National Geographic Society.)

The first spacewalk. I would fall for nearly fourteen minutes—four minutes and thirty-six seconds of which were in virtual free fall. (Courtesy: National Geographic Society.)

"Minute and thirty-five seconds."
I was going to make it.
"Sixty thousand!"
It was 94 degrees below zero, but I was—with the exception of my right hand—relatively comfortable inside the partial-pressure suit and all my undergarments.
"Beautiful stability!"

As I fell through 50,000 feet and back into the troposphere, I began to be aware of the increase in the density of the atmosphere and could feel myself slowing down. I was now traveling *only* 250 miles per hour. The sensation was wonderfully welcome. I was beginning to get some fogging in my helmet faceplate, but it didn't worry me too much at this point. I could feel the constriction of my pressure suit beginning to subside.

"Awful bright. Thirty thousand. Three minutes and thirty seconds."

The sun was still brilliantly intense, reflecting off the tops of the clouds.

"Four minutes."

All I had to do was make it through the clouds, and I would be home free.

"We're going into the overcast."

The tops of the clouds were right at 20,000 feet.

"Into the overcast!"

I'd never fallen through thick clouds before, and I found myself pulling up my knees reflexively as I went into them. It went momentarily dark.

We had calculated that the aneroid would open the main canopy at about 17,000 feet—four minutes and thirty-seven seconds into the jump. I had my left hand on the D-ring and was ready to release the main if I needed to, but it deployed at 4:36, one second early.

"The main chute opened! Right on the button!" I was through the clouds and into the light. Jubilation began to overcome me as the ground came rushing up.

"Ahhh, boy! Lord, thank you for protecting me during that long fall."

The only damper on the whole thing is that I wasn't able to cut the instrument kit away with my bad hand and had to land with it. It made for a pretty rugged crash landing. Thirteen minutes and forty-five seconds after leaving the gondola 19 miles in the sky, I had stopped moving. I was back on Earth. I was alive. We'd done it. After a year and a half of preparation, we'd actually pulled it off. Mission accomplished.

My crew landed in a helicopter about 100 feet away, and several of them came running up as if they couldn't believe it, huge smiles on their faces. As they huddled around me, Dr. Richard Chubb got to work on my hand. The blood pressure in my right arm was very low. The hand was chalky white, but it improved steadily. After a few hours passed, I was as good as new.

We piled in the chopper and flew back to Holloman. We had just landed, and I'd done an impromptu press conference with the small group of reporters who'd shown up when an Air Force public-relations guy came hustling up.

"Captain, you're wanted in Los Angeles for a live interview with Walter Cronkite. We need you to get there as fast as you can." We didn't have to keep anything quiet any longer. The Air Force wanted publicity now that we'd managed to avoid disaster.

I got out of my uniform and put on a flight suit, then jumped in a T-33 and flew nonstop to Los Angeles International Airport. I did a live remote right there on the ramp at LAX, with Cronkite in the CBS studio in New York, for the East Coast six o'clock news. Then I boarded the airplane and returned to Holloman. I had a rendezvous scheduled with my crew, and I didn't want to miss a minute of it. We headed straight to the bar and held our debrief session. It lasted about five hours, and

Dr. Chubb attends to my right hand. If I'd informed my ground crew about the failed pressure glove, they would have ordered me to abort the flight. I made a calculated decision to assume the risk. (Courtesy: National Geographic Society.)

I think everyone who was there that night would agree that it was one of the wildest debriefs in history. We were beyond elated. Not only had we done something not many people thought we could pull off, but we'd made an important contribution to the future of aviation. We'd proven that it was possible to survive escape from an aircraft or spacecraft from extreme altitudes. It was a very proud moment for all of us associated with Project Excelsior.

The only real mysteries were the pressure glove and the choking sensation I'd experienced in free fall. The first one was easy: a postflight inspection revealed that the glove's inflation tube had cracked wide open. The choking was trickier. The next day George Post ran a "hang test," suspending himself in the suit from an overhead hook to try and duplicate the problem. We discovered that a steel cable securing the helmet to the pressure suit was riding up and forcing the helmet against his throat. We weren't entirely sure we had it figured out, but it was the best explanation we could come up with.

Not only did *Excelsior III* set the mark for the highest manned balloon flight, but nobody had ever been outside of a pressurized cabin at anything approaching 100,000 feet. We'd shown NASA that a space walk was possible. We'd demonstrated to all our military aircrews that the MC-3 partial-pressure suit was effective in conditions beyond anything most of them would ever experience. My top speed in free fall was measured at 614 miles per hour, on the verge of Mach 1. And we'd done it all for a fraction of what rocket travel was going to cost the nation in the future.

Although I'd set an unofficial record for the longest and highest parachute jump and the longest free fall in history—I free-fell for a total of four minutes and thirty-six seconds—the international aviation commission, the Fédération Aéronautique Internationale (FAI), never recognized it. That was just fine with me. Because Excelsior was an emergency escape program, setting records was never our mission. I had refused to give the FAI permission to install their measurement and recording equipment in the gondola or to pay one of their onsite observers. I didn't believe the American taxpayers ought to be asked to foot the bill so that we could establish a world record. Besides, the Air Force's instrumentation was an order of magnitude more accurate than anything the FAI would have used. The whole procedure seemed silly to me.

About a year after the flight of *Excelsior III* in 1960, Russian Army major Yevgeny Andreyev jumped from a two-man balloon at 83,500 feet—with an FAI barograph aboard—and became the official world-record holder. Although the Soviets covered it up, Col. Peter Dolgov, the other jumper on that flight, died from decompression when the faceplate on his helmet failed at altitude. Of course, we didn't learn about this incident until many years later. Their entire objective had been to capture the altitude record. Both of the Russians were veteran skydivers with thousands of jumps to their credit. In contrast, my jump from *Excelsior III* was only my thirty-third parachute jump. For us, the whole business had been about saving lives—period. I honestly didn't give a damn about the record.

They did finally put me in the *Guinness World Book of Records* for the highest parachute jump, and every year since 1960 I've been approached by someone who announces that he (or she) intends to break my record. Most of these people are just glory seekers or daredevils, but there have been a few serious projects. Skydiver and adventurer Nicholas Piantanida was fatally injured in an attempt to set a new free-fall record in 1966. He invited me to join his project, but his cavalier attitude worried me, and I stayed away. I have seen a long parade of others since then. My free-fall mark, unofficial though it may be, has stood for fifty years. Some say the record will never be broken. I don't believe that, but I do know this: if it was easy, somebody would have done it by now.

In my estimation, Project Excelsior's biggest contribution to aviation and aeronautics was the stabilization chute on the BMSP. We had figured out how to counteract the forces of flat spin, but we'd done it in a way that didn't significantly retard a jumper's descent. That was fundamentally important. At the higher altitudes at which our crews were going to be operating, an ejecting pilot's primary goal would always be to get down into warm, breathable air as quickly as possible. We'd built and tested a system that stopped a body's tendency to spin even as it travels at mind-boggling speeds. Our system is still being used today. Every ejection seat system in the world uses the 5-foot diameter stabilization chute that we developed and tested.

In January 1966, Bill Weaver and Jim Zwayer, Lockheed test pilots, lost control of their SR-71A at 80,000 feet. They had reached an airspeed of Mach 3.1 when the aircraft began to break up. Zwayer did not survive, but Weaver, who blacked out, was somehow separated from the aircraft, which still had the ejection seat inside the cockpit. Weaver regained consciousness during his descent and landed safely beneath his multistage parachute. He later credited the stabilization chute for saving his life by preventing his body from spinning and tumbling while he'd been incapacitated. It was precisely this scenario—emergency escape at extreme altitudes—that had obsessed the Excelsior team from the beginning. We all were gratified to see our work pay off this way.

I received most of the glory for Project Excelsior's achievements, but the truth is that the whole endeavor was the end product of Col. Stapp's vision and courage. Without his confidence in my ability to perform and without his willingness to bet his career on the project, we'd never have gotten the chance to attempt it. Without Stapp, there'd have been no Excelsior.

Life magazine put me on the cover, and *National Geographic* gave me a spread. I went on *The Ed Sullivan Show* and *What's My Line?* and *I've Got a Secret.* I was awarded the Harmon Trophy in a White House ceremony with President Eisenhower. The Air Force hooked me up with aviation writer Martin Caidin, and we produced a book about the project, titled *The Long, Lonely Leap.* It was an exciting time. It was especially meaningful that a number of the Mercury astronauts—most of them friends of mine—made public statements about the value of our program. Gordon Cooper told the press that what we'd done was "absolutely vital." I thought it was important that our work be seen as having contributed to America's race to the moon. My favorite comment came from Alan Shepard. A reporter asked him if he'd have attempted the jump from 103,000 feet. "Hell no!" he answered. I always liked that.

Whenever I got the chance and somebody would listen to me, I'd make sure to tell them about Col. Stapp. He would never seek any personal credit for these projects, so I considered it my job to ensure he was recognized. If something had gone wrong and I'd been killed, they would have buried me, but they would have hounded Stapp forever.

We had intended to keep going and send up *Excelsior IV.* We'd already done a fair amount of planning, and there was a sense of momentum among the team. There was more we wanted to learn, new equipment and techniques we wanted to test. George Post was going to be aboard for that flight. But not even Col. Stapp could get approval for another

The Harmon Trophy. With President Eisenhower in the White House. The other trophy recipient that year, Capt. Joe Jordan (to Ike's right), had set his own altitude record in an F-104: 103,395 feet. The tall man, second from left, is Gen. Bernard Schriever of the Air Force Systems Command.

balloon and another launch. I guess Gen. Schriever felt that we'd pushed our luck far enough. He refused us the funds to continue. I felt bad for George. He really wanted a shot, and there's no question he would have performed marvelously. By this point, preparations for Project Mercury were going full bore at NASA, and people were beginning to turn their noses up at the idea of manned balloon flight.

After the project was canceled, I received a call from the Smithsonian Institution in Washington asking if they could have the gondola for their museum. I told them it didn't belong to me, that they'd have to make their request to the Air Force. It turned out that plans had already been made to exhibit it at an Air Force Association convention in California that September. The Smithsonian was told it could take possession after that. We cleaned and painted the gondola and then loaded it onto a C-123 for transport to San Francisco. The plane laid over in Denver that night and left the next morning. Flying over a remote stretch of Colorado, it crashed, killing everyone onboard. The gondola was recovered from

```
PTNVL 657 NO 21  ROBERTSON MO 17  AUG 60

                                            1960 AUG 17  16  39
         KITTINGER
  CAPT. JOE JITTINGER, USAF

  WADD

  WRIGHT-PATTERSON AFB

  DAYTON OHIO                                    LB.      RLB

                                              WWRD

  GOOD SHOW, JOE, THE NEWS OF YOUR CONTINUED           AUG 17    12:54

  PENETRATIONS OF THE SPACE ENVIRONMENT ARE

  MOST ENCOURAGEING.


  GOOD LUCK AND BEST PERSONAL REGARDS


  /SIGNED/  CARPENTER, COOPER, GLENN, GRISSOM, SCHIRRA, SHEPARD, SLAYTON


  PROJECT MERCURY


  SENT ONE   1136A CDT PLS ACKN
```

Kudos from Project Mercury. NASA, as an organization, was always reluctant to acknowledge the contributions that the military high-altitude projects made to the U.S. space program, but the pilots who formed the original astronaut team always let us know how much they appreciated our work.

the crash site and brought back to Wright, but it was pretty banged up, so we spruced it up as best we could and repainted it. We had it in a warehouse, awaiting transport to Washington, when the building burned down. I guess we'd exhausted all the gondola's good luck on the project. The Smithsonian never received its exhibit.

Many years later the Air Force pulled out the diagrams and specs for the Excelsior gondola and quietly rebuilt it from scratch. It hangs in the Air Force museum in Dayton today, but what you see there is not the actual gondola that took me to 102,800 feet—it's a replica. The Air Force has never owned up to the true story of the Excelsior gondola, but I guess now the cat's out of the bag.

It was during the middle phase of Project Excelsior that NASA's Project Mercury was ramping up, and I had serious thoughts about volunteering. After all, I was one of the few people who'd actually been up there. I went to Col. Stapp and asked for his thoughts on the matter. As always, he was honest. He said that in his opinion I would certainly qualify for Mercury and had an excellent chance of making the cut, but he also told me he didn't want to lose me on Excelsior, that my leaving would set the program back a year or so. I thought it over. Not only did I owe Stapp more than I could ever repay, but I was making real contributions right where I was. I decided to stick with the Aero Med Lab and push ahead with the emergency escape work. I never regretted that decision.

Project Excelsior wasn't the only thing I'd been working on in Dayton. I still had the original High Dive gondola: a two-passenger, pressurized vehicle. It was spacious and beautifully designed, and it was just gathering dust. One day I received a phone call from a guy named George Nielson at the Smithsonian Astrophysical Observatory in Cambridge, Massachusetts. He'd heard about the gondola, and he wondered whether it would be possible to take a telescope up with a balloon. I was immediately curious, so I flew to Boston the next week to discuss it with him. His idea was to raise an astronomer up high enough to get above the haze and turbulence of our atmosphere in order to conduct some real cutting-edge celestial observation.

I took the idea to Stapp the next day.

"I need you to answer one question for me, Joe," he said after thinking it over for a minute or so. I could tell he was intrigued. "What will the Aero Med Lab get out of this?"

"Well, sir," I told him, "we could do a lot of basic science that would really be phenomenal. For the first time in history, we'd be able to look at the stars and planets from beyond the atmosphere. No scintillation, no haze. Just imagine, sir."

He stared at me.

"So the Aero Med Lab wouldn't really get much out of it, right?"

"No, sir," I admitted. "It wouldn't. Not directly. But we would be using a different approach on the life-support systems and incorporating a new pressure suit and helmet."

"Well, I'll tell you, Joe," he said, sighing a little. "I think we ought to do it. Go ahead and put it together."

Nobody else in his position would have done it, but Stapp could see that this project was going to supply some needed research and be great for space engineering. He didn't hesitate.

We founded Project Stargazer in 1958. There were lots of tough problems right from the beginning. The biggest challenges were the gyro-stabilization system and the star tracker. The telescope would be positioned on top of the gondola, so we needed complete stability. But because men would be moving around inside the gondola, it wasn't exactly going to sit still. It was a puzzle. I discussed it with Dr. Alan Hynek, who was the director of the Smithsonian Astrophysical Observatory, and the chief scientist for Project Stargazer took me to see Dr. C. S. Draper, who was chief of the MIT Instrumentation Laboratory. Draper was an absolute genius. He invented the autopilot and later did the guidance systems for Project Apollo. After we briefed Draper, he introduced us to a twenty-six-year-old engineer, Dr. Winston Markey, and agreed to lend him to us for Stargazer, so we had the best minds in the country working with us right from the start.

We had talent, but we had little money and limited options when it came to hardware. We had to get our balloons from the Air Force Cambridge Research Laboratory, which really set us back. These folks were *not* Winzen Research. I gave them requirements for a balloon that could lift a four-ton payload to 90,000 feet, which was pushing the state of the art pretty hard. They made us five balloons to test, and every one of them blew up. It took them almost four years to get an envelope that would hold together. It was extremely frustrating.

Our centerpiece instrument was a 12.5-inch Cassegrain telescope built to our specifications. We found an astronomer who was working for the Navy civil service, Bill White, to design and carry out the science agenda. We were lucky to get him, not only because he was a real pro at what he did, but because he turned out to be a joy to work with. That makes a difference on these kinds of projects. The plan was for the two of us to ascend together. I'd fly the balloon and handle all the communications, and Bill would look at the sky and record everything.

By the time we finally got the whole package ready to fly, it was December 1962. (NASA had nearly completed Project Mercury by then. John Glenn and Walter Schirra had already orbited Earth.) We launched from Holloman and reached a peak altitude of 87,000 feet. We stayed up there eighteen hours. In spite of all the hassles we'd had with the program, the mission went off almost flawlessly. We experienced a few minor technical glitches, but Bill was able to work through his entire agenda. He got to see the cosmos with a clarity that astronomers had only dreamed of. We were pretty cold the entire flight, but I'm not sure Bill ever noticed. He was like a kid on his first camping trip.

One astronomer referred to Stargazer as "the greatest breakthrough . . . since Galileo." That might have been a little over the top, but our project made some real contributions. It prefigured NASA's Hubble Telescope by decades. We immediately began putting the finishing touches on plans for a follow-up flight, but we had a new problem to deal with. Stapp had been transferred again, and I was now on my own at Wright. My support and cooperation began to dwindle almost immediately. Bill and I did manage to get back out to Holloman for another flight a month later, but moments before launch an electrical charge that allowed us to separate the balloon from the cargo parachute detonated prematurely, and our balloon went sailing off into space without us. We had to scrap the mission. It was maddening. And embarrassing.

I called my friend John Glenn at NASA. I needed some high-profile organizational muscle if we were going to get the right people

Project Stargazer. Bill White and I after the completion of our landmark astronomy flight. Few people remember it, but our project was a precursor to NASA's Hubble Telescope mission. (Courtesy: United States Air Force.)

and systems in place to make another flight. I told Glenn the whole story. He sympathized and said the one thing the Mercury astronauts had worried about was the inadvertent firing of some minor piece of equipment while they were in space.

"Joe," he said, "I'll give you access to any of the NASA engineers you want to help you fix your problem. Just say the word."

I went straight to the Air Force Cambridge Research Lab and told them their termination system had nearly killed my project. I was steamed, and I let them know it. I threatened to take our entire program to NASA, which got their attention, although the truth was I really had no other option. The chief engineer took responsibility for what had happened and guaranteed to deliver a solution.

A couple of months later, with a redesigned system and a new balloon, Bill and I were back in the gondola at Holloman ready for our return trip to the stratosphere. We had a full slate of observations and experiments, and we were chomping at the bit to get Stargazer off the ground once again. Then a couple of minutes before we were to be released, BAM! A damn squib fires, and there goes our balloon. Twice in a row! I won't try to describe my emotions as we climbed out of the capsule that morning.

I needed Stapp, but he could no longer help me. When I returned to Dayton, I was notified that the project had been killed. The news was hardly a surprise. There was no funding to continue the program, and it was pretty clear that NASA had a lock on space research dollars and personnel at that point. Project Stargazer was finished, as was—it turned out—manned scientific ballooning beyond Earth's atmosphere. There would never be another military or science-oriented, lighter-than-air flight into the upper stratosphere with a man aboard. We could almost feel the ground shifting beneath us. An era had ended. From now on, we'd be doing our space research in rockets. NASA had the budgets, the glamour, and the political clout.

My life was about to take another fateful turn.

5
Combat

✳   ✳   ✳   ✳   ✳   ✳

My first operations officer for Project Stargazer had been Capt. Jerry Carlisle, formerly an experimental test pilot and a graduate of the Test Pilots School at Edwards AFB. Early in 1962 he came to me and said that he had an opportunity to be assigned to a secret project. He was obviously pretty excited about it. I hated to lose him on Stargazer, but I wasn't going to stand in his way, so off he went. I had no idea where he was headed. A few months later he returned to Wright-Patterson, flying a T-28 with guns. He couldn't tell me where he was stationed, only that it was classified. I started right away trying to figure it out and pretty quickly determined that he'd been assigned to the Air Commandos at Hurlburt Field near Fort Walton Beach in Florida. Needless to say, I was intrigued.

After the aborted attempts to get Stargazer back up, and with Col. Stapp out of the picture, there were plenty of folks in Dayton after my butt, so the natural thing for me was to return to my roots. I was a fighter pilot, and I wanted to get back in the cockpit. I'd still never flown in combat and decided that I wanted that experience; I felt that I owed it to the United States Air Force. I went to the personnel office and asked how to volunteer for the Air Commandos. I filled out some paperwork, filed it, and got an approval back a few days later. I was instructed to report to Gen. Schriever. In his office, I explained my situation. Schriever was skeptical but wished me well. "When you get through with this fling," he told me, "let me know, and we'll get you back in the Systems Command."

When I arrived at Hurlburt the following March, I immediately volunteered for duty in South Vietnam and signed up to fly the T-28. After all, I had plenty of experience in single-engine fighters. It seemed a no-brainer, so I was disappointed when I was given the assignment to fly the B-26, but it made some sense because I'd flown B-26s at Holloman. Checking out again in that airplane and going through combat training at Hurlburt turned out to be a complete blast. Next we went to the gunnery ranges and started delivering ordnance and shooting guns day and night. It had been ten years since my last gunnery training in Europe, but I felt that I was back in my element. One of the biggest thrills was the low-level navigation training. Right on the deck at 200 miles per hour! It was as far from balloon flight as you could get, and it really made me appreciate the navigators who flew with us. They were pros and never showed the slightest concern no matter how low we flew on the cross-countries or how hard we pressed the targets on the gunnery ranges. Navigation training in a strike aircraft was a real opportunity for those guys who might otherwise have been looking at comparatively unchallenging duty on a C-130—or, even worse, a Strategic Air Command bomber.

The original Air Commandos (1st Air Commando Group) were a collection of Army aviators who had served in Southeast Asia during World War II. They had provided air support for the British campaign in Burma. President Kennedy reformed the group in April 1961 at Gen. Curtis LeMay's suggestion. It was the first United States Air Force unit to concentrate on counterinsurgency tactics and to train specifically for combat in Third World countries. It was a unique organization: the only all-volunteer unit in the Air Force. I have to say that my time in the Air Commandos ruined me for the rest of my Air Force career because having experienced true teamwork with no "union rules" made it difficult to go back to the status quo. I would never again be able to get used to the regular Air Force with its "stan eval" and checklists ad nauseam. Our morale was off the charts. Ditto our patriotism. By God, we were proud to be Americans, proud to be in the United States Air Force, and damn proud to be in the Air Commandos. But what really distinguished the Air Commandos at Hurlburt was the caliber of the men. We worked hard, we trained hard, we fought hard, and we played hard. Everything in that outfit was 100 percent, 100 percent of the time. (I have genuine sympathy for the current Air Force officer—no stag bars, and everybody worrying about that extra drink affecting performance ratings. I can't imagine that it's much fun anymore.)

At Hurlburt, we studied the principles of guerilla warfare, counterinsurgency, and the history of Vietnam. It was fascinating stuff. Some of the detachment was headed to Central America, and those guys studied Spanish. The rest of us were headed to Vietnam, so we studied French. Except for me. By the time I got there, the French classes were already full, so they stuck me in a Spanish class. *Hola, Señor Charlie!*

The U.S. mission in Southeast Asia was a noble effort—at least initially. The objective, to help a small country repel Communist invasion, was one we all believed in. I personally couldn't wait.

I said good-bye to my family—an emotional time for all of us because my sons were old enough to understand that I wouldn't be back for many months—and departed for Bien Hoa in September 1963. The landing at the main Saigon airport was an eye-opener. The scene was right out of a John Wayne movie. When we came off our C-141, aircraft were buzzing all over the place: helicopters, H-21s and Hueys, T-28s, C-47s, RB-26, airliners. Everybody walking around the ramp carried either a rifle or a pistol, and they all were decked out in fatigues or some sort of camouflage. The flight line was a furious hive of activity. I found my way to base operations and arranged for transport to Bien Hoa in the back end of a U.S. Army truck.

My check-in at the Bien Hoa Air Base opened my eyes a little wider. This place was a bare-bones facility—absolutely no frills. It was located in a rural area some 30 kilometers north of Saigon. We lived in hutches, each of which housed eight to ten pilots and navigators. These structures had concrete floors but no real walls. The bathing and toilet area was in a little building about 50 yards away. Three hanging lights illuminated the hutch. We kept our personal effects in footlockers. There was a one-room officers' club, no fancier than the hutches, where we could get a hamburger and visit the bar. We had an open-air theater that showed movies each evening and served as a chapel on Sunday.

I was made operations officer upon my arrival, and because the commanding officer spent most of his evenings and weekends in Saigon, I became the de facto commander of the B-26s. We flew several types of missions with that airplane, our orders usually coming from 7th Air Force in Saigon. Before we went into action, we had to receive a fragmentary order, or FRAG—a teletyped air-operations order specifying the type of aircraft, takeoff time, communications frequencies, ordnance load, Forward Air Controller (FAC) call sign if appropriate, and information relating to the mission itself. The FRAGs we received might indicate supplying direct support for an Army operation, working with FACs on suspected targets, providing helicopter escort, or—in the case of C-123s—spraying Agent Orange. We flew approximately three-quarters of our missions in daylight. The ordnance varied according to mission. We typically carried four cans of napalm along with a full load of .50-caliber ammo and twelve 110-pound fragmentation bombs in the bomb bay. On certain occasions, we carried four 500-pound bombs.

Our night missions were part of what was called the Strategic Hamlet Program. After sunset, the South Vietnamese would secure their hamlets; anyone still moving around outside was presumed to be Viet Cong (VC). If the village came under attack, the villagers would call—on radios provided by the United States Army—for help from our fighter aircraft and lay out burning oil pots arranged to form an arrow pointing

at the enemy position. We would then drop napalm cans or fire our machine guns at those locations. These missions seemed to be very effective. The locals were certainly appreciative of what we were trying to do.

One of our worst days during my tour came on a Thursday in the spring of 1964. Black Thursday.

Bien Hoa, South Vietnam. The Douglas B-26 was the first airplane I flew in combat. It had seen limited action toward the end of World War II but had been a workhorse in Korea. Unfortunately, it wasn't very well suited to its role in Vietnam. (Courtesy: United States Air Force.)

Two of our best B-26 pilots and several helicopters were shot down over the Mekong Delta on a close air-support mission. The entire base wanted revenge, and we put a lot of aircraft in the air in the sad days following that incident. During one of these retaliation flights, I was hit in the left leg by a bullet while I was making a strafing pass. The bullet didn't do much damage—the thick checklists in my leg pocket absorbed most of the force—but I bled just enough to be awarded a Purple Heart.

Not long after my arrival in Vietnam, I got pretty close with the commander of the U.S. Army helicopter detachment, Maj. Al Hayes. His unit was also stationed at Bien Hoa, and we frequently crossed paths in the officers' club at dinnertime, where we would discuss tactics. Not long after I arrived there, Hayes told me he'd lost a chopper to ground fire on a recent air-infiltration mission. I suggested that in the future we ought to use B-26s to escort the choppers. He agreed, and a few days later he called me about an upcoming mission. I met Hayes on the flight line the day before, and we flew an Army L-19 over the landing zone at about 5,000 feet. We didn't loiter over the area because we wanted to avoid giving away our interest in that particular terrain. We made one more pass before returning to base to discuss tactics for the next day's mission.

In the meantime, Hayes made a request through channels that his choppers receive a B-26 escort. When the FRAG came through that evening, I put my name on the mission. The plan was for me to arrive at the landing zone fifteen minutes prior to his arrival with ten choppers—all filled with South Vietnamese Army personnel. In accordance with the tactics Hayes and I had developed, I dropped my napalm on the north side of the village and made repeated gun passes on the surrounding area. Our theory was that if enemy forces were stationed nearby, they would be drawn to the landing zone. Hayes and his men then landed south of the village, off-loaded the troops, and got out with no hits. If they had encountered resistance, I still had a full load of bombs along with my guns. The whole operation went off without a hitch, and Hayes was elated. From then on, B-26s escorted the helicopters, typically doing some aerial reconnaissance the day before.

On some occasions, the FRAGs would specify the Viet Nam Air Force (VNAF) A1-Es and Gs instead of my B-26s. Hayes hated that because he could never get a face-to-face briefing with the VNAF pilots prior to the mission and didn't trust them to support his troops aggressively.

One day I received a summons to report to the director at 7th Air Force headquarters. It was my impression that this gentleman hadn't been out of Saigon much; he certainly knew very little about our operation in Bien Hoa. He was not very friendly from the outset. He told me that they were getting too many requests from the Army for B-26 support, and he didn't like it. I explained that since both Hayes and I were located at Bien Hoa, we could closely coordinate on these dangerous missions. I also explained that the B-26 had a big advantage because it could carry such a large and diversified ordnance load and had the capability to stay on station for four hours. The centerpiece of my argument was that the Army choppers had received zero battle damage when escorted by our B-26s. We had a perfect record. How could you argue with that?

This guy looked at me for a long moment and sniffed.

"You don't understand, do you, Kittinger?" I guess he felt as if he had to put me in my place. "We here at the 7th Air Force determine how we're going to provide air power to the Army."

I replied that although I had no authority over who the Army requested for their missions, if they were asking for B-26s, then we must have been doing a good job for them. I took a chance and offered him an opportunity to observe a briefing and a seat in a B-26 cockpit on an actual mission. It didn't surprise me that he never showed up. Most of the headquarters weenies wanted no part of actual combat. They preferred the comfort and safety of an office chair in Saigon. The only real problem with Army and Air Force cooperation in Vietnam was located right there at the headquarters level. When given the opportunity, Army and Air Force units worked extremely well together. There was rarely any friction.

At the time I arrived in country, Brig. Gen. "Buck" Anthis was in charge of all U.S. air operations in Vietnam and Thailand. In my opinion, this guy was a real joke and, frankly, a discredit to the Air Force. (Gen. Paul Harkins, the Army commander, wasn't much better.) Gen. Joe Moore later replaced Anthis; Moore was a breath of fresh air, and it was a huge relief to all of us when he arrived and took command of the skies. Gen. William Westmoreland took the Army command at about the same time. These two had absolutely no problems with regard to roles and missions, and they changed the whole complexion of our military involvement in Vietnam.

Westmoreland and Moore knew who the enemy was, and it sure wasn't another branch of our own service.

Maj. Hayes at Bien Hoa was a very good commander. Working together, the two of us made some real breakthroughs with the problem of how to provide close air support for a helicopter infiltration. But it wasn't all business between us. On plenty of occasions, I got to fly with him in the Huey. He gave me a little instruction, and pretty soon he was allowing me to take off and land in the chopper.

One day we had a mission briefing scheduled in Saigon for Hayes, me, and four of my pilots. Since none of my men knew about my chopper practice, and they all were quite aware that I wasn't qualified to fly one, Hayes and I cooked up a little fun. When everybody was assembled, Hayes turned to me and said, "Joe, would you like to try flying us to Saigon in the chopper?" I hesitated and then said, "Aw, what the hell? I've never flown one of these things before, but it can't be too damn difficult if you Army guys can do it." I climbed into the pilot seat on the right side, fumbled around a little, and started the engine. Hayes went through the pretakeoff checklist and indicated the chopper was mine. Without hesitation, I took off. Only once did I glance back to see the pure terror in my pilots' eyes. I made a perfect landing at Tan Son Nhut Air Base and just got out and walked away. Neither Hayes nor I ever said another word about it.

I flew every chance I got while I was in Vietnam, and because I felt personally responsible for the readiness of the B-26s—it was a difficult airplane to maintain; we had to change spark plugs after every mission—I was reluctant to take the overnights in Saigon that most of the officers allowed themselves. After I'd been at Bien Hoa for five months, the commander called me in and ordered me to take a few days off. Rather than head to one of the typical recreation spots such as Bangkok or Sydney or Hong Kong, I decided this time off would be a great opportunity for a different kind of adventure. I'd always wanted to participate in a ground operation. We flew support missions for our soldiers and for the South Vietnamese Army all the time, and I wanted to get a taste of what their lives were like, so I made some inquiries and arranged to accompany a South Vietnamese Army mission that was scheduled to last five to seven days.

I had brought a folding-stock .30-caliber carbine with me from Florida, and I always had it with me in my B-26. I had two banana clips installed and a sack of additional clips loaded with ammo. Hayes flew me out to the helipad at Ben Cat with my weapon and a rucksack, where I was met by Army major Al Buckley, the advisor to a Vietnamese ranger battalion. We piled into his Jeep along with his Chinese driver and a U.S. Army corporal who was the radio operator and drove into the little village. Ten trucks loaded with Vietnamese soldiers met us there. We parked at the head of the convoy and got out. Buckley and I went into a small, open-air shop and ordered bowls of soup. As we sat eating, another Jeep with three soldiers pulled up and parked in front of our vehicle. This annoyed Buckley because we were supposed to be the number-two vehicle in the column behind the commander's Jeep, which had yet to arrive.

"Damn it," Buckley said. "I'll have to go over the column order again tonight. These guys just don't listen."

When the Vietnamese commander pulled up in front of the column, Buckley introduced me to him. The commander had been trained in France after World War II and had fought at Dien Bien Phu, the 1954 battle in which the Communist forces of the Viet Minh finally defeated the French. His English was excellent. I paid for the soup, and the battalion set out, with our Jeep number three in line. As we rolled out of Ben Cat, Buckley asked me if I had a round in the chamber of my carbine.

"No," I said.

"Well, put one in the chamber." He was firm on this. "If we're fired on, there won't be time."

I complied. I double-checked the safety. The Jeep was very crowded with the mounted radio in back. I didn't want any unintentional fireworks.

As soon as we'd gotten out of the village, we drove into dense jungle that surrounded both sides of the road. About a mile from Ben Cat, we took fire from the south. We piled out and hit the dirt, firing into the jungle in the direction of the attack. By the time the excitement had died down, I realized that I'd fired more than sixty rounds. It had happened so fast I'd hardly been aware that I'd shot at all.

When we got up to take stock of our situation, we found that the three soldiers in the Jeep directly in front of us in the column were dead. It was the Jeep that had taken our spot while we'd eaten our soup. They took bullets that should have been for us. As the convoy started up again, I chambered a round—without being asked this time.

We eventually arrived at a compound in the jungle that was guarded by Vietnamese sentries. We rolled up into our mosquito netting that night and got a little fitful sleep. The next morning the U.S. Army radio operator was so sick that they called a chopper in to extract him from the fort. Not much later the Vietnamese soldiers in the fort launched a mortar attack on an area to the north of the compound. I was fascinated watching the 81-millimeter mortar operation. The soldiers didn't speak English, but they asked in sign language if I wanted to drop a few rounds. Of course I did. I wanted to experience it all.

About noon, we loaded up the vehicles and drove about 10 miles north. Buckley warned me to be on the lookout for VC who'd been reported in the area. The convoy stopped, and we climbed out, about one hundred of us, and headed into the jungle on foot. As we started out, I noticed that each of the Vietnamese soldiers had a live chicken tied to the top of his rucksack. I was amazed that these chickens never made a peep. Each day as we'd stop for lunch, a few of the chickens (one for each five-man squad) would be killed, chopped up—bones and all—and thrown into a pot along with some green vegetables and served with rice and fermented fish sauce called *nuớc mắm*. Buckley and I stuck to our GI rations.

On our first night in camp, the commander pulled Buckley and me aside and informed us that he suspected his group included a few VC sympathizers. He suggested that only one of us sleep at a time since we could be targets. That was a hell of thing to discover now that we were out in the jungle with these guys. It finally dawned on us that one of the VC sympathizers had likely gotten word to the enemy that the Americans would be in the second Jeep in the column as we pulled out of Ben Cat—that had been the original plan. The best we could figure, that bowl of soup we stopped for had saved our lives.

As we clawed our way through the vegetation the next morning, I could feel the tension in the air. There was no talking, no noise—only the sounds of us moving through the jungle. It was eerie. My head was on a constant swivel, my carbine loaded and ready. I never really rested

With Vietnamese rangers. My tense week on patrol in the jungle made me appreciate the pilot's life.

the entire five days, even at night. The slightest unfamiliar sound was cause for alarm. I expected to be shot at any moment.

On the last day, Buckley and I decided to give the Vietnamese guys a treat. We opened several cans of chili we'd saved, heated it all up, and ladled it out so that all the soldiers could get a little sample. The Vietnamese are extremely polite people, but when they tried our chili, most of them made faces and started pouring their fish sauce on top of it. I think some of them may have thrown the chili out when we weren't looking.

When my stint with the rangers was over and I caught my chopper back to Bien Hoa, I congratulated myself on having had the good sense to join the Air Force, and I gave thanks once more to that little bowl of soup.

On the last day of October 1963, we received an unusual FRAG. It called for a B-26 with napalm and bombs to be on station near Saigon at 2:00 p.m. the following day. That was the extent of it—no mission objectives, no FAC, nothing. Not knowing what it was all about, I scheduled myself for the mission, as I always did when we received new or unfamiliar orders. When I arrived in Saigon the next afternoon, I couldn't believe my eyes. VNAF fighters were bombing the royal palace and shooting up gunboats. I contacted the 7th Air Force command post and asked what the hell was going on. They said, "We have no idea! *You* tell *us!*" So I gave them a running account over the VHF radio. Only later would I learn that what I had witnessed that day was the coup against President Diem, sponsored by our Central Intelligence Agency and State Department and, of course, carried out with full knowledge of the 7th Air Force headquarters staff—which explained the FRAG order the day before. They knew exactly what was going to happen, and they wanted an aerial narration of the event.

I had been airborne for four hours when my fuel began to get critical. I returned to Bien Hoa, but by that time the Vietnamese Army had barricaded the runway and taxiway, which prevented me from landing. I proceeded back to Saigon and landed there, still with my full load of ordnance. A Vietnamese Army vehicle with .50-caliber machine guns escorted me to the parking area. I had a VNAF private in the back seat of the B-26, and that poor little guy was scared to death. He knew just enough to know that something bad was going on, and he decided to stick to me like a shadow.

As we entered the new officers' club at Tan Son Nhut, I headed to the bathroom with the VNAF private right behind me. That guy stood just a few feet away from me in the bathroom the whole time. He didn't speak a word of English, but he figured I was his best bet, and he wasn't going to lose me. After a hamburger and a Coke, I was paged by 7th Air Force Operations. They'd lost contact with a U.S. Army helicopter. By now it was dark. I rounded up my crew—including my Vietnamese shadow—and we took off after the chopper, which had last been heard from about 60 miles north–northeast of Saigon. When we arrived there and made contact with the chopper crew, it turned out they were down working on a small mechanical problem and didn't require assistance. I reported back to headquarters and, once again low on fuel, headed back to Bien Hoa, only to find those damn barricades all over the runway. I made several requests to the tower to get the barricades removed. No response. So I buzzed the hell out of the tower until they cleared the runway. We all were pretty glad to be back on the ground and out of the mess around Saigon.

It had been an entertaining day for me, but a sad one for the future of South Vietnam. Who knows what my VNAF shadow thought? Diem had not been much of a national leader, but as things turned out, he was better than the alternative. Following the overthrow of Diem—who was assassinated along with his brother in the back of an armored personnel carrier on November 2—the South Vietnamese government withered. My country was responsible. The United States had sanctioned the assassination of a foreign leader and the ouster of an elected government. This chapter in our history was, quite simply, despicable.

One morning three weeks later, as I was shaving, one of the men at Bien Hoa asked me if I'd heard the news. President Kennedy had been shot in Dallas. Lyndon Johnson was our new commander in chief. Some of us there had the sense that we were literally holding down the fort while the rest of the world lost its mind. I stayed buried in my work: the B-26s, the missions, the United States Air Force.

The Douglas B-26 had been designed and built during the latter stages of World War II and saw only limited action in 1944–45. For its day, it was extremely fast and carried a lethal weapons system. It was used extensively during the Korean War for night interdiction missions, mostly as a light bomber releasing ordnance from a straight-and-level configuration. In 1961, the B-26 was selected to be employed as a fighter bomber for strafing, dive bombing, and releasing napalm—purposes for which it had not been designed and was not well suited. They were first flown in Vietnam in 1962, and a few were lost in combat. There was a suspicion that some of the losses were due not to enemy fire but to the wings shearing off during high-G pull-offs. Then, in the spring of 1964, a B-26 at Eglin AFB in Florida crashed spectacularly during a night firepower demonstration. As the pilot pulled up following a napalm release, the wings folded in front of thousands of spectators. The crew was killed, and the Air Force decided to ground all the B-26s, so those of us flying them in Vietnam were grounded indefinitely, too.

After a few days, we pilots and navigators came up with a plan. We petitioned headquarters to allow us to continue flying the B-26 missions with the restriction that bombs would be released only in straight-and-level flight. It wasn't long before we received approval. Because we didn't have Norden bomb sights on these aircraft, one of our navigators came up with the idea of positioning a navigator in the plane's rear compartment and having him tell the pilot when to release the bombs. The pilot identified the target and relayed a description back to the navigator. The pilot then opened the bomb bay doors, and the navigator would look down and get a visual on the target. We were usually 1,000 to 2,500 feet above the ground, which kept us just out of the range of small-arms fire. The navigator then estimated the release point and told the pilot when to drop the bombs. We called this procedure the "Flintstone Bomb Release System." It was stone-age crude, but pretty effective once we got the hang of it. From our point of view at least, it beat the hell out of sitting around the base waiting for something to happen.

In spite of our efforts, in April 1964 orders came down that all B-26s were permanently grounded—to be returned to the Philippines or to the United States—and all the crews were sent home.

In May 1964, back at Hurlburt Field, I received a call from someone who identified himself as the counsel for the Stennis Senate subcommittee in Washington, D.C., asking me to testify about my experiences in South Vietnam. I flew to Washington about a week later, arriving the day before the Senate hearing was scheduled and discovered that I was one of ten pilots from the 1st Air Commando Wing who'd been called to testify. This group had flown the T-28, the C-47, the U-10, and the B-26 in Vietnam. An Air Force general met us and immediately escorted us to a large conference room in the Pentagon. The ten of us had never been together prior to the meeting and so had not had an opportunity to discuss our individual experiences or our feelings about the war. The room was full of civilians who I guessed were on Defense Secretary Robert McNamara's staff, and they did not appear to be all that friendly. At the conference table with us were several very young lawyer types with their briefcases. Oddly, the atmosphere bordered on hostile.

The general welcomed us to the Pentagon and Washington and announced that we would be appearing the following morning in front of Senator John Stennis's Preparedness Investigation Subcommittee of the Armed Services Committee. On the panel would be, among others, Senators Barry Goldwater, Stuart Symington, Leverett Saltonstall, and Margaret Chase Smith. As recent returnees from Vietnam, we would be questioned about our experiences in Southeast Asia and would be asked to give our assessments of the war's progress. By the way, the general said, almost as an aside, he had assembled for our information all of

Secretary McNamara's recent public statements about the war. He told us he thought it might be helpful for us to be aware of the secretary's point of view. Copies of these statements were handed to each of us. It seemed pretty obvious that we were being asked not to contradict McNamara in our own testimony.

We were a little shocked by what was happening. We sat there at the conference table in silence for an hour or so and read all the statements. Much of what I read contradicted the facts as I knew them, and the statements definitely did not reflect my view about how the war was going. I'm sure all of us looked pretty uncomfortable as we considered what we felt we were being asked to do. I think that the civilians in the room were taking our measure and beginning to understand that we were not likely to be very good lackeys for the Defense Department. After the meeting at the Pentagon, our group of pilots was driven to a nearby motel. That evening, over some adult beverages, we began to get to know each other, and we speculated about how all this was going to play out. As a group, we'd seen many things and been in many unusual situations, but the byzantine world of Washington politics was unfamiliar terrain.

The next morning, the general picked us up at the motel and escorted us to the Senate hearing room. At about five minutes before nine, Senator Stennis entered the room and motioned for the general to approach the dais. Stennis was an impressive man; he radiated power. A Democrat from Mississippi who'd been elected to the Senate in 1947, he would later become chairman of the Armed Services Committee and would even have a supercarrier named after him.

"And just why are you here, General?" Stennis drawled.

"Sir," the general replied, a little sheepishly, "the secretary thought that perhaps these Air Force officers might desire some legal counsel while appearing before the committee."

"Boy," Stennis scolded, "get out of my committee room! These officers will not require any legal counsel while appearing before this committee, and frankly I consider this an insult."

The general ducked his head and began to back away.

"Wait a minute, boy," Stennis said to this United States Air Force general. "What is your name? I want to remember your name the next time you come up for promotion."

Wow. All of us pilots sat stone still. After watching Stennis chew out a general, we wondered what fate awaited the likes of us lowly captains and majors.

A few minutes later the committee members filed into the room and took their seats. Senator Stennis, in a gentlemanly and amiable manner now, welcomed us all and announced that the purpose of the hearing was to determine how the war was going from the point of view of aviators who had been there and seen the fight firsthand. He said he had read all the reports from the secretary of defense and the Air Force brass, but that he wanted to hear from those who had actually flown in combat. He told us that all he wanted was the truth as we saw it and assured us that there would be no repercussions for our testimony. His was a friendly subcommittee, he went on, and he wanted to thank us for our service to our country. Stennis sounded kind of like a friendly uncle who just wanted to hear your side of the story.

I was the second pilot to testify, but all of us told essentially the same story. One by one we placed our hands on a Bible and were sworn in. We were asked to state our name, rank, and the organization to which we were presently assigned. We were then asked when our most recent combat tour in Vietnam started and was completed, what type of aircraft we flew, and what the nature of our combat missions was. It didn't take long to understand that these senators knew exactly what was going on in Vietnam and that they really only wanted our testimony on the record to substantiate what they already knew.

After the preliminaries, we all were asked the same big question, and it was a doozy: "Are we winning the war in Vietnam?" That's what this whole thing really came down to. Without having rehearsed our answers or even having agreed in general terms about what we intended to say, all of us replied the same way: "No, sir."

At that point, we had lost 250 Americans in Vietnam and spent more than a billion dollars. (We would eventually lose nearly 60,000 Americans.) The committee asked for our recommendations. Again, we answered as one. Have Congress declare war on North Vietnam and turn the operation over to the military—or else withdraw completely. Half measures were a sure path to disaster.

Since 1960, the United States had been sending advisors to Vietnam to help the South Vietnamese military fight the guerilla war being conducted by North Vietnam. During 1962, the number of advisors on the ground increased significantly. The United States Air Force sent personnel to Vietnam initially under the aegis of a program called Farm Gate. These pilots were flying both fighter bombers and reconnaissance missions. We were officially there to train South Vietnamese pilots, but as far as we could tell, there was never any serious intention to train anybody. That was just a cover story, a farce. Every aircraft on a combat mission had to carry a South Vietnamese Air Force enlisted man. In the B-26 that I had flown, the South Vietnamese airman took the seat behind the navigator. There was no way he could even monitor the controls, much less touch them. These poor guys couldn't speak English, so they had no idea what was going on, and most of them were petrified. They definitely did not want to be up there. For our night missions to defend the hamlets, our aircrews used to wait together in full flight gear in air-conditioned trailers so that we'd be ready to roll the moment we got a scramble signal, and the Vietnamese observers often took that opportunity to try and climb out the rear window when we turned our backs. I finally had to confiscate their boots when we went into the trailer; most of them were afraid of snakes, and I knew they wouldn't go traipsing around outside—especially at night—without their boots. When we received the signal to go, we'd throw their boots to them as we ran toward the aircraft. The desertion rate for these guys was sky high. One of our crews actually discovered its Vietnamese observer smoking pot *during a mission*!

One night in Sóc Trăng, guerillas began firing mortars at the airfield. Two United States Air Force pilots who were sitting at the bar immediately jumped up, sprinted to the flight line, took off, and flew around trying to locate the mortar position. But once the two aircraft were in the air and no longer available as targets on the ground, the mortars stopped. When the commanders at Air Force headquarters in Saigon discovered that these pilots had taken off to counter enemy action without a Vietnamese airman in the rear cockpit, they threatened the men with courts-martial. Luckily for everybody, cooler heads prevailed, and the charges were dropped.

McNamara had made frequent trips to Saigon and was well briefed. I attended two of these briefings myself. There's no way he could have avoided knowing what a ridiculous environment American servicemen were operating in. But Gen. Anthis, the Air Force chief in Vietnam at that time, was completely out of the loop, as was the overall Army commander, Gen. Harkins. They both were busy fighting intraservice battles and didn't have much of a clue about the realities of the tactical situation, and they could always be relied upon to tell the secretary of defense what he wanted to hear.

In spite of the increasing number of American forces, combat aircraft, and "advisors"—both from the Air Force and the Army—it was evident to everyone there that we were in fact losing the fight. The beginning of the end, or perhaps the end of the beginning, came when President Diem and his brother were assassinated. A series of successors was installed, but the war effort suffered horribly due to the political instability. The South Vietnamese government was thoroughly corrupt, and all its generals were on the take. By the spring of 1964, there was simply no denying that the Communist forces were winning.

Only half of the ten military aviators completed their testimony to the Stennis committee on that first day. When the hearing adjourned, the Air Force took us all straight to the Pentagon and put us back in that conference room with the same crowd. The general who'd been chewed out by Senator Stennis wanted to know what types of questions we'd been asked, who'd asked them, and what we'd said. The Defense Department clearly wanted and expected to hear that we'd parroted the McNamara party line.

After hearing the gist of our responses to the committee's questions, these people didn't exactly start to warm up. They seemed especially unhappy to hear that we'd told the committee how we felt about the rules of engagement (and particularly about the stipulation that each aircraft on a combat mission include a South Vietnamese airman). McNamara had been lying to the public to justify the presence of the Air Commandos in Vietnam by saying we were running training missions. The truth, of course, was that we were helping fight the enemy because the South Vietnamese didn't have the forces to do it themselves.

Our largely civilian audience became positively unglued when they heard we'd told the senators that we were losing the war. If they'd had the power to run us all out of the Air Force, there's no question they would have done it on the spot. I pointed out that we'd put our hands on the Bible and sworn to tell the truth. I think that response just made them angrier. They kept us in there for three hours, and not one minute of it can be described as pleasant.

The following day went pretty much the same: testimony before the committee, then a debriefing at the Pentagon. By this time, the whole thing felt like a stage play. Everyone knew what we were going to say, but we all had to go through the motions in order to get the testimony on record. As we left the Pentagon that second day, the general made the rather ominous comment, "We'll be seeing you later." None of us was sure what that meant, but I had a strong sense that all of our careers might now be in jeopardy.

Three weeks later that same general showed up at Eglin AFB, where we were ordered to meet him at base operations at 6:30 in the morning. He took us all into a conference room, dropped a briefcase on the table, and informed us that he had with him the preliminary findings of the Stennis subcommittee. As was the practice, the committee had given the secretary of defense and the Air Force chief of staff the opportunity to review the findings before they were sent on to the full Senate and to President Johnson. I asked the general about the purpose of his visit to Eglin. He blanched and told us that if there was anything in the report that we found objectionable, the secretary would be willing to challenge it on our behalf. He was giving us a chance to change our story. At that point, he handed each of us a copy of the report and left the room. It didn't take us long to see that the record was an accurate account of what we'd said to the committee—which completely contradicted what McNamara had been telling Congress and the media. Before calling the general back in, we all agreed that we would stick together and make no recommendations for any changes.

The report clearly stated that we were losing the war in Southeast Asia and contained a recommendation from the Armed Services Committee: admit defeat and withdraw all forces or declare war on North Vietnam and win it.

We called the general back in. I was the spokesman. I told him that we'd read the report carefully and had no recommendations for changes. We were happy with it. We could see right away that he was shocked. I don't think he ever really understood who we were or what we represented. This outcome was not at all what he'd hoped for. He quickly collected the copies of the report, packed his briefcase, and left in a huff.

The following week I received a call from a Mr. Kimball, the Stennis subcommittee counsel. "Senator Stennis asked me to call you and thank you again for telling the truth," he said. "He also asked me to tell you that if there should ever be any repercussions for any of you from the Air Force or the Department of Defense as a result of your testimony, you should contact Senator Stennis at once." Oh, he added, there was one final message from Stennis: "There's absolutely no reason to worry."

"Well, if there's no reason to worry," I asked, "why did the senator have you call me?" We both laughed about that.

The subcommittee report was forwarded to the president through the office of the secretary of defense. The result? The president made the decision to escalate the conflict *without* a declaration of war from Congress. In the ensuing years, President Johnson and Secretary McNamara would personally direct tactical operations from the White House and the Pentagon. This approach was one of the great tragedies of Vietnam. With the report from the Stennis subcommittee, history had given the president a golden opportunity and plenty of political cover to make the right decision. We'd lost only a couple hundred men to that point. In my opinion, from that day forward, Lyndon Johnson was directly and personally responsible for the agony our country would suffer for the next eleven years. If Congress had declared war—the guerilla incursions into South Vietnam had provided all the justification necessary—and turned the management of combat operations over to the military, the whole thing could have been wrapped up in two weeks. If we truly believed that China or Russia would enter the war, and we were unwilling to confront them, the only sensible option was total withdrawal. We were losing the fight in 1964 and would continue to lose in spite of the commitment of two hundred thousand troops and the death of sixty thousand U.S. soldiers. Historians tell us that before his assassination, President Kennedy understood the fatal mistake the United States had made by sanctioning the coup that removed Diem and that he was already resolved to begin bringing the troops home.

In the end, all our efforts were in vain when South Vietnam was overrun by the North in 1975. It all might have been very different if President Johnson and his defense secretary had possessed the wisdom to accept the recommendation of ten honest Air Force pilots.

Beginning in 1962, at the request of the Air Commandos, Mark Engineering in Los Angeles had begun a project to completely modify the B-26 for combat. All of the problems we'd experienced with the airplane were eventually solved. New R-2800, dash-52 model Pratt and Whitney engines with new propellers were installed. These engines had more horsepower and reliable low-tension ignition systems. They had more boost on takeoff and reversible props that allowed for safer and shorter landings on the pierced-steel planking runways we used, especially when the runways were wet. Tip tanks gave us more endurance, and external bomb releases gave us more ordnance capacity. Eight .50-caliber machine guns were installed, along with new lighting, instrumentation, and radios. But the most important aspect of the redesign was a new wing configuration that ensured structural integrity in combat and bomb delivery. The A-26 was a great aircraft and a joy to fly—and it was just what we needed. We never experienced a wing failure during the five years it was in service.

I started flying the A-26 in 1965 and was transferred from Hurlburt to England AFB in Louisiana in January 1966, where I was made operations officer of a newly formed A-26 squadron. About half the crew were combat veterans who were familiar with A-26 operation; the rest were eager volunteers. We flew gunnery missions during the day, and because we knew we'd be flying primarily at night in Vietnam, we flew sorties and practiced with strobes and flares at a night-tactics range near Fort Polk, about 70 miles away.

In a matter of weeks, we were ready to deploy to Nakhon Phanom (NKP)—or, as we referred to it, "Naked Fanny." I volunteered to lead the first eight A-26s across the Pacific. It was a great honor. To assist us, we had two C-97s from the Georgia and Tennessee National Guards, which transported our crew chiefs and some spare parts. Because of the long overflights ahead, we had an 800-gallon fuel tank installed in the bomb bay of each aircraft and a 55-gallon oil drum with a hand crank and engine selector valve installed in the rear seat. We departed on June 9, 1966, flying nonstop from Louisiana to Travis AFB in Napa, California. We had a lovely morning for our flight to Hawaii the next day. Once an hour we'd pump a gallon of oil into each engine. Ten and a half hours later we landed at Hickam AFB near Honolulu. Our next legs took us to Wake, Midway, Guam, and the Philippines, and we had a blast at every stop. We landed all ten aircraft right on schedule on June 15 at NKP in the northeast corner of Thailand on the Mekong River and were met by the rest of our detachment, who greeted us with a full supply of cold beer.

Right away we started preparing the A-26s for combat. We had trained for nighttime missions, but some clown at headquarters in Saigon decided that we needed to fly over the combat area in daylight first. Our targets consisted of the logistics roads coming through Laos from North Vietnam, popularly known as the Ho Chi Minh Trail. On a daytime overflight on the very first day, one of our crews was shot down and killed by ground fire. Let me tell you, that got our attention real quick. The A-26 was fast and maneuverable, but it couldn't outrun antiaircraft fire from .50-caliber or 23-millimeter guns. The enemy gunners had a big advantage during the day; they could see us, but we couldn't see them. At night, however, the advantage was all ours—and we were much more accurate than the jet fighters who had to release their ordnance from an altitude of 5,000 to 10,000 feet. In the A-26, we were practically right on top of our targets.

There were four interdiction targets on the Ho Chi Minh Trail: Alpha, Bravo, Charlie, and Delta. These areas, or choke points designed to snarl traffic, had been turned into sand piles as a result of frequent bombing. The idea was to intercept enemy vehicles and destroy them as they attempted to traverse the choke points. The road was easy to spot as it snaked through Laos on its way into South Vietnam, but we also had radio navigation devices and radar to help us locate specific targets.

The ordnance aboard our aircraft varied. We continually sought out the best mix for our environment. We always carried two racks, one on each wing, with six flares in each rack. We carried a full load of .50-caliber ammunition, which amounted to two hundred rounds per gun. We had great versatility and plenty of options with those guns. We had no tracers in the ammo that would help shooters on the ground spot us. Our primary targets were supply trucks.

I would take the first mission of the night. We'd drop flares on the choke points and then make a visual pass looking for trucks trying to make their way through. If we found targets, we'd drop cluster bomb units or napalm, or we'd fire our guns, depending on the situation. If we hit a moving truck, we would never claim a kill unless we could see the truck burning. Those trucks burned diesel fuel, which is not very flammable. I'm sure we destroyed twice as many trucks as we claimed simply because they didn't always burn very well. On a few occasions, I could actually see the spilled diesel pooling up around the truck but just couldn't ignite it. The trucks usually traveled as singles, but sometimes we'd find a convoy of three or four together. Six was the most I ever saw at one time. They were slow and used low-beam tactical road lights, so they could be hard to spot, but once we spotted them, they were in a world of trouble. There aren't too many things in this world I would less rather have been than a truck driver on the Ho Chi Minh Trail in 1966.

NKP seemed like the end of the world, and the conditions there were primitive. The jungle heat was miserable, but other than in the briefing room the only air conditioning to be found was in the officers' club, where we could get a cold bottle of Pearl beer for ten cents. It was a popular place, and one day Sgt. Carlos Christian, my first sergeant, came to me with a problem.

"Sir," he said, "we've got *ten thousand* empty beer bottles. We need to get rid of them."

I thought for a minute and came up with an idea.

"Here's what you do," I told Christian. "Tonight, bring 'em all down to the flight line. I'll take it from there."

So that evening they brought down two pickup loads full of empties. I had my crew close the bomb bay doors on my A-26 and dump all those bottles right into the bomb bay. I taxied out, the airplane piddling beer all over the taxiway, and took off. I flew into North Vietnam, just on the east side of the mountain pass, dropped down to about 50 feet, and deployed the load of beer bottles right onto the Ho Chi Minh Trail. I really got a kick out of that. It was just the start. I repeated the mission about once a week. We'd load up the bottles, and I'd make a precision drop right onto the trail. It was a good morale booster for the guys at NKP. I suspect that glass cut up quite a few truck and bicycle tires. We laughed, imagining the enemy trying to figure out our new secret weapon: Pearl beer bottles. I guess the only folks who didn't appreciate these missions were the crews that had to clean up my airplane each time I brought it back reeking like a brewery.

One evening I was scrambled earlier than usual because of a high-priority target in one of the choke-point areas. I arrived there about an hour before sunset. There was still plenty of daylight, which didn't make me happy. A forward air controller hit the target site with a rocket to mark it for me, and I followed in behind. I was halfway down the final approach, heading for the target, and just as I started firing my machine

My men loading the A-26 in preparation for a beer run. I dropped thousands of empties onto the Ho Chi Minh Trail.

guns, I saw four strings of continuous bullets heading for me. They had me wired. The bullets obviously came from a four-barreled gun, and it had me in its sights. I continued shooting until I had to break off because the ground was coming up, and right then I realized my aircraft had been hit. I pulled up and did a battle damage check. It was extensive. What I really wanted to do was go back down after the target with my guns, but instead I climbed up to about 5,000 feet, entered a steep dive, and dropped all of my cluster bomb units. I splattered the target.

In the meantime, I had lost both my generators and had to use my battery, aware that it would run down pretty quickly. I had no hydraulic power and was leaking hydraulic fluid from both engines. I could see damage to both engine cowlings. When I was established on the route back to NKP, I saw a massive thunderstorm between me and my destination. I made the decision to divert to Ubon, an F-4 fighter base about 80 miles south of NKP on the Mekong. It was completely dark by the time the battery quit. My navigator, who had done a bang-up job during the emergency, had to hold a flashlight on my instrument panel so I could see what I was doing. The night was absolutely black. We had no navigation instrumentation, no lights, no radio, no hydraulics, no transponder. We were flying in and out of the overcast, holding a compass heading to the base, when we suddenly had a break in the clouds. I looked down and saw the Mekong and the town of Ubon. I knew we were almost there.

I had no way to alert anybody at Ubon that we were coming in. We watched for returning F-4s and dropped down toward the runway in the pouring rain. About one mile out, on final approach, we extended the landing gear with the emergency system. Without electric power, we couldn't be sure the gear was down and locked. Without hydraulics or lights, with no flaps, we came in hot and practically invisible in the downpour. I had to use the emergency brakes but managed to get us slowed down and off the active runway. The guys in the tower told us later that they never had a clue an A-26 was even in the vicinity until they heard our tires hit the runway. When the fire and crash personnel got out to us, I asked for a gun crew because we had hot guns and some ordnance left in the bomb bay. I offered to assist them in downloading the guns, but the sergeant told us not to worry. "I know how to download .50-calibers," he said a little sarcastically.

My navigator and I proceeded to the officers' club. I bought the first four martinis. It was sometime after the fifth one arrived that I got a call from the gun-crew chief. He wanted us to return to the flight line and help them download the guns. I guess the job turned out to be a little trickier than he'd suspected. We had volunteered to help, he'd turned us down, and now—after five martinis, or was it six?—I sent word that we were no longer available. I suggested he call our gun shop at NKP and ask for help there. It had been one hell of a mission and a very close call. I made it thanks to an awful tough airplane, a damn good navigator, and a generous portion of my trademark good luck.

My second tour ended in January 1967, and I was really glad to get back home. My boys were teenagers now, and I could take them hunting and fishing. It was a great time, but we were together in the States only for a season. In June, I was transferred to Germany, where I received the best assignment I ever had: air liaison officer to the 10th Special Forces. The 10th was an elite Army group down in the Bavarian Alps that was trained and equipped for unconventional warfare. I was a lieutenant colonel by this point and was stationed in Bad Tölz with a group of about five hundred of the best troops in the United States Army. It was an absolutely first-class operation. It had a parachute jump team, and I volunteered for it as soon as I arrived. I was a little out of my league since the rest of the team had hundreds of free falls to their credit, and I had only about fifty. We put on demonstration jumps all over Europe and had a rip-roaring time wherever we went.

The team had a long-standing tradition. Before any jump, we'd agree on a target. Whoever landed farthest from the target had to buy the beer that night. I was at a clear disadvantage due to my relative inexperience. We'd get ready to jump, and some sergeant would always shout: "Hey, Colonel, you got your money with you?" I was a pretty good sport about it—I bought a lot of beer that year—but after a while it started to tick me off. So one day on a jump in Garmisch-Partenkirchen at the commemoration of a new little-league baseball field, I decided I was not going to allow myself to lose again. They always let me jump last so I'd see the mark I needed to beat, and on this day I really studied the technique of every guy who preceded me. We were jumping from an H-34 helicopter, and the target was second base. One guy landed behind home plate, another in shallow centerfield. After I left the chopper, I really focused and made sure I had a good approach. I came in perfect, but I could see at the last second that I was going to overshoot second base just a bit, so I collapsed my chute and stuck myself right on the bag. The landing was a little awkward looking, but I nailed it. As I came to rest, I realized right away that I'd snapped my leg.

The jumpmaster came running up. He knew what had happened.

"You broke your leg, didn't you, Colonel?"

"I sure did," I said.

"Can you walk?"

"No, I don't believe so."

So while the rest of the jump team joined up in formation and marched over to a little reviewing stand where the local bürgermeister gave an hour-long talk and then some general gave another hour-long talk, I stood at attention on second base. When the whole thing was over, they called an ambulance for me.

I had a jumpsuit on over my civilian clothes, and while I was sitting in the hospital in Munich, waiting to be examined, a female Army major on the medical staff walked in and frowned at me.

"Where are you from, soldier?" she asked.

"Well, ma'am," I said, "I'm from Bad Tölz."

She frowned again, deeper this time.

"You damn special-forces people," she said, shaking her head. "In the wintertime you bust your asses skiing, and in the summertime you bust your asses jumping. I wish you knew how much trouble you cause us."

She went on and on. Finally, I interrupted her.

"Ma'am, excuse me," I said a little sheepishly. "What time is cocktail hour?"

I thought she might explode.

"Cocktail hour? *Cocktail hour, soldier? Where the hell do you think you are?*"

I would have kept stringing her along, but my leg was really starting to hurt by this point. I pulled out my ID.

"Ma'am, enough of this crap," I said. "I need somebody to set this leg, and I want it done now."

They took me to a very nice intensive care room, and I was treated pretty well from that point on. Every evening my special-forces buddies sent a guy down with a couple of bottles of cold beer. Five days later I was discharged from the hospital and—with my leg in a cast—rejoined the jump team's grand tour of Europe. Over time, I was able to hit the targets with some reliability. At least I didn't have to buy the beer every time.

That winter they put us on a C-123 at ten at night with a 60-pound rucksack and an M-16, and they flew us from Munich into the mountains of northern Norway for a secret exercise. We flew for six hours and made a blind night jump into a total whiteout. We plowed 10 feet or so into the snowbank when we landed. It was impossible to see anything, but we managed to get ourselves organized and get our gear packed onto two sleds that had been dropped along with us. Then we all strapped on skis and slalomed 12 miles down the mountain, where we rendezvoused with a group of Norwegian troops.

We spent the next three weeks in the snow, training with the Norwegians. We instructed them on how to fire our weapons, and they showed us how to fire theirs. We did joint training in winter survival techniques. We lived in snow caves and tents and practiced mountain operations. We worked on crevasse rescue, first aid, and communications techniques. The whole experience was fantastic. Except for the Air Commandos, the special-forces guys were the best troops I ever served with.

From Bad Tölz, I went to joint headquarters in Stuttgart, where I worked on special-operations problems involving the Army, Air Force, and Navy. I was there for two years. Joe and Mark attended excellent armed service schools, and we all went skiing and touring the countryside whenever I could get away for a couple of days. We had some marvelous times together and really bonded as a family. The boys were proud of their father, and I was proud of them. As much as I enjoyed my assignments in Germany, though, I was torn. It was impossible not to think about the war in Vietnam, still raging in 1970. I knew what our troops were going through, and from the news we heard, it didn't sound as if things were going to be wrapping up anytime soon. I was a forty-two-year-old lieutenant colonel, but I was a fighter pilot. Finally, I decided that I wanted to go back one more time.

I volunteered for my third tour.

Joe was a junior in high school and wanted to stay and graduate in Germany. Both boys had friends there and had adjusted well to life in Europe, but in the end we returned to America as a family.

After receiving training in the F-4 Phantom at Davis Monthan AFB in Tucson, Arizona, I left once again for Southeast Asia. This departure was especially tough. Joe was a senior in high school by this time, president of the Honor Society and a few weeks away from becoming an Eagle Scout. I was painfully aware of what I was giving up.

Shortly after I arrived at Udorn Royal Thai AFB in May 1971, the wing commander, Col. Lyle Mann, called me in and asked me if I thought I could maintain discipline in a squadron and uphold appearance standards in accordance with Air Force regulations. When I answered that I could, Col. Mann said that he had a squadron commander who was not cutting it and that he would like to offer me the opportunity to see what I could do. It was then that I received command of the 555th Tactical Fighter Squadron, the Triple Nickel, the most celebrated squadron in the theater. I was obviously elated.

This would be my first experience in a management situation where

I would be responsible for the execution of Air Force regulations and directives as well as maintenance of staff discipline. I had more than seventy-five officers—pilots, navigators, and administrative officers— and three hundred enlisted men. The Triple Nickel had twenty-five F-4 Phantoms flying combat missions every single day and night.

After the change-of-command ceremony, I called all of the men together, enlisted men as well as officers, and assured them that together we would continue to be the best damn fighter squadron in the United States Air Force. Remembering Mann's complaint about appearance standards, I told them what I expected. Mann had been particularly concerned about haircuts and facial hair. I told the men they had two days to get in compliance with Air Force regulations. The only dissenter was the ranking navigator on my staff, a major who decided to test me by refusing to get a regulation haircut. I had a private talk with him and gave him another day. He showed up for work the next morning with the same haircut and a defiant look on his face. I could see that the junior officers were watching this confrontation play out. I called the offender into my office, along with my administrative officer, told him to stand at attention, and gave him a direct order to comply with Air Force grooming regulations. If he failed to do so, I made it clear, I would bring court-martial charges against him.

McDonnell Douglas F-4 Phantom in Thailand. It was quite a step up from the B-26s I flew on my first tour in Southeast Asia to this supersonic fighter with a top speed in excess of Mach 2. (Courtesy: United States Air Force.)

"Do you understand, Major?" I asked.

"Yes, sir."

I then instructed my chief of staff to prepare a written statement docu-menting the proceedings and had the major sign it. I told him he had one hour to fix the problem. Thirty minutes later he was back with a regulation haircut. This issue may seem trivial, but if I had let this major get by with violating standards and ignoring my direct order, I would have been quickly replaced as squadron commander, and I was not going to let that happen over a couple of inches of hair. I learned that it's not always possible to be the good guy. You have to comply with your superior officer's wishes, regardless of your own feelings. The majority of the men understand this.

Initiating disciplinary action against anyone is the last thing any commander wants to do, but there are times when there's just no alternative. A unit's morale depends on decisive action that is fair, prompt, and consistent. We had an F-4 mechanic on our flight line at Udorn whom I'll call Staff Sgt. Jones. He was sharp and always did a good job. One month he was awarded a ride in the back seat of a Phantom for winning Best Airman in the Squadron. Since I spent hours on the flight line each day, I got to know all the men and learned a lot about their lives. Sgt. Jones in particular had impressed me. Then one day, my maintenance supervisor, Chief Master Sgt. Lucien, pulled me aside to tell me that he was having trouble with Sgt. Jones. The news was a double surprise: first, that Jones was seen as a problem, and, second, that Lucien hadn't been able to take care of it and felt that he needed to come to me. I figured the problem must be something pretty serious. Sgt. Jones had apparently become infatuated with a local girl, and his work ethic was starting to slip. He was showing up late for work and failing to keep up his personal appearance. Lucien even suspected that Jones might be using drugs, which really floored me.

The next day Sgt. Lucien showed up in my office with Jones in tow. Lucien explained that Jones had been late for work three days running. I asked Jones if he had anything he'd like to share with us. He said nothing, avoiding eye contact.

"Sgt. Jones," I said, "you really disappoint me and leave me no choice but to initiate disciplinary action if this happens again. Do you understand?" He said he did.

The following morning Sgt. Lucien called to say that Jones was absent without explanation for the morning formation. I asked for Jones to be delivered to my office whenever he showed up. In the meantime, I called the staff judge advocate officer, explained the problem, and asked that paperwork be prepared to bring charges against Sgt. Jones. I hated like hell to do it, but I had no alternative. The next day Jones was brought to my office. I took him right over to the staff judge's office. He was fined $150, given a suspended bust, and restricted to the base for one month. If he kept his nose clean and straightened up, I made it clear I'd rescind the order, but if there were further problems, he would lose a stripe and the Article 15 would be entered on his official record. Sgt. Jones didn't say a word. He just signed the papers.

On the way back to the squadron area in my Jeep, I told Jones how disappointed I was. "I thought you were more of a soldier than this," I said. "But if you'll straighten up, all will be forgiven. Are you capable of that? Do you want to get back in step with the rest of the squadron?" He said yes, but he never looked me in the eye. My confidence in him wasn't very high at this point.

About a week later, Master Sgt. Gerald Roy, my first sergeant, came into my office. Roy was a great soldier and an invaluable help to me. He had his finger on the pulse of the squadron and always knew what was going on. He told me he'd heard rumors that Sgt. Jones was breaking the imposed confinement to base and had been sneaking into town to spend evenings at his girlfriend's place. I knew I had to do something. We couldn't let the enlisted men see an order being ignored without consequences.

The next morning I had Sgt. Roy and my administrative officer, Capt. Bud Smith, take positions at the two gates that provided access to our base. I wanted to catch Sgt. Jones in the act of reentering the base. Two mornings went by with no success, but on the third morning Sgt. Roy saw Jones coming back through the gate. That was enough for me. I called the staff judge, a major, and told him to pull a stripe from Sgt. Jones. The major said he would investigate and get back to me. There was no need for an investigation, I said. My first sergeant would sign a statement detailing what he'd seen, and we would have it delivered immediately to the staff judge's office.

A little later I received a call from the major, who asked to see me. I gathered up Sgt. Roy and Capt. Smith on my way. When we arrived, the staff judge informed me that he could not follow up on my recommendation to remove a stripe from Sgt. Jones. He said that when he had questioned the sergeant, Jones had insisted he had *not* broken his restriction to base and that Sgt. Roy was mistaken.

I thought for a minute, then told the major that in light of what he'd told me, I wanted to prefer charges against my own Sgt. Roy for making a fraudulent statement.

"Someone is lying here," I explained, "and since you've assured me you have Sergeant Jones's word on this, then Sergeant Roy can't possibly be telling the truth." The staff judge smiled. He understood immediately the point I was making. He brought Jones back in and ordered him to put his earlier statement in writing, at which point Jones recanted. He lost his stripe, and I dropped my request to prosecute Roy. The lesson for me and for my first sergeant was that you should always have a witness or hard evidence in hand when bringing charges against someone. Whether we like it or not, in the legal arena a man's word is rarely enough.

An effective commander is required on occasion to think outside the box. It is a skill that can't be taught, but it's one a good leader must find a way to learn. One morning in July 1971, I was at my desk looking through the day's mail when I found a letter from Maj. John Kiker. He'd been one of my instructors during my F-4 training in Arizona, and my respect for his ability and judgment was unsurpassed. His letter said that a lieutenant from his squadron, a Charles DeBellevue, had been assigned to the 432nd Tactical Fighter Wing, to which the 555th was attached, and would be arriving shortly in Udorn. Kiker said that DeBellevue was very good and that I should try to get him assigned to my squadron. If Kiker thought enough of this DeBellevue to go to all this trouble on his behalf, I knew I had to have him, so I went over to the wing personnel office and explained to the sergeant on duty what I wanted.

The sergeant thumbed through his paperwork and shook his head.

"I'm sorry, Colonel," he said, "but it looks like DeBellevue has been assigned to the 13th Squadron." The 13th was the other F-4 squadron at Udorn.

I decided to press my case. John Kiker's word on this DeBellevue was about the best recommendation I could have.

"Sergeant," I said, "as you're very aware, the Triple Nickel is known as the MiG-killing squadron, and we need the skills this particular lieutenant possesses. You wouldn't want the North Vietnamese to win this war because you wouldn't make a slight change in assignments, would you?" I lowered my voice for emphasis. "We both know this guy would be wasted over at the 13th."

The sergeant winced and explained that the 13th had already been informed that DeBellevue would be reporting, and it would look bad for his boss to have to admit a mistake if they reassigned the new lieutenant to my squadron. I repeated my assertion that the Triple Nickel needed this guy and informed the sergeant that I wasn't going to give up. With that, I left for lunch at the officers' club.

After I had something to eat and time to consider the problem, I went to the base exchange and bought a case of Budweiser. I took the case over to the personnel office and slid it under the sergeant's desk while he was at lunch. About half an hour later, I received the call I wanted.

"Colonel," the personnel sergeant told me, "you sure know how to get to a guy."

Chuck DeBellevue was subsequently assigned to the Triple Nickel, where he belonged. He went on to shoot down six MiGs—the most MiG kills in the air war over Vietnam. I will always be indebted to Maj. Kiker for the recommendation and to the personnel sergeant for being a beer drinker.

I eventually had more than three hundred enlisted men in my squadron at Udorn. It was a fine group of dedicated professional soldiers who did their jobs under harsh conditions in the jungles of Thailand. I had very few personnel issues. One of the saddest concerned a lovesick tech sergeant on his third consecutive tour of duty.

I had received information indicating that this particular individual was not sending his wife and family sufficient funds to pay the bills. I talked to the man about it, and he promised me that he would increase the amount he was sending home each month. Then one day I received a letter from him requesting another year's assignment at Udorn. Knowing that he'd already been in Southeast Asia for three years and that his family was having problems back home, I denied the request. He was due to leave for the States on January 15, 1972. When I found out he'd missed the flight, I asked 1st Sgt. Roy to have the man report to me.

"Sergeant," I said to the man in my office the next morning, "I expect you to be on the C-130 tomorrow, or you will lose a stripe." I had him sign a document to that effect, but I promised him that I would tear it up once I received word that he'd made the plane. This guy had put seventeen years into the Air Force and had never been in any kind of trouble before. I wanted to save him.

Later that day, Sgt. Roy gave me a little more background. It seemed that our technical sergeant had a girlfriend in downtown Udorn who went by the name of Honey Child. "Sir," my first sergeant told me, "they say her face would stop a freight train. She gets falling-down drunk with him every evening. He says he loves her, sir." I called Chief Master Sgt. Lucien in and addressed Lucien and Roy together: "I expect him to be on that plane in the morning, and I'm holding you both responsible for making sure that happens. No excuses." They knew from my tone that I was dead serious.

As soon as the man's shift ended that evening, Lucien and Roy escorted him to his room, but when they went to pick him up the next morning to take him to the plane, they found he'd climbed out the window during the night and gone to town. He missed the flight again. When Lucien and Roy finally found the AWOL tech sergeant, they hauled him right into my office. Because he had no excuse for disobeying my direct order, I informed him that he was going to lose a stripe, and, furthermore, that if he didn't make the next morning's C-130, he'd lose another one.

"Do you understand?" I asked him.

"Yes, sir." But as he got ready to leave, he turned to me. "Sir, Honey Child wants me to tell you that she's put a hex on you for sending me away."

Lucien and Roy hauled the guy straight to jail at Security Police and had him locked up for the night. They both watched him get on the plane the next morning.

By the fall of 1971, the North Vietnamese had become more aggressive with both their air and ground assaults. They stockpiled supplies at the border of Laos and the demilitarized zone (DMZ) and brought their surface-to-air missiles (SAMs) and MiGs farther south, which put us at a real tactical disadvantage because the rules of engagement didn't allow us to bomb the enemy airfields or to attack supply ships or facilities in Haiphong Harbor. There was no way we could win the war this way. Misguided politicians and ineffectual military leaders had tied our hands. It was horribly frustrating for our fighting men.

Luckily, we had Gen. Jack Lavelle, chief of the 7th Air Force, on our side. Vietnam was Lavelle's third war, and he was a hero to all the fighter pilots. When we flew escort for the F-4 reconnaissance flights in the North, we were put in a "protective reaction" stance, which meant that we were allowed to try to destroy any SAM or antiaircraft sites that fired at us. We were happy about this change in status because it gave us a chance to inflict real damage on the enemy—even if it was in seeming violation of the official rules of engagement. Gen. Lavelle's superiors were aware of what we were doing and initially raised no objections. Word eventually got out and political pressure came down the chain of command. Lavelle was reprimanded, and the protective reaction raids stopped. It's a shame there weren't a few more Jack Lavelles around.

The North Vietnamese would occasionally land a MiG at a small airfield nestled in the foothills near Quan Lãng on the western edge of southern North Vietnam, just north of the DMZ. On the morning of November 8, 1971, I happened to be in the 432nd Wing intelligence center for a briefing when we received word that a MiG-21 had just landed at Quan Lãng and that we were cleared to bomb the location. I volunteered to lead the mission and was quickly approved. I made a call to the Triple Nickel and requested three additional F-4 crews for an immediate combat mission. I also ordered a reconnaissance aircraft to prepare for takeoff. I had the crews assembled in about fifteen minutes and had the fuses on the bombs set to detonate on ground contact, the most effective way to inflict damage on any aircraft parked at Quan Lãng. I didn't care about blowing a hole in the runway—the North Vietnamese could repair a hole in no time. I wanted to kill that MiG.

Aware that the enemy monitored our frequencies, we maintained total radio silence. Four strike F-4s, along with an F-4 reconnaissance aircraft, were rolling down the runway a few minutes later. I leveled off at about 50 feet above the ground with the others lined up off my right wing. We'd been briefed that the MiG would be hidden in a grove of trees at the west end of the dirt runway, even though on our first pass over the field I couldn't find it. I went to afterburner and pulled up hard, setting up for a bomb run. The other F-4s pulled up in sequence. I got set up and came in for a perfect release. Just as we pulled up, I got a signal that a SAM radar site was tracking us, but we were in and out so fast that the enemy had no time to launch any missiles.

After the last bomb from the last strike F-4 hit the ground, I made a call for all my flight to check in. I received no answer from the number three aircraft, flown by Bruce Gillette. This mission was Bruce's last before returning home. I sent the rest of the flight back to base and turned back to look for a column of smoke in case Bruce had gone down, but just as I got back over the target area, I heard Bruce's voice. He'd been on the wrong frequency and had just gotten it squared away. I went into a 6-G diving turn to get the hell out of Dodge.

When we reviewed the recon film later, we discovered that in fact there'd been no MiG on the ground at Quan Lãng, but we'd definitely sent a message to the enemy not to tug on Superman's cape too hard. It had taken guts for Gen. Lavelle to approve that strike, and we hoped that it was a harbinger of a new attitude in the Air Force. Maybe the politicians were going to let us try to win this war after all. Instead, the opposite occurred. The politicians prevailed, and Gen. Lavelle was fired. In my estimation, Lavelle was the most effective leader we had during the entire air war. It was just a damn shame.

A couple of weeks later, Gen. John D. Ryan, the Air Force chief of staff, showed up and demanded a briefing on the raid at Quan Lãng. I delivered the briefing personally. When Ryan finished looking through the reconnaissance photos, he had one question.

"Why in the hell didn't you hit the runway?"

In my mind, it had been a perfect bomb run, and the photos bore that out. I was insulted by the general's question.

"General," I said, "our target was a MiG, not a dirt runway. If we'd put a bomb dead center on their runway, they would've had it repaired in a matter of minutes."

Ryan frowned. He still didn't understand that I was not just the briefer, that I had led the raid myself.

"Did the pilot use the Dive Toss system?" he asked. This radar-assisted system released bombs automatically according to radar distance to the target, dive angle, airspeed, and type of bomb. Unfortunately, it wasn't usually very accurate.

"No, sir," I said. "We didn't use Dive Toss because we wanted to hit the target."

It was pretty clear the general didn't appreciate my response.

"Damn fighter pilots," he barked. "They don't use the equipment we give them—no wonder they miss the damn targets."

"General," I told him, "we hit the target dead on."

He glared at me. "And just how do you know so much about this particular mission?"

I told him. He looked at me a moment longer before dismissing me. Our wing commander, Charlie Gabriel—Charlie had been in my fighter squadron in Germany in 1952 and would go on to become Air Force chief of staff—told me that he'd never heard a junior officer speak to a general the way I had. The general's aide told me the same thing. But no one ever accused Gen. Ryan of being a great leader like Gen. Lavelle, so I didn't worry about it for too long.

From the moment of his first rat race as a cadet, every fighter pilot dreams of one thing: becoming an ace. The number of enemy aircraft kills required to qualify as an ace has varied over time, but in my day the number was five. As squadron commander of the Triple Nickel, I coined a phrase that described my activist philosophy: *you can't kill a MiG sitting on the ground.* Every time I took off in an F-4, getting a MiG was my goal.

When we weren't in the air, we spent a lot of time talking about how to engage the enemy and how we could put ourselves into position to shoot down a MiG. We knew the North Vietnamese MiGs were directed into combat and controlled by ground radar. We also knew that they monitored our tactical frequencies and were generally aware of our location and intent. Every day we were provided with a communications code that we would use to coordinate with the various controlling agencies that guided our aerial combat procedures. Since we knew the enemy was listening, I came up with the idea of using a code signifying that the following message was bogus. In the right situation, this tactic might give us a chance to throw the enemy off guard and maybe get the jump on them.

At Udorn, we had four F-4s on ground alert twenty-four hours a day. At any given time, our alert building housed eight aircrews and eight maintenance personnel, everybody rested and ready to scramble. One day in March 1972, I scheduled myself for alert duty. After preflighting my aircraft, I sat down with my weapons system officer (WSO), Lt. Leigh Hodgson. I'd never flown with Hodgson before, and I briefed him on the way I flew the F-4 and on tactics and crew coordination. Maj. Roger Carroll and Capt. David Harris, who would be my wingmen, were also present.

That evening at about eight the klaxon horn went off. We hustled out to our aircraft, made a formation takeoff, and began our climb to altitude. Ground radar informed us that MiGs were in the air over Hanoi, heading for northern Laos. This scenario was not uncommon. In fact, it had almost become a game. The North Vietnamese MiGs would penetrate Laotian airspace and then withdraw as soon as our F-4s got up and into position. It was their way of tweaking us, and they'd been pretty effective at it. This time, however, I had a plan. As we were heading toward our orbit area, I got on the radio and announced that I was heading to the tanker for refueling. I instructed the other aircraft to continue to the orbit area. As I left the tanker in the clear, I informed my wingman that I would replace him in the orbit while he refueled.

Just as I'd planned, as soon as the other F-4 left the orbit, the MiGs turned back into Laos, assuming they were safe. When I had confirmation of that, I used the bogus code and announced that I was having trouble with my tanks, that they were not transferring fuel properly, and that I would have to return to the tanker. I hoped the enemy would conclude that all the F-4s had vacated northern Laos. That's when I dived for the deck. There was no moon that night, and we were over mountainous terrain. I dropped down to about 700 feet above the peaks and pushed the engine up to full power. In order to remain invisible, I did not light my afterburners. My WSO, Hodgson, was absolutely fearless. He knew how close we were to the mountain tops, but he just continued working the radar set.

We could see the MiG on our screen, but we didn't lock our radar on him right away. The MiGs had a detector that signaled when they were being tracked by enemy airborne radar. We were charging straight at him, and he was heading right for us. We had a closing rate of more than 1,000 miles per hour. Then, at the last moment, we locked up on him, and I fired a missile—which promptly fell off and failed to ignite. I fired again. This time the missile dropped off the rails and veered off-course to the right. I only had one AIM-7 (an air-to-air missile) left at this point, and the MiG was closing hard. I squeezed the trigger. I knew there wouldn't be much time for the missile to arm after it was launched. I was going to need a bit of luck.

Seconds later the MiG exploded in front of us. Just moments before I'd gotten him, he had fired two missiles at us. I put the F-4 into a 6-G turn to the left and stayed low. Both of his missiles just missed.

We were in pretty high spirits on our return flight to Udorn. I called ahead to the command post and asked them to get a replacement crew to stand alert for me after I landed since I was going to be busy writing out my postflight reports. I now had my first kill under my belt. Four more and I'd be an ace. I was thankful for the entire team's professionalism: my WSO, my wingmen, the controllers on the *Lockheed Constellation*, and the flight crew. Everyone did an outstanding job. During the Vietnam air war, the success rate of the AIM-7 Sparrow missile was only about 30 percent, so a pilot needed not only a great team but a bit of good fortune to get a kill. On that day I had both.

In celebration of my kill—the 114th MiG shot down by American pilots in the war—my squadron managed to park my Jeep *inside* the officers' club. I never figured out exactly how they did it since it was too large to fit through the door or any or the windows, but the Triple Nickel made its reputation doing the impossible.

Drive-in service. In celebration of my MiG kill, the men managed to park my Jeep inside the Udorn officers' club.

In the spring of 1972, our fighter wing at Udorn began to increase our daily number of missions. The F-4 Phantom is a superb fighter, but it was extremely difficult to maintain—especially in the conditions we faced in Southeast Asia. With a force of twenty-four F-4s in my squadron, we could usually schedule only about twenty-one or twenty-two sorties per day. With our twenty-seven crews, we could easily have flown forty combat missions a day if we'd had aircraft ready to go, but we never did. As a consequence, in response to the invasion, we could increase our output by only three or four missions a day. It was frustrating for all of us because the North Vietnamese Army had troops and tanks out in the open and would have been sitting ducks for our fighters. The weather was always a problem, with monsoons and multiple layers of clouds stacked up to 30,000 feet in some cases, but we were fighter pilots, and we solved problems.

On April 2, an EB-66 was hit by a SAM just south of the DMZ. Only one crew member, a crusty fifty-three-year-old navigator named Lt. Col. Gene Hambleton, survived. The next day all of the aircrews were briefed on the situation and informed that Hambleton, whose call sign was Bat-21 Bravo, was in contact by radio. The account of Hambleton's ordeal would later be celebrated in at least two books devoted to his story.

The Triple Nickel had three aircraft instrumented with the LORAN-D navigational system (LORAN stands for "LOng RAnge Navigation"). The LORAN used low-frequency transmitters and three ground stations that combined to provide an accurate position of the plane's movement across the surface below. The onboard computer would then provide guidance information to the pilot, allowing him to place his bombs on a specific point on the ground. In those days before geographical positioning systems, it was the best such system we had, and we relied on it whenever cloud cover obscured our view of the target.

On April 10, a full week after Bat-21 Bravo had gone down, I was assigned to drop bombs on enemy elements that he was reporting were advancing on his position. I had two triple-ejector racks with 500-pound bombs, one rack on each wing. Because of the thick overcast, I was concerned about dropping my bombs so close to his position. This guy had managed to survive ejection and an enemy that was hot on his trail, and I sure as hell didn't want to drop anything on top of him. I was above the clouds at 18,000 feet, right in the optimum range for the SAMs that we knew were being launched in the area. I had Bat-21

Bravo on the radio, and I alerted him when we were ready to release our bombs. I told him I was going to release three at a time and gave him a countdown so he'd be able to take cover. This stuff was going to hit very close to where he was.

When the first bombs hit, Bat-21 Bravo was ecstatic. We apparently knocked out some of the enemy. He wanted the next drop even closer to him. I was impressed with the confidence he had in us. My navigator and I recomputed for the next drop and came in for a release of our remaining three bombs. This time Bat-21 actually shouted into his radio. We'd hit right smack on the target. He wanted even more bombs, so I called airborne command and requested additional aircraft. After refueling, I led four F-4s back to the area. When we arrived, I called Bat-21 on the radio again and heard him say that this time he wanted the bombs 100 yards *closer* to his position. I led the F-4s to the target, and each dropped its bomb on my countdown. I waited anxiously after each pass to hear Bat-21's voice, sure that at some point we were going to nail him, but once all the bombs were gone, he was back on the radio, crowing about our pinpoint accuracy.

I returned to the tanker, refueled again, and returned with three Marine A-4s that were waiting for me. Again, we dropped ordnance all around Bat-21, a little closer to him each time. When the A-4s had dropped everything they had, I asked Bat-21 if he needed more support. He said no, we'd taken out all the enemy he could see. He thanked us for our work, and I returned to Udorn. I hated to leave the poor son of a bitch out there, but by this point I'd been airborne for more than six hours and had made five aerial refuelings.

The next day, April 11, a brave ground team rescued Bat-21 Bravo. The entire operation was controversial because of the manpower and ordnance expended on behalf of a single soldier, but I was happy to have contributed to the survival of one of our own. I knew I'd hope for the same level of effort if I ever had the misfortune to be the man on the ground.

6
Hanoi

*   *   *   *   *   *

On March 31, 1972, the North Vietnamese Army came rolling
across the DMZ in force, and the entire complexion of the war
changed overnight. It was a full-on invasion. Whole divisions
with tanks and artillery. Conventional warfare. The enemy was finally
out of the swamps and the jungles and out into open country where
we could get at him. We'd drawn down much of our ground forces by
this point, but we still had plenty of air power on tap. This aggressive
escalation was exactly what we'd been waiting for—in my case, for nine
years.

We started going after targets around Hanoi and Haiphong in a
serious way. These were "heavy" missions, with maybe 150 airplanes:
F-4s, A-4s, F-8s, F-105s, Wild Weasels to take out the SAM sites and other
significant targets such as bridges and fuel depots, all accompanied by
tankers, chaff planes, and reconnaissance planes. And the MiG combat
aerial patrols, or MiGCAPs—they were the Triple Nickel's responsibility.
We were up there above the fray, watching and waiting. Hunting. Our
assignment was to keep the Soviet-built fighters off our aircrafts' backs.
We didn't carry bombs—we carried air-to-air missiles. And we killed
MiGs. From 1966 to 1973, the 555th had thirty-nine confirmed MiG
kills, more than any other squadron in Southeast Asia. In fact, we still
hold the modern record for MiG kills by the Air Force or the Navy. Our
unofficial motto was: World's Largest Distributor of MiG Parts.

On May 10, we went north on one of these heavy missions. I was
the element lead of a four-ship MiGCAP. The MiGs were up that day,
but my flight always seemed to be where the MiGs were not. I listened

to the various encounters on the radio but never did see any MiGs or have any radar contact. It was very frustrating for me because I lived for these fights, and the fight that day represented the most intensive air-to-air combat with the greatest loss of aircraft of any in the entire air war. We lost two aircraft from our own fighter wing. One of them was flown by Maj. Bob Lodge. A MiG-17 snuck up his butt. Bob had been our fighter-wing weapons officer, and he was one hell of a fighter pilot. He had three MiG kills to that point and, without a doubt, would have become the leading ace in Vietnam. So I'd not only missed the action—and my chance at a second MiG—I'd lost two crews and four of my good friends. It was a black day at Udorn.

I sent word to the wing commander that evening. I felt as if I had a score to settle. Charlie Gabriel was a good guy, and I knew he'd give me a fair hearing.

"Sir, I'd really like to fly tomorrow. We just lost Bob Lodge and Roger Locher. If we have a heavy tomorrow, I want to be in there." (We would later learn that Locher, after his shoot-down, managed to evade the enemy for twenty-three days before being rescued.)

About an hour later, Gabriel called back with my answer.

"Sorry, Kittinger," he said, "request denied. I'm going to lead that MiGCAP tomorrow myself. I need you back here on the ground."

When the FRAG came in at two the next morning, I called the colonel, resigned to my status: "Sir, you've got a heavy, and your takeoff time is 10:30. Your MiGCAP is called 'Oyster Flight.' Good luck."

That's when I got the good news.

"You're going to have to go ahead and take it." The colonel sounded frustrated. "I'm too tied up with these summary courts and taking care of the survivors of yesterday's tragedy. You go on and get 'em, Joe." Which is how I came to lead the Oyster Flight on May 11, 1972, exactly seventeen days before what was to have been the end of my final tour of duty in Southeast Asia.

It would turn out to be the hairiest mission of my career.

As squadron commander for the Triple Nickel, I made a practice of flying as many different types of missions as I could. I had resolved never to ask any of our pilots to do something I hadn't already done myself—an ethic I'd picked up from Col. Stapp back at Holloman. Contrary to accepted practice, I also made a point of flying with a different WSO on each mission in order to get to know my men better and to give all of them a chance to get comfortable with my procedures. Most of the F-4 pilots flew with the same backseater on every mission, which allowed them to establish coordination and procedures. They would work as a team and build up confidence in each other. I had flown with Lt. William "Tiny" Reich—Tiny was about 6 feet 3 inches tall—on the May 10 mission, and he'd done a great job. Now I informed the scheduling officer that I'd decided to use him again because of the time that would be required to brief a replacement—forty-five minutes that I didn't have. It was the first time I'd ever flown with the same WSO on consecutive missions. Unfortunately, it wouldn't turn out to be a very lucky deal for Tiny.

As with all such missions to the North, we had to refuel on a tanker following takeoff. After refueling and departing the tanker, I headed for the rendezvous point over Hanoi. A Navy ship stationed in the Gulf of Tonkin was the controlling agency for this mission. The ship had all kinds of listening devices and good radar capable of detecting MiGs leaving the airfields. On the mission frequency, "Red Crown" (the call sign for the Navy vessel; my call sign was "Oyster") announced that MiGs were aloft over Hanoi and very close to our position. My flight was spread out in a tactical formation slightly north of Hanoi, orbiting at 30,000 feet, and we were watching for those MiGs. We had just turned back south when we heard Red Crown. By this time, our external fuel tanks were dry, so we jettisoned them and pushed up our power to increase airspeed.

I suddenly spotted a smallish aircraft several miles in front of us, although I couldn't positively identify it as a MiG. The Navy's A-4 was small like a MiG, with a delta-type wing, and had a similar profile from the rear. The first rule of aerial combat: *never shoot down a friendly aircraft.* It's always better to bypass a kill than to shoot down a buddy. I asked the other members of my flight if they could identify what we were seeing, but nobody could. I pushed up the power and gave chase. The unidentified aircraft headed north and then turned back to the south. I was on his butt now. I was almost positive I had a MiG. Almost. He made a slow turn to the west, then to the north. I stayed right on him. I called Red Crown and told them I was in pursuit of an unidentified aircraft, and if they could identify it as a MiG, I could kill it. But Red Crown couldn't make the identification either.

"Stand by, Oyster 1."

Such is the nature of the fighter pilot's job. I increased the power to full afterburner to try and close the gap. I was in excess of Mach 2 at about 22,000 feet and constantly checking all quadrants to make sure enemy aircraft weren't converging on us as we chased this bogie. I had just checked my wingman's position, and he was in good shape to clear my tail—or so I thought.

I was slowly gaining on the unidentified aircraft and instructed Tiny to lock up the radar on it. I had already armed the fire-control systems and needed only to pull the trigger to fire the missiles. I was ready. I continued to close in steadily on our prey. I asked again if anyone could identify the aircraft. I told my wingman that if I overshot and the target turned out to be a MiG, he should go ahead and shoot it down in case I was no longer in position. I didn't care who got him—just as long as we got him.

And then I heard the panicked voice of my wingman.

"Oyster Lead, break right!"

I immediately jerked the stick to initiate a right bank and put a brutal 8 Gs on the aircraft. The next thing I knew, we were hit by an aerial missile. That fast. The guy had snuck up from below and gotten me. It happens before you know it. There was no guesswork about it. I understood instantly that this strike was the real deal: we'd been fatally hit, and we needed to eject. My airplane had gone crazy—tumbling and spinning and rolling.

I attempted to pull the face curtain, which was the preferred method of high-speed egress from an F-4, but due to the terrible G forces I couldn't manage to extend my arms above my head to initiate the ejection sequence. I was pinned to my seat. Next I tried to use the under-the-seat handle to eject, but it took me several tries before I could even get my hands on it. At this point, I was in excess of Mach 1 at 18,000 feet, and what was left of the F-4 was a mess of hardware and fire.

The ejection sequence runs like this: the rear canopy goes, the front canopy goes, the backseater ejects, then the pilot ejects. If the pilot were to eject first, he'd burn up the backseater with his rocket blast. The whole process is over in half a second.

I was finally able to time the rolling Gs and get a grip on the handle. I pulled up with everything I had, and then boom: I found myself in midair, shot out of the spinning, tumbling jet. The forces twisting my body as I sailed free were like nothing I'd ever experienced. It was just a sudden violent chaos of wind and pain. I was getting a taste of the punishment Col. Stapp had experienced on his final sled run at Holloman back in 1955.

Moments later I separated from my seat. I was in free fall now and for the first time became aware that I'd lost my helmet in the windblast. I knew the aneroid was set to open my parachute at an altitude of 10,000 feet, so I assumed a skydiving position, face to earth, trying to stay focused and looking for the ground, and fell until the chute opened. I glanced up to check my parachute canopy, then started scanning the skies for signs of Tiny. I finally spotted him about 2 miles away, coming down beneath his chute. I could see that his head was chin down, and he looked limp. Damn. I tried to maneuver myself toward him so that we'd land as near to one another as possible. Then I heard a strange, almost surreal, sound: bells ringing. Like church bells. Vietnamese villagers ring bells to alert each other when something unusual happens. My F-4 had already hit the ground a few miles away and was now burning furiously. Below me, all I could see was an endless rice field. It was three in the afternoon, and I was roughly 30 miles northwest of Hanoi. There was absolutely no cover anywhere, though I could see what looked like a small village maybe a mile from where I was going to come down. It wasn't a great situation. For the first time, I began to think about the future. The days and weeks ahead. Months? Years?

As I approached the ground, I could see people, lots of them, in peasant clothes and coolie hats, running toward my landing spot. I knew I was in real trouble, especially when a guy took a potshot at me with a rifle. I couldn't locate any trees or anything that might provide even just a bit of concealment. It was a pretty helpless feeling. I didn't want to break an ankle, so I concentrated on a good landing position. I landed fine but was immediately gang-tackled by a gaggle of farmers, many of them women and children, all of them frantic and shouting. I couldn't move, and I couldn't talk to these people. I had no opportunity to get to my pistol or my Randall knife. Dozens of hands stood me up, keeping a grip on my arms and legs, and removed my weapons. They were screaming and spitting at me. One of the women clawed at me and tried to tear off my flight suit, but she couldn't make much progress because my pistol belt was still attached. Then the whole crowd went to work on me. They cut off the pistol belt and stripped off my flight suit. By this time, about two dozen people were surrounding me. An old woman, maybe about seventy, with a single black tooth in her howling mouth, took a swing at my throat with a small machete. Then a little boy took a whack at me. They both missed, but only by inches. Under the circumstances, I had to consider myself lucky. Even though it was about all I had going for me, *I was alive.*

A few moments later a soldier with a rifle showed up and took charge. The first thing he did was make me lower my underwear so that he could check my rectum for a weapon. Then he had me remove my boots and tied my arms tight behind me. He tied my feet with a rope about 18 inches apart so I could walk but not run. As we started out of the rice paddy, the soldier's rifle still trained on me and prodding me in the back, individuals stepped out of the crowd and took swings at me with their fists and sticks. It was at this point I realized I had a pretty bad gash on my left shin that was bleeding, probably from a piece of shrapnel picked up before leaving the F-4. I called the soldier's attention to my wound, but he simply motioned for me to keep moving.

We eventually got to a road where a Jeep-type vehicle was parked. The soldier shoved me into the back and ordered three of the locals to ride with me. We drove maybe 5 miles to a small village, where I was hauled into a mud hut and had my feet bound together. I was thinking about Tiny and wondering what had happened to him. I couldn't be sure that he'd even survived the ejection. I said a prayer for Tiny. As darkness fell, I was struck again with the thought that, in spite of my predicament, my own luck had held up. So far, at least.

A while later they blindfolded me and crammed me into another vehicle. It was a four-hour ride to Hanoi and not a very comfortable one. It was hot, and I was developing a terrible thirst. I was hogtied on the floor and tended to by a bunch of North Vietnamese, who punched and kicked me the whole way. We finally stopped, and they removed the bindings on my feet—but not the blindfold. They marched me into some sort of compound, unlocked a door, and shoved me into a small room. Later, somebody came in to untie me and remove the blindfold.

The cell was 10 feet by 10 feet, windowless, bare except for a small table and illuminated by a single light bulb suspended from a piece of wire too high to reach. My captors would slide aside a block of wood attached to the outside of the door whenever they wanted to look in on me. After I'd been there about thirty minutes, I had visitors. Three soldiers. They brought me a small bucket to use as a toilet. I motioned that I needed something to drink and showed them the bleeding wound on my leg. They understood but remained expressionless. It was as if they were sizing me up, inspecting the day's catch. After a minute, they left and locked the door. I was horribly thirsty.

I sat on the floor and reviewed my predicament. Twenty-four hours earlier I'd been in the officers' club in Udorn enjoying a big, juicy steak and a cold beer. Tonight I was a member of the It'll Never Happen to Me Club. U.S. prisoners of war (POWs) had been a constant topic of discussion in the Triple Nickel. We knew they were up here in Hanoi, but we had no information about how they'd been treated or precisely where they were kept. We suspected some had been killed. Many of us wore POW bracelets with names of pilots who were missing in action (MIA). In fact, I'd had one on when I'd come down in the rice field. It had the name "Maj. Kenneth Johnson" on it. Ken was a Triple Nickel pilot who'd been shot down in December 1971 during my command of the squadron. That bracelet confused the hell out of the soldier who'd captured me. He kept asking for my name and shaking his head when I told him. He pointed to the bracelet. He thought I was Ken Johnson. We'd never forgotten the POWs, and it was a small source of comfort to think that somebody might soon be wearing a bracelet with my name on it.

I thought back on all the survival schools I'd attended and all of the literature I'd read about being taken prisoner. I tried to recall all that I'd learned about resisting interrogation and about the Geneva Convention. I understood that everything would hinge on how I handled my initial experience with the interrogation process that was surely to come. I prayed that I would find the strength to stick to my principles and that I would survive this ordeal. I was worried about what might happen, but I told myself that I would rather die than give in. By this time, the enemy knew that I was a lieutenant colonel and a fighter pilot, and I imagined that I would probably be something of a prize for them. I was determined not to allow myself to be exploited for whatever propaganda purposes they might dream up.

In my mind, I reviewed the training sessions in which students had been interrogated. I recalled that once a person starts to make concessions to the interrogator, regardless of the reason, it gets harder and harder to resist. I made up my mind to stick strictly to the requirements of the Geneva Convention, to give them only my name, date of birth, rank, and serial number.

I was acutely dehydrated by this time, and my leg was killing me. It was a long, miserable night. About an hour after sunup, three North Vietnamese entered my cell, bringing with them two chairs. I later found out that one of the men, an older guy, was the camp commander, another was an interrogator, and the other was a guard. The guard remained standing while the other two sat in the chairs. I stood at attention.

The interrogator, the only one who spoke English, asked me to identify myself.

"Lieutenant Colonel Joseph Kittinger," I replied. "Serial number 260-74-6890. Birth date 27 July 1928."

The interrogator asked me where I was stationed and what wing I was assigned to.

"North Vietnam signed the Geneva Convention. All I am required to give you is name, rank, and serial number."

As the translation was given to the camp commander, I could see that my response did not make him very happy. I imagined he'd heard it once or twice before. He glared at me for a moment.

"In accordance with the Geneva Convention," I continued, "you are required to provide medical treatment to wounded prisoners of war."

The commander and the interrogator conferred. It was a long, animated discussion, but I remained at attention. When they stopped talking, I told them I was thirsty and needed water. I realized later that it was a mistake to ask for anything. They talked a while longer, then picked up the chairs, left the room, and locked the door behind them.

I waited, hoping someone would return with some water so that I could at least wash out my leg wound. About five hours later, the door opened, and the interrogator entered with two guards. By this time, my tongue was so dry and swollen that I found it difficult to speak.

"Where are you stationed?" he asked. "What organization are you assigned to?"

I repeated my name, rank, serial number, and date of birth.

"Do you want food and water?"

I hesitated. "Yes."

"If you will answer my questions, we will bring you some water."

"In accordance with the Geneva . . ."

The interrogator cut me off. "You must not repeat that statement!" His expression was grim. "The Geneva Convention applies to military prisoners of war, which you are not. You are a Yankee pirate. You are a criminal and will be treated as a criminal. If you do not answer my questions, you will die in this cell. Do you understand?"

With that, they left me alone. I had no reason to doubt the threat. I prayed. There was no other relief.

I learned later that there were four separate prison facilities in Hanoi. Earlier in the war, American captives had been stashed in makeshift facilities all over the countryside, but following the dramatic raid on the Son Tay prison camp by Army Special Forces and the Air Force in November 1970, most POWs had been moved to secure sites in the capital. French-built Hoa Lo, where they'd brought me, was the biggest penitentiary in all of North Vietnam. It was the one nicknamed the "Hanoi Hilton" by the American POWs who'd preceded me and who were presumably somewhere nearby. If they were still alive. Virtually escape proof, surrounded by a 16-foot concrete wall topped with protruding shards of broken glass and electrified barbed wire, monitored by four guard towers, the compound covered an irregularly shaped city block in the metropolitan heart of the city. The place had a few trees and a garden, along with a long central courtyard, but you'd never have mistaken it for a real Hilton. Hoa Lo was steamy, filthy, and infested with ants and scorpions and mosquitoes. The rats were everywhere, and they were huge—literally the size of cats. It was where most of the American prisoners were kept, and it would be my home for most of the next year.

About two hours after my initial interrogation, the camp commander reentered my cell, this time with a new interrogator. It was immediately obvious to me that they'd decided to try a good cop/bad cop routine. The new interrogator announced that the prison was being run by the Benevolent Society of North Vietnam and that all prisoners were treated humanely. Then they left. About thirty minutes later, the door opened again, and a guard brought in two small bowls, one containing about a pint of water, the other full of a suspicious liquid that I guessed was some sort of soup. I spent a moment debating whether to drink the water or use it to cleanse my wound. I was concerned about infection, but decided to drink. The soup was vile, but it was all I had—so down it went.

After a while, the "good cop" interrogator returned and asked if I felt better. I reminded him that I needed medical attention. He silenced me with a wave of his hand.

"We still have some questions to ask you for our records."

I started to repeat the name, rank, and serial number mantra, but he cut me off. The smile had melted off his face.

"You have a bad attitude," he said and left the cell. I would hear this comment hundreds of times during my incarceration. I began to wonder where Tiny was and if he was still alive. I said another prayer for him.

And yet another for myself.

The next morning they brought me some more water and another bowl of soup. At about 10:00 a.m., the original interrogator appeared and began peppering me with questions. I gave him the same litany, citing the Geneva Convention.

"Does your wound hurt you?" he asked.

"Look," I told him, "you are *required* to provide me with medical attention."

He glared at me. "Not for criminals," he said, flashing a sadistic smile. That was it. He took his chair and left. The whole thing was getting a little ridiculous.

The truth was the wound hurt like hell, and I could see that it was becoming infected. Now that I'd had some water, I was able to urinate into the wound, trying to wash out some of the dirt and puss. That became my routine over the next few weeks, and it seemed to help. At least, the infection didn't seem to be getting worse or spreading.

Each morning the North Vietnamese would come into my cell and ask me questions that I would answer the same way. I knew that they were becoming more irritated with me. I think they were hoping that my wound would get worse and that by denying me sufficient water to irrigate it, they could weaken my resolve, but I was determined not to give up. I was going to push these guys as hard as I could and resist for as long as I could.

As time goes on, solitary confinement becomes a truly miserable experience. All my life I had filled my idle time with books, and being locked up with nothing to read and no stimuli was very depressing. I started playing mental games to keep myself occupied. I revisited my childhood, thought back through all the aircraft I'd ever flown, all of the places I'd visited. There was fortunately plenty to remember. Anything to keep from dwelling on the dismal fix I'd found myself in. I thought back on my balloon training, on the Manhigh and Excelsior and Stargazer days. I began to think about what it would take to make a solo flight around the world in a balloon. It was kind of a romantic, crazy idea—but what a glorious trip that would be! It was one of the last great adventure challenges out there, and I saw no reason why I shouldn't be the one to do it. There were a million things to consider with such a flight, and I had time to consider them all. I came up with a balloon design that would take advantage of solar heating and nighttime cooling, the gondola setup I'd need, the entire life-support and communications system, the weather-reporting resources I'd want access to, a navigation strategy, and on and on. This fantasy project kept me alert and mentally occupied. As the days and weeks ground on, I continued to review and modify these plans until not only did I begin to believe that they *might* work, I became convinced that they *would* work—just as soon as I could find my way out of this hellhole.

My mother was a devout Christian. Way back in February 1949, just a month before I left home to pursue my career in the Air Force, she had sat me down and handed me a piece of paper that had the Twenty-third Psalm written on it. She told me she didn't worry about me entering pilot training because she had faith that God would take care of me, but she said she wanted me to memorize that psalm so that I would have it available if I ever got into a situation where I would need it. Because I could see that it was important to her, I did as she asked and committed the psalm to memory. I hadn't thought much about it in all those years since then, but one evening in my cell in Hanoi it all came rushing back. It seemed to fit my predicament perfectly, especially—for some reason—the part about lying by still waters. I repeated the words to myself, and they brought me great relief. It seemed to be Scripture written especially for a POW. I thanked my mother and hoped that I would see the day when I could tell her how much her gift to me had helped. My family would not learn for many months that I had survived my shoot-down. It hurt to imagine what they might be going through. I thought of my wife and my boys, my parents, and wished I could somehow get word out to them. Some of the POWs were allowed to write letters home, but that was a privilege I would never enjoy.

One day, one of the North Vietnamese asked if I wanted something to read. If I could have one book, he asked, what would I choose?

"The Bible," I replied. I guess that psalm was on my mind. I had never really had time to study the Bible, and this seemed like the perfect opportunity.

"That's what all you American criminals want," my captor said, looking genuinely puzzled. "Why is that?"

I just looked him in the eye. There was no way he could ever understand.

I was pretty sure the day would come when the North Vietnamese would get fed up with my refusal to answer their questions. They didn't seem to be big fans of the Geneva Convention, and it was clear their patience was wearing thin. I'd been in their faces from the beginning, and I assumed there would be reprisals at some point. One day the bad cop came into my cell accompanied by a very muscular guard and his assistant. I knew what was about to happen wouldn't be good.

The interrogator addressed me. "We will no longer take your attitude. You have insulted us. We insist that you answer our questions."

I stood at attention, maintained my defiance, and gave him the same routine: name, rank, serial number. The funny thing was, they already knew the answers to all the questions they'd been asking me. Three days after my capture, *Stars and Stripes* had run a piece on me—"Daredevil Pilot Lost in Dogfight over North Viet"—and these guys had a copy. They knew I was a lieutenant colonel who'd been in Vietnam off and on since 1963, that I was a squadron commander with 483 combat sorties and a MiG kill. They even knew about Project Excelsior. I found out later that the North Vietnamese had mostly stopped torturing POWs in Hoa Lo well before I arrived there, but I seemed to be a special case to them.

The interrogator motioned to the big guard, who forced me onto the floor. With the help of his assistant, the guard bent my arms behind me and tied them to a steel bar, bringing the rope ends down and tying my feet to a second bar. It quickly became very painful. When they tightened the rope, it winched my legs up and forced my abdomen down. It felt for all the world as if my spine were coming apart in splinters. I guess they'd worked out this whole routine pretty carefully because I'd never experienced pain like this before. I was actually hoping that the pressure would snap a bone and force me to lose consciousness. At a certain point, I knew that I wouldn't be able to take it much longer and was ready to give up, but at that instant, before I could say anything, they loosened the ropes and relieved the pressure. My prayers had been answered. They left me tied to the bars, though, and the muscles in my arms were on fire.

The interrogator asked me again if I was willing to cooperate. I took a deep breath, shook my head, and the big guard tightened the ropes. In a matter of moments, I was in such agony that I couldn't even think straight. Before I knew what I was saying, I told them I'd answer their questions. The guard took the ropes off. My arms were still burning. I stood back up at attention. The interrogator asked me what squadron I belonged to. Along with the *Stars and Stripes* article, I knew they had my flight suit with the patch of the 555th Tactical Fighter Squadron.

"555th TFS," I said. Jesus, I hated like hell to say it.

He then asked me what organization I belonged to. I felt as if I needed to hold on to something, so I told him I couldn't give him that. He said something in Vietnamese to the big guard, and the guy hit me twice, one fist to the left side of my head and the other to the right. I could feel blood oozing from both my ears. I thought at first the eardrums were ruptured. The interrogator informed me that they would be back to resume the rope treatment and suggested that I had better demonstrate an improved attitude, or things were liable to get much, much worse.

It was something to think about, and, believe me, I did.

Each time I was interrogated, I stood at attention facing the wall about 5 feet in front of me. I would look past the interrogator at the wall. During one of the torture sessions, even though I'd stared at the wall for hours at a time, I suddenly noticed a small cross that appeared to have been etched into the surface. I could only assume that it was the work of a previous POW. However it got there, that little cross was a lifeline to me at a time when I needed all the help could get. It seemed to me literally a godsend.

The tropical heat in Hanoi was oppressive, and mosquitoes were everywhere. My leg wound grew progressively worse. It was now a festering mess about 10 inches long and 4 inches wide. I could barely stand to look at it. The only treatment I could apply were the daily urine baths. I was filthy. My wardrobe consisted of the underwear I was wearing when I was shot down. I was also a little depressed that I'd had to give up the information about my squadron during the torture session with the big guard. I was disheartened. I'd always considered myself to be strong, and now I felt weak and useless. I felt as if even God had abandoned me.

I thought of a fellow Air Commando, Burke Morgan, an A-26 navigator who'd run the Air Commando survival school at England AFB back in the swamps of Louisiana. That training had been grueling. They used to take the Air Commandos and the U.S. Army Special Forces guys down there, and about half of them would flunk out in the first few days. That's how tough it was. Burke used to brief us on interrogation and prison life. Burke was a true warrior who had gotten killed in 1967 on a night mission over Laos in an A-26, but now I found myself talking to him. I told him I was going to hang in there. No matter what they did to me, I wouldn't let them break me. I promised him I wasn't going to disappoint him or let my country down.

"I swear I'm not going to give them anything else, Burke," I told him. "Not one goddamn thing."

The next morning I had visitors. The muscular guard threw me on the floor and once again tied my arms and feet to the bars. There were no preliminaries this time. The guy just came in and got to work.

"So, has your attitude changed?" the interrogator asked me.

I told him my attitude was perfect and that I was within my rights as a POW. I also invited him to kiss my ass. The guard tightened up the ropes. I started praying for the strength not to give in, but the pain overwhelmed everything. You can't think. Time stops. I couldn't help it. I screamed. I told them I'd answer their questions.

The guard loosened the ropes a little but let me know he was ready to cinch them up tight again at a moment's notice.

"What organization are you assigned to?" The interrogator looked at me calmly.

I gave him some generic information he could easily have gotten without my cooperation: "The 432nd Tactical Fighter Wing."

"And what type of aircraft do you fly?"

Once again, he didn't need me to tell him this. The damn thing was all over the rice paddy not far from where I'd been captured. But we were playing a game. He'd won; I'd lost.

"F-4," I said.

The smug interrogator signaled to the guard to let me out of the ropes. I'd given them what they'd wanted, which was my humiliation. They'd tortured me for a total of about ten days, and they had succeeded in breaking me. I had succumbed to the pain. I felt compromised. I had gone beyond the requirements of the Geneva Convention. In my estimation, I had failed to live up to the Code of Conduct of the American Fighting Man, which reads in part: "WHEN QUESTIONED, SHOULD I BECOME A PRISONER OF WAR, I AM BOUND TO GIVE ONLY NAME, RANK, SERVICE NUMBER, AND DATE OF BIRTH." The code goes on to say that prisoners should avoid answering further questions *to the best of their ability*, but I wasn't willing to give myself an out based on that. I was embarrassed, and I was disappointed in my own failure of will. In spite of the fact that I hadn't given them any valuable information, they now had the satisfaction of knowing that their torture techniques had worked on me and of knowing that I knew they could come back and use their ropes again at any time. I'd let myself down. That night, for the first time in my life, I felt myself sliding into depression.

The next day I was moved into a smaller cell, perhaps 5 feet by 8 feet, in an area the prisoners referred to as Heartbreak Hotel; it functioned as a kind of receiving and processing area in the center of the compound. Instead of a door, there were bars. Along one wall was a concrete platform outfitted with metal leg stocks. There were five other cells in the row along with mine, but as far as I could tell, none of them was occupied. I kept hoping that because I'd answered their questions, they'd let me see a doctor. My leg was getting worse, and it was starting to worry me. It stunk something awful, and this stench—along with the pain—made the wound hard to ignore.

On my second day in Heartbreak, the guard took me to a small room at the end of the hall where there was a large bucket of water to bathe in. What a relief! I was given standard-issue POW clothes, and I gladly put them on after getting myself cleaned up. This was my reward for telling them things they already knew. The guard had warned me not to try to look outside, but when he left the hallway, I pulled myself up onto the sill and managed to get a glimpse of the world beyond. That simple act of defiance did wonders for my peace of mind. Right outside the window, an Asian man with a big coolie hat was sweeping the ground. He saw me and gave me a V sign and a thumb's-up signal. A thrill ran through me. I would later learn that this man was Thai Army Special Forces Master Sgt. Chaicharn Harnavee, a fellow POW; he'd been a prisoner for seven years. I also found out that after seeing me, he immediately informed the senior ranking American officer in the prison, Air Force colonel John Peter Flynn, that he had gotten a look at the new POW they'd all heard being tortured the night before.

Three days later they brought in somebody new and put him in a cell in Heartbreak next to mine. It was nighttime. I couldn't see the guy, but when the guards had gone, I decided to investigate.

"Who are you?" I said. He was just around the wall, but I wanted to make sure they hadn't put a North Vietnamese in there to try and get information out of me. There was a long silence before I got an answer.

"Who are *you*?" he asked. He sounded American, but I still wasn't sure.

"You first."

"No, you first," he said back.

We sat in silence for several hours before the guy reached his hand out of his cell and stuck it out where I could see it. It was a black hand! Black skin! I knew he couldn't be a Vietnamese.

"My name is Joe Kittinger," I said immediately.

"Colonel Kitt!" he said. "It's Jim Williams."

Jim was a guy in my squadron. A backseater. We'd flown together. I couldn't believe it. One of my own. It turned out that Jim had been shot down and captured nine days after my incident. There's no way you can imagine how good it felt to have somebody I knew and trusted—not only a member of the United States Air Force, but a member of the Triple Nickel—in there with me just a few feet away. Even though we couldn't actually look each other in the eye, we had a wonderful little reunion just sharing our stories and giving each other the comfort of a familiar voice. Later that same evening, the guards transferred both Jim and me to a room containing a bunch of other prisoners. Room 5 it was called.

I can't really convey the scramble of emotions that had built up in me after a month in solitary—thirty-two days to be exact. Inside Room 5 were more than two dozen other aviator POWs. I saw three more members of my squadron, including Tiny Reich, who had survived his ejection without serious injury and been immediately captured. I'm not sure I've ever been so glad to see anybody in my life. The whole bunch of us started talking all at the same time, trying to bring each other up to date on how we'd come to arrive in Hoa Lo and how we'd been treated. Besides myself, only one other recent POW had been tortured. I guess we were the stubborn ones, or maybe we just had the worst "attitudes."

Room 5 was about 70 feet long by 20 feet wide. It had open areas and barred windows. A small room at the back had a hole in the ground that served as the toilet. At night, we placed individual wooden pallets on the floor to sleep on. During the day, we stacked the pallets upright so we could move around freely. Outside of the room was a small enclosed area beyond which we understood the "older" POWs were imprisoned.

The POWs had been divided into two groups, and the North Vietnamese worked hard to keep us separated and to block any communication between us. The POWs who had been shot down prior to December 1971, when the United States resumed operations in the North, were affectionately known as the FOGs, Fucking Old Guys. They had endured the harshest conditions. Apparently sensitive to the scorn of the international community and perhaps fearful of reprisals, the North Vietnamese had improved conditions in their prisons after Ho Chi Minh's death. The rest of us were the FNGs, Fucking New Guys. All the men in Heartbreak Hotel with me were FNGs, and our wing of the prison was known as New Guy Village.

One of the things we'd all learned in our survival training was the necessity of maintaining a military structure as POWs. This understanding came largely out of the experiences of American prisoners during the Korean War. It was crucially important to keep up an established chain of command even behind bars. As such, the senior ranking officer (SRO) would be the overall commander of the POWs, regardless of branch of the service. The SRO would represent all the prisoners to the enemy organization, even though the North Vietnamese refused to recognize our military structure and made it clear they gave it no credence. I'd never given much thought to this requirement during my training days.

You never imagined that you might actually become a prisoner some-day. In Hanoi, though, we resolved to have an SRO for every room and an SRO for each group. It was quickly determined that as a forty-four-year-old lieutenant colonel, I was not only the oldest man there, but the one with the highest rank and should therefore serve as SRO for all the FNGs. I had never desired any command position less, but I kept this feeling to myself. It was an awesome responsibility, and it weighed on me from the first moment. The SRO was charged with advocating for the health and welfare of all the POWs and for making decisions on their behalf. It involved disciplining the men when necessary and hold-ing them accountable for their actions. I had to take the responsibility seriously because everyone's well-being and the group's morale were at stake.

The next day, after being transferred to Room 5, I was taken to see a medic, who cleaned my leg wound, applied some salve, and dressed it. Nevertheless, it was clear that the medic expected me to lose the leg to infection. Over the next three weeks, he tried a variety of medicines and gave me three shots of penicillin. Finally, he doused the wound with sulfur powder. That seemed to work, and my wound gradually began to heal, but it would be three months before I was sure that I'd be able to keep the leg.

A few days after I was moved to Room 5, an Air Force aviator named Brian Seek who had been badly burned was brought into our room. This poor guy was in shock and didn't respond to suggestions or questions from anyone. There was a vacant look in his eyes, and he walked around like a zombie. He was obviously in terrible pain and needed medical attention, so I went to our cell door and called out, "Bao cao!" This is how we summoned the guard. A rough translation from Vietnamese would be, "I have something to report." One of the English-speaking guards eventually showed up and asked what I wanted. I demanded to speak to the camp commander about the burned man. It was the North Vietnamese's practice to ignore any request from an SRO, so the guard instructed another POW in our room to dress for an interview. All of us had been issued one pair of short pants, one pair of long pants, one short-sleeve shirt, and one long-sleeve shirt. When they wanted us to dress for an interview, they gave us a certain gesture that meant we were to put on the long pants and long-sleeve shirt. So the man who'd been selected dressed up and relayed my request for medical attention, but nothing happened.

That evening we discussed our options. We didn't have many. We weren't in a position to make demands. We couldn't carry around protest signs like the demonstrators back home. We took meals twice a day, once at around nine in the morning and again at about four in the afternoon. They gave us rotten pumpkin soup with an occasional green leaf in it and a portion of bread. It was a starvation diet, but we were happy to get it. It kept us alive. As we talked, we decided that our only leverage was to stage a hunger strike until Seek received medical help. We were taking a big chance because it would be simple for them to allow us to starve ourselves to death. But we knew that Seek was going to die soon if we couldn't get him some help, and we were determined not to let that happen.

After some debate, I put the idea to a vote. We needed 100 percent solidarity on this because we all would suffer if we decided to go forward with our plan. The vote was unanimous: we wouldn't eat until our man received medical attention. No dissenters.

The guard brought our food the next morning as usual, but we left it untouched outside the door. When the guard saw what was happening, he went off to consult with his superior. After a while, he returned and took the food away. We kept trying to get a prison official to talk with us. We shouted "Bao cao! Bao cao!" again and again. When the evening meal came, we left it outside the door uneaten. We were fortunate that the guards never shut off our water. (We found out later that when the FOGs had tried a similar tactic sometime earlier, their water supply *had* been cut off.) After three days, one of the guards instructed me to put on my long clothes for an interview. By this time, we were really feeling the effects of not eating.

Once again I found myself standing at attention in front of a visibly upset camp commander. He was elderly and spoke no English, so an interpreter had to translate for us.

"Why don't you eat?"

"We don't eat," I said, "because we have a man who is very sick and needs medical care. You are obligated to provide care for this man."

"This is not a capitalist prison!" he lectured me. "You do not dictate what we do. You have no rank here. You are criminals. We do not respond to requests from those with bad attitudes, and we do not respond to strikes."

I tried to reason with this man. "All we want is medical attention for an injured soldier. Nothing more." I reminded him again that we were entitled to such treatment under the Geneva Convention.

"*You are not soldiers!*" he screamed. He was apoplectic. "*You are criminals! You have no rights!*"

His next comment was hilarious. After consulting with his guards, he said: "If we do decide to provide treatment to your injured criminal, then you must not think we are doing this because the rest of you are refusing to eat. We do not respond to such attitudes! And you must not tell anybody that we have listened to your request."

I had to suppress a smile. "Naw, we won't tell a soul."

The commander dismissed me, and I was returned to Room 5. Not much later, some guards came and took Brian Seek away. They brought him back a few days later, and we could see that his burns had in fact been treated. He was still in bad shape, but at least we now felt as if he had a chance to make it. In my opinion, these men who were willing to give up their meager portion of food saved a fellow soldier's life. We all ate our ration when it was delivered the next morning. We felt that we'd earned it. Bad pumpkin soup never tasted so good.

The next day I was taken to see the camp commander again.

"Your man is very lucky," he told me. "We were going to send him to an insane asylum."

I believed him. I also believed the next thing he said.

"You would not want to be in one of our insane asylums."

Being an SRO was a humbling experience. I was responsible for our overall stance, our discipline, and our conduct—not only for those in my room, but for all the FNGs at the prison. Even though the North Vietnamese didn't recognize our command structure or my status as SRO, they were acutely aware of it. Whenever one of our captors gave any of our prisoners an order, the prisoner was supposed to respond that his orders came only from Col. Kittinger. I prayed for guidance every night. As American servicemen, we were set on maintaining the integrity of our military structure. It was what we were trained to do, and we felt a powerful obligation to acquit ourselves as well as humanly possible under the circumstances, whether we ever got out alive or not.

We started holding a church service each Sunday morning. We appointed a different POW each week to conduct the service. The man selected typically spent considerable time preparing the sermon. The sermons always did us a world of good. We would open the service with the Pledge of Allegiance, then sing "God Bless America" and a few church songs. We didn't know the second verse of any of the hymns, so we just repeated the first verse. After the first such service, the North Vietnamese took one of the POWs aside and informed him that religious services were strictly forbidden. From that point on, we turned our backs to the cell door during our services, but we kept them going. Whenever a new prisoner was brought into our group, his first Sunday service was guaranteed to bring a tear to his eye. The services always reminded us of home, family, and freedom.

I also instituted a daily calisthenics session for first thing in the morning. I appointed Jim Williams, who was a strong, athletic guy, to lead the exercises. Our sessions lasted about thirty minutes. The guards claimed that these routines amounted to a forbidden military formation, but we mostly just ignored them and kept right on with our workouts.

Communication between rooms was accomplished by means of a "tap code." A FOG had devised the code years earlier, basing it on a code invented by American prisoners in Korea. It was easier to learn and use than Morse code, and every new prisoner was taught the code as part of his orientation. There was even a visual shorthand for the code that looked something like a third-base coach sending signals to a batter. We practiced all the time to keep our code skills sharp. It was our language, and everyone was expected to become fluent.

As the SRO of the FNGs, I learned that a special "high-level" communications protocol would allow me to communicate by means of a written note with the FOGs' SRO across the compound. (We enlisted the help of the Thai prisoner I'd seen sweeping the courtyard to serve as our courier.) Because we seemed to be annoying our captors with our Sunday services and daily calisthenics, I wanted to find out if the FOGs were doing anything similar and, if so, what the consequences had been. So, using ink made of coal dust and a small sheet of coarse toilet paper, I composed a note to Col. Flynn of the FOGs and described the situation. (Flynn was the highest-ranking military officer to be captured during the war. I was eager for any guidance he could provide.) We wanted to coordinate with our brothers on the "other side" as much as possible.

We had a place where we'd hide our notes, under a particular rock in the courtyard, and the Thai POW, Chaicharn Harnavee, would retrieve the notes in the course of his duties and deliver them to Col. Flynn. You had to hand it to Harnavee—it took a lot of guts to be our middleman. There was little doubt that if the guards had ever caught him, he would have been executed. (The North Vietnamese would not free Harnavee until nineteen months after the last American prisoners were released. The Thai and South Vietnamese POWs were gallant warriors, and we were proud to have served with them. They suffered grievously at the hands of our captors.)

I didn't sleep very well as I waited for a return message. I was hoping for some good advice. Three days later I received a note back from Col. Flynn. It read: "It appears that what you are doing is adequate. GBU. SKY."

"Sky" was Flynn's call sign. "GBU" was short for "God bless you"; it was the salutation on all our tap code communiqués and written notes. His reply wasn't really too informative and pretty slim in the way of guidance, but at least I'd made contact, and it sounded as if Flynn was OK with our basic stance.

You have a lot of time to think in prison. You find yourself replaying the events of your life and making plans for a future that sometimes seems hard to believe in. Some things that seemed so important previously become trivial, and others that you'd barely considered begin to consume your thoughts. It can be hard not to dwell on the horrors of the present or to get lost in useless fantasy.

I spent a lot of time thinking about my sons. They were great boys, and I was incredibly proud of them. They'd been moved around from base to base, and that's not an easy life for a child. Their father hadn't been around as much as I knew they'd have liked, but they had always seemed to understand the situation, and they both had a knack for making the best of it. I assumed that Joe had graduated from high school. I knew that he'd received an ROTC scholarship and would be heading to the University of Colorado in the fall. I wanted to let my sons know how much they meant to me, and I vowed that when I returned, I would make sure they'd never have cause to doubt it.

We all dealt with the empty days and empty nights in our own ways. Keeping ourselves entertained and mentally alert was something we worked at. Fortunately, we were a group of mostly educated men. We had Annapolis graduates and Air Force Academy graduates; the majority of us had college degrees. Every day one of us was assigned to provide a briefing on a topic of our choice, something we had special knowledge of. One day we might have a lecture on the Roman Empire or the paintings of Rembrandt. We learned about philosophy, geography, mathematics. We put on skits and re-created movies. We heard songs and poems. We told jokes. It didn't matter. Anything to occupy our minds and remind ourselves that we had real lives beyond the walls of Hoa Lo.

One of my duties as SRO was to organize the FNG escape committee. The Code of Conduct reads: "I WILL MAKE EVERY EFFORT TO ESCAPE AND AID OTHERS TO ESCAPE." It was a tricky thing to contemplate because there had been a few escapes and attempted escapes from the POW camps in Vietnam, and they had usually resulted in brutal retaliation against the remaining prisoners. We had heard that prisoners had even been tortured to death following escape attempts. It was vital that the group involved in escape planning be small in number and that the individuals be unknown to each other so that if anyone were caught trying to escape and subsequently tortured, he would have only limited information to divulge. I designated one man, a Navy lieutenant commander, as chief of the escape committee. I made it clear that any escape attempt must involve all prisoners at one time, leaving no one behind in camp to be brutalized and pay the price for the rest. There could be no exceptions to this rule. But the grim truth was that escape and evasion for most Americans in Hoa Lo (and elsewhere in North Vietnam) was little more than a dream. Even if we could manage to get outside of the prison compound, it would be nearly impossible to blend in with the populace—especially in a crowded metropolis such as Hanoi. Escape from prison sounds adventurous and exciting, but it never seemed very practical to me. Still, given the possibility of spending the rest of our lives in the Hanoi Hilton, we needed to be prepared for all contingencies. And so we were.

As POWs, we did everything we could to antagonize our captors. It was almost a sport. Every week or so we would be taken outside to an area that contained a huge pile of coal dust, maybe 500 pounds of it, and we were instructed to make coal balls from the dust. Now, this might not be the average person's idea of a good time, but to us the fresh air and camaraderie were the equivalent of a holiday at the beach. It's just that we didn't want to prove ourselves *too* efficient at our job.

We'd sit around the pile and each of us would add a little water to a handful of coal dust and use our hands to form little balls about 4 inches in diameter. We were grown men making mud balls. The Vietnamese used them in their cook stoves. It would take about a minute or so to make a coal ball. We'd stack them in a little pile. But every time somebody would add a ball to the pile, somebody else would take a ball away and crush it back down into dust. We'd work hard all day, but our pile of thirty or so coal balls never seemed to grow. The guards could see us going at it, everybody busy making coal balls, but they could never figure out why our production never grew. Fooling the guards was tremendously satisfying for all of us. We laughed our butts off at their stupidity. Much of the captive-captor relationship comes down to a battle of wits, and in that battle most of our North Vietnamese guards were fighting unarmed.

One day I was taken in for interrogation and asked if I'd like to write a letter home. Up to that point, this privilege had been denied me. We'd never been able to figure out our captors' rationale when it came to allowing letter writing and receiving mail from home. Some of the hard-core resisters had been allowed to write, whereas some of the more compliant prisoners had not.

"Of course I'd like to write a letter," I said, "and I'd like to receive packages, but I won't do it unless you allow all of my men the same privileges."

Well, that was pretty much that. I was never allowed to write, and I doubt our captors were ever serious about letting me do that. It was part of their game, and the game had no end.

When the American actress and political activist Jane Fonda visited Hanoi in July 1972, she was given a tour of what the North Vietnamese called their War Museum. In the course of the tour, Ms. Fonda remarked: "Every American should see this museum." Her hosts thought so much of this suggestion that they started parading small groups of POWs through the facility. Those of us inside Hoa Lo had no idea this was happening, or we would have been better prepared when our summons came.

At about seven o'clock one evening in September 1972, the guards entered our room and instructed all of us to put on our long clothes. This marked the first time they'd asked us to do so as a group; this procedure was usually for one POW at a time prior to interrogation, so we knew something was up. We were led outside, loaded onto a bus, and driven a few miles to a nondescript building. A large contingent of guards ushered us inside. There were guns everywhere. Once inside, we were herded into a large room and seated at a big, round table. There were about thirty of us. Four or five bowls of candy and cigarettes had been set out on the table. In the background, half hidden behind a curtain, we could see a movie camera and so were aware that we were being filmed. Their deception skills were never very sophisticated.

A North Vietnamese officer informed us that we were in the War Museum and that they were going to give us an opportunity to experience all the exhibits. They said they wanted us to see evidence of the destruction wrought by the United States on innocent civilians and hospitals. We all sat straight up. Nobody smiled, and nobody took any of the candy or cigarettes. As the SRO, I spoke up and told them that we had no interest in any of their propaganda exhibits. Someone barked an order, and one of the guards jerked me out of my chair and forced me to the floor. Then they grabbed the man sitting next to me. Bill Talley was a big guy, a former football player, and very strong. It took six of them to wrestle Bill to the floor. When it became apparent that the guards were losing the battle, more joined the pile.

"OK," I said. "That's enough. Stop."

Bill was fighting them, but I could see they were going to hurt him if the struggle continued much longer, and I ordered him to stop resisting. He would never have given up otherwise. There was no reason he should get injured over this. He complied, which was gratifying to me; Bill was a POW, but he was still a soldier. I believe my order saved him from serious injury.

Once everything had calmed down, they marched us into another room that contained the first exhibit. There was some amateurish English-language documentation accompanying it, but at my command all of the POWs pivoted, turning their backs and refusing to look. At this point, I guess the guards realized that we weren't going to cooperate with their "tour" and weren't going to give them anything useful for their film, so they loaded us back on the bus and returned us to our cell at Hoa Lo. We'd become more trouble than we were worth. I was proud of how we'd handled ourselves. We'd remained professional soldiers, a military unit, and we'd maintained our discipline and integrity. And—significantly, in my mind—we'd come back in one piece without any serious injuries. The North Vietnamese certainly didn't get much value out of our visit to their museum. It was always funny to me that they imagined we had any regard for Jane Fonda and the other Americans who came to North Vietnam at the enemy's invitation. I suspected, though, that I was going to pay a price for my actions as SRO.

Sure enough, on December 3 I was taken to another section of the compound and put into a small room. I was given food and water but left in solitary confinement. They gave me a strip of mosquito netting that I wrapped myself in at night to keep from being devoured by insects. I had no light at all after the sun went down. When I looked out the edge of the door one time, I could see the camp commander standing there staring at me. The situation was more than just a little unnerving. He knew how to get to me if he really wanted to. He knew I hadn't forgotten those ropes.

But I was confident of one thing. By removing me, our captors had not deprived the FNGs of a leader. We had talked about this as a group. We knew the rank of every man in our section of the prison, and we knew who would pick up as SRO if I left and who would pick it up if that guy left. They'd never be able to break our chain of command. When it became evident that I'd been separated from the FNGs, Cdr. Ron Polfer, U.S. Navy Vigilante pilot, took over. I learned later that Polfer gave the North Vietnamese the same static they'd gotten from me.

Our system worked.

Very early on the morning of December 18, American B-52s began bombing Hanoi. It was a blessed day. No sound was ever more welcome than the sound of those beautiful bombs exploding all around us and shaking the foundations of Hoa Lo. Even though I couldn't talk to them, I was sure that every American in that place had the same reaction, and I knew it was the beginning of the end for North Vietnam. The POWs had held our own presidential election six weeks earlier, and Richard Nixon had won around 97 percent of the votes inside the Hanoi Hilton.

We believed that he would press the war, and this bombing was the proof. I crawled up onto the window sill and peered up into the night skies. I could see the SAMs being launched and actually saw one B-52 take a direct hit and explode into flames. About an hour later I was moved to a cell in a different corner of the prison compound, where they kept me in isolation for another five days. I found out subsequently that some of the newly shot-down B-52 crews had been brought into the area where they'd been keeping me. A whole new tribe of prisoners would be joining us.

Two days before Christmas I was taken to a wing of the prison I'd never been in and put into a room where a number of the FOGs were housed. In that room was the SRO of all the American POWs, Jack Flynn, with whom I'd been able to communicate only by means of secret notes. Alongside Flynn were Jeremiah Denton, James Stockdale, Jim Hughes, Howard Rutledge, Jim Mulligan, and David Winn. These guys were legendary. Except for brief glimpses through the fences separating us, I'd never actually set eyes on a FOG until now, and none of them had ever seen an FNG in the flesh. We were two different species, but the same genus. I can only speculate that the commander moved me in with this group because he and the guards were tired of my antics as SRO of the more recent prisoners. I was the first FNG to be so honored. I'd been a pain in their collective rears for too long, and relocating me was their way of burying me.

My new prison mates had been incarcerated for as long as seven years. That was a hell of a thought for me. Twenty-five hundred days. I could barely imagine it. I represented their first chance to talk to someone who'd been living out in the world they'd left behind. For the next forty days, I was grilled about news of the world, military tactics, fashion, television, movies, music, politics, sports. I was able to describe for them what it had looked like when Neil Armstrong and Buzz Aldrin had walked on the surface of the moon. Each man had his own specific interests and his own questions—and the questions never ended. It was an incredibly gratifying experience to be able to feed information to these brave men who were so hungry to reconnect with what they considered their *real* lives, the *real* world.

One of the FOGs took me aside and confided that he'd received a photograph of his son and that the boy's hair was down over his shoulders. As a professional soldier, it was hard for him to reconcile the idea of his own son looking that way. He told me, "When I get out of here, I'm going to kill that kid." I knew he was kidding, but I could also see he was really bothered by it. I tried to paint a picture for him of all the changes that had taken place back home since he'd been taken prisoner, and I assured him that his son's hairstyle was not an uncommon thing at all. Months later he would joke with me that I'd saved his son's life.

During my forty days with the FOGs, I received an honorary title: Great White Hunter.

North Vietnam—Hoa Lo in particular—was infested with rats. Large rats. VERY LARGE RATS. I'd never seen anything like it. They were everywhere, including all over the courtyard outside of our cell. Reverting back to my gator-hunting days with my brother in Florida, I devised a way to trap these monsters. We had a metal tub that we used to wash our clothes in, and one evening just before the guards locked us into our cell for the night, I set the tub out in the yard and propped it up with a stick. I tied one end of a piece of string to the stick and brought the other end into the cell with us. I'd placed a few crumbs of bread underneath the tub for bait. At sunset, I took up a position looking out into the courtyard and sat there with the string in my hand. I waited patiently for about an hour, and one of the large rats finally appeared and slowly nosed his way beneath the tub. When he got all the way to the crumbs, I jerked the string, bringing the tub down on top of him.

The trapped rat went berserk scrabbling around inside the tub. The thing was so big that it was able to drag the tub several feet across the courtyard, struggling to find a way free. I thought: Now you know what it feels like! The sound of the tub scraping across the ground brought a guard running into the yard. He stood staring at the overturned washtub making its way across the ground. He had no way of knowing what was inside it, only that it was making quite a racket. By this time, all of the FOGs were crowded around the window watching this little drama. The guard had raised his rifle and kept it trained on the tub. Finally, he got the nerve to lift up the edge of the tub, and when he did, the rat jumped straight up out of there—but not as high or as fast as the guard himself. We howled. The guard was embarrassed and angry, but there wasn't much he could do.

The next night I trapped another rat, but this time the guard just ignored the commotion. Over the next few weeks, rat trapping became a great diversion for all of us. My cell mates appreciated it and would volunteer for sentry duty, keeping an eye on the tub and announcing incoming bogies whenever a rat appeared, but I retained the honor of pulling the string that trapped the Communist rats.

You had to take your entertainment where you found it in the Hanoi Hilton. Options were severely limited. Jeremiah Denton and I played gin rummy every day and kept a running tally. Our cards were made from tiny squares of toilet paper. At the end of our forty days together, Denton owed me a whopping eleven cents, which he dutifully paid by personal check following our release.

After the bombing of Hanoi on December 18, 1972, which was followed by a few less-spectacular raids in the succeeding days, we all were convinced that the war was coming to an end. In fact, the Paris Peace Accords would be signed a few weeks later. In anticipation of our release, we had a number of quite detailed discussions about what we should do and how we should comport ourselves when the day finally came. These sessions helped prepare me for some of the decisions I'd be faced with in the weeks ahead. My time with the FOGs had been like POW graduate school for me. I'd learned a great deal and been able to sync up with Jack Flynn in case I was ever reunited with my FNG cohorts.

On January 20, guards took me to an interrogation room where several North Vietnamese, including the camp commander and a photographer, were waiting. Oddly enough, they all had smiles on their faces. They were uncharacteristically polite as they sat me at a table and offered me candy and cigarettes. Then the interpreter read aloud a statement in English. He announced that the pilot who'd shot me down over the rice field ten months earlier was in the room. The interpreter gestured toward one of the men, who grinned and nodded at me. They'd brought two aerial combatants face to face as if it were a great historical event that required preservation for posterity. The photographer clicked away. The only problem was that I didn't believe any of it. Something didn't seem right about the guy they were claiming was the MiG pilot who got me.

"OK," I said to the interpreter. "Can he describe the incident?"

The mood in the room changed instantly. They all seemed surprised.

"It should be an easy question," I said.

The man began to talk, and the interpreter relayed his words to me. The monologue went on for several minutes. The description was quite detailed, but it was immediately obvious that this was *not* the man who'd shot me down. Nothing about his account was even close to accurate. When he finally wrapped up his speech, I sat forward and looked right into the camera.

"He is not telling the truth," I said, pointing at the man. "It's all a lie. I was there, and I know what happened."

They stared at me.

"I'm not even convinced he's a pilot," I went on. "But I can tell you one thing for sure: this man is a fraud."

There was confusion until the interpreter explained what the word *fraud* meant. The commander ordered the photographer to leave. Then he glared at me and said something I couldn't understand, but I could guess. Some sentiments are universal. I was pretty sure that he had plans for me.

On January 30, I was removed from the cell where the FOGs were housed and transferred from Hoa Lo to a facility known as "the Plantation Gardens," where all 150 of the FNGs were now housed. The Plantation, just a few blocks from Hoa Lo, had once been the official residence of the mayor of Hanoi. On the grounds was a small palace. It was the showcase facility for American POWs that all the visiting delegations and journalists were shown.

Now that I was back with my group, I was also back in the role of SRO for the FNGs at the Plantation, and there was an issue awaiting my decision that I felt had to be dealt with immediately. Col. Flynn had found two of the men at the Plantation guilty of cooperating with the guards and therefore of collaborating with the enemy. Serious stuff. I sent word to both men, who were in another cell, that I was divesting them of their rank. However, they were transferred back to Hoa Lo shortly after my arrival.

I also found out that a number of POWs previously held at the Plantation had accepted special privileges and had been given luxury items such as Bibles, guitars, and chess sets. Some of the men had been seen playing volleyball with the guards. It was this facility that Jane Fonda and other gullible visitors, including former U.S. attorney general Ramsey Clark, had seen. The North Vietnamese had wanted

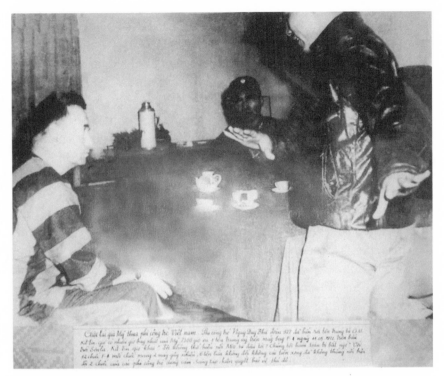

In Hoa Lo Prison, Hanoi. During my time as a POW, I was confronted with a man who claimed to have shot down my F-4 over North Vietnam. This photograph appeared in the Hanoi newspapers. The caption (translated into English) reads: "The older American invader was defeated by the young Vietnamese Pilot Nguy Duy Cho, Group 927. He shot down Lt. Col. J. W. Kittinger, who had a lot of flight time (even) for an American—7,300 hours—and 1st Lt. flying an F-4 as wingman on May 11, 1972, over the skies at Son La, Kittinger stated: 'I don't know where that MiG came from. We were completely taken by surprise.' With twelve F4s plus two more (aircraft), six individual dogfights could not change the outcome—they could not overcome the pair of aircraft flown by the young pilots using sensitivity, creativity, and determination to preserve our capital city." I informed my captors that the man was a fraud, but the papers didn't print that.

to demonstrate their humanity and prove to the world how well the captured Americans were being treated. The visitors had toured a couple of spruced-up "display" cells. (Most everyone remembers that Fonda, while in North Vietnam, made broadcasts denouncing American belligerence and encouraging American soldiers to lay down their arms and that she returned to the United States insisting that rumors of torture and maltreatment were exaggerations if not fabrications. But not everyone remembers that she called us, the POWs, liars and hypocrites. Those were her exact words: "liars and hypocrites." Fonda was a traitor to our country and in my estimation should have been formally charged with treason as our Constitution provides for those who give "Aid and Comfort" to an enemy of the United States.)

I immediately issued an order to all POWs at the Plantation that they were forbidden to play volleyball or any other games with guards under any circumstances, and I demanded that any gifts be immediately returned to prison officials. I was aware that some of the men regarded me as a hard-ass, but we weren't civilians, and we weren't free agents. We were still a military unit of the armed forces of the United States. When I learned that these disgraceful activities hadn't ceased immediately upon my order, I followed my original order the next day with a threat to have anyone who cooperated with our captors court-martialed upon return to the United States. That did the trick. The fun and games stopped, and the special gifts were returned.

Shortly after my arrival at the Plantation, the camp commander summoned me for another meeting. This action was highly unusual because for the first time they indicated they recognized my status as SRO. The commander seemed friendly that particular day, which made me a little nervous. As I'd come to expect, candy and cigarettes were spread out on the table between us. He announced, smiling, that he had decided to bring in some dancing girls to entertain the prisoners. He said he wanted to prove once and for all what a civilized and humane country North Vietnam was, and he said he wanted us to be able to experience their native culture. While I was with the FOGs, Col. Flynn and I had discussed how to handle these kinds of conversations and offers. I refused the goodies and said that we weren't interested in dancing girls or any other form of entertainment. Instead, I asked to be provided with the status of all the missing POWs. I had memorized the names of the ones we knew about and rattled them off for the camp commander. We suspected these men had been killed, but we felt it was our duty to continue to press for word on their status. As always, my questions were dismissed.

The commander returned to his plan to bring in dancing girls. His eyes lit up, and he seemed quite excited by the prospect.

"We have no interest in your dancing girls," I told him.

He asked what we would do if he brought the girls in and assembled the POWs in the courtyard. I told him I'd order the men to turn their backs on the dancers. (If he tried to film it, I intended to have the men offer the old "one-finger" salute. The North Vietnamese knew what the finger meant, and they didn't like it.) He snorted and motioned to have me returned to my cell. I could tell he was disappointed. On the way out, I inquired again about the missing POWs. For just an instant, I thought he might order me shot on the spot.

With the signing of the Paris Peace Accords on January 27, 1973, the North Vietnamese finally released the names of all the prisoners. This was the first time that some of our families found out that we were still alive. Not much later, each POW received a Red Cross package. It was like a lifetime of Christmas mornings in one shot. The packages were individually addressed, and that's how we all learned of our promotions. When I was shot down, I was a lieutenant colonel, but my Red Cross package was addressed to "Colonel Joseph Kittinger." It was the same for all of us. Lieutenants were now captains, and captains were now majors. It was a real morale boost.

The best part was inside those boxes. There were snacks, cigarettes, candy, and, most important to us, two paperback books in each package. The entire camp stayed up all night reading. You'd read a book and pass it on. It didn't matter what it was: it was something to lose yourself in. For us, those little books were truly the Great Escape.

Now that we were in a less intimidating facility, I made sure our actual escape plans were updated. The Plantation was right near a river, and the fences, like the camp itself, were rather run down. I felt as if the chances of a successful escape were quite a bit greater than they'd been at Hoa Lo. Still, I cautioned the man I'd put in charge of the escape committee, the same Navy officer who'd been given that responsibility earlier, that no one could be left behind. Not one soul.

"If one goes, we all go." That was the requirement for any escape scenario. We had a few cowboys who remembered the World War II movies and believed it ought to be every man for himself. But we'd all suffered together, and I was determined that if the peace accords fell apart, we'd make our attempt at freedom as a unit. We'd fight our way out together, and, if necessary, we'd die together. To my way of thinking, growing old in North Vietnam was not an option, and I briefed the men on this. "If I come to you one night and say, 'It's now!' you get up and march out with us. Nobody stays behind." I felt that with our numbers and with the weapons we could acquire from the guards, we would at least have a chance. Any outcome would be better than rotting in that prison for the rest of our lives.

All of the training I'd received on survival as a prisoner had stressed the importance of looking out for your fellow POWs. A number of American prisoners during the Korean War had become psychologically isolated and had given up. Some of them died. I stressed to all the FNGs that we had to be vigilant and make sure that we never fell victim to this sort of thing. I also told them to beware of what our training had referred to as "self-induced punishment," which amounts to blaming yourself or feeling sorry for yourself to the point that you surrender your spirit or begin to sympathize with your captors.

One day the senior officer of the room next to mine initiated a conversation through a crack in the wall. He was concerned about one of the men in his room who had become withdrawn and had stopped participating in discussions and group activities with his fellow POWs. The officer and his other cell mates had tried to cheer the guy up, but nothing had worked. I asked to have the man brought to the wall the next day so I could talk to him. The man's name was John.

"John," I asked the next morning at the wall, "do you know who you're speaking with?"

"Yes, sir, Colonel Kittinger."

"Do you know my role here?" I asked.

"Yes, sir," he replied. "You're the SRO."

"John," I said, "with me on this side of the wall is Ron Polfer. You know Ron. On your side of the wall is the senior officer in your room. Do you acknowledge that there are two witnesses to this conversation, to what I'm about to tell you?"

"Yes, sir," he said, sounding a little confused.

"I am going to give you a direct order, John," I said. I was not going to let this man deteriorate any further. "I'm ordering you, as of this moment, to start eating the food you're given and to start taking part in activities with the other POWs in your room. If you do not obey this order, I am hereby informing you that I will have your ass court-martialed when we return to active duty upon our release. Do you understand, John?"

There was silence for a moment. Finally, John said he understood and would comply. The next day the senior officer reported that John seemed to have changed his attitude and was back in the swing of things—back to being a soldier. This is an example of why it's critical for POWs to look out for their fellow prisoners' welfare and to maintain a command structure. There are times when the only effective motivator is a direct order from a superior. We were prisoners, but we were still soldiers, and our survival as a group depended on our working together and maintaining military discipline. During my tenure as SRO in Hanoi, with as many as 150 men in my command, only a couple of them caused me any real trouble. That's a pretty damn good ratio, and it's testimony to the caliber of the men and to the training we'd all received. Every night as I lay on the board that served as my mattress, I prayed for the wisdom to carry out my role in a way that would result in the greatest benefit for those men. Being a prisoner is inherently stressful. It's an especially difficult role for a professional warrior. I am extremely proud of the POWs I knew and lived with in Hanoi. I'd like to think I served them well; I know they served their individual services and their country with honor.

A few days before we were released, I had another session with the aging camp commander. This time he was surrounded by all of his officers. As always, I asked about the status of the missing POWs, and, of course, he ignored me. It was not his favorite subject, and I was not his favorite captive. As he began to discuss the arrangements for our release, I told him that as SRO I had the responsibility to be the last one to leave captivity. It was very important to me. I explained that this protocol was part of our military tradition. He gave me a funny look, as if he thought I'd finally gone off the deep end, and knew right then that he would never respect my request to be the last one out.

He didn't. On March 29, 1973, I boarded a bus along with a group of my fellow POWs, and we were driven through the streets of Hanoi on the way to the airport. We were able to see the ruin our bombers had inflicted on the city. The railroad stations had been reduced to rubble, and most of the bridges were gone. In just ten days, our bombers had really torn that place to shreds, and seeing the devastation made me wonder why we hadn't done that back in 1964. But there was no

jubilation on our bus. We were mostly quiet, thinking about what we'd
gone through and the friends we'd lost.

When we arrived at the airport, we were taken off the bus and
marched past a desk where North Vietnamese officers sat alongside
a United States Air Force colonel. I saluted the colonel and climbed
up into the C-141 waiting on the ramp. It was a powerfully emotional
moment. It felt exactly like a dream. I had fantasized about this day for
eleven months, and it was just a little hard to believe it had finally come.
I knew the FOGs had boarded this same C-141 about a month earlier,
and I found myself wondering if they'd felt the same emotions as they'd
come face to face with their freedom after so many years behind bars. I
can't tell you how much I admired those guys. What the FNGs had faced
in Hanoi was nothing compared to what the FOGs had endured. They
were my heroes and still are. We taxied out and began rolling down the
runway. At the moment the wheels lifted off, a spontaneous roar went
up from all the POWs on board. Cheering, tears, the whole thing. Some
of the men were hopping around like kids. It was raw emotion from
front to back.

The otherwise routine flight from Hanoi to Clark Air Base on Luzon
Island in the Philippines was an unforgettable experience for all of us.
It was still hard to process the fact that we were free, that it wasn't some
kind of slipup, a bureaucratic snafu. About thirty minutes before we
landed, I was informed that, as SRO, I would be expected to make a
few remarks on behalf of the men when we got off the plane at Clark. I
honestly can't recall my exact words, but it was something to the effect
that we all were proud and happy to be free once again. I think I was
a little numb. I know that I added: "God bless America." The rest is a
blur.

We had a big crowd waiting for us when we arrived, and they all
cheered as we walked toward the buses. We sure hadn't expected that.
We waved, but I imagine we were a pretty sorry-looking bunch. When
we were taken to the base hospital, the hospital commander took me
aside and reminded me that I remained the SRO in charge of these
POWs, which took me by surprise.

"Sir," I said, "we are no longer in prison. As far as I'm concerned, I
am no longer the SRO." I looked him in the eye. "Sir, I hereby resign."

"But you can't resign, Colonel Kittinger. These are your men."

"Why can't I resign?"

"Because you have one more order to give them."

I'd had it up to here. I was a free man again. I'd been hounded by cowardly North Vietnamese bullies for almost a year, and I didn't intend to let this clown push me around.

"Bullshit, Colonel," I said. "Whatever it is, *you* give 'em the damn order."

The colonel sighed, but he wasn't going to back down.

"The first group of POWs that came through here went to the officers' club, and a few of them got drunk. They got disorderly and threw up all over the place. It was a disgrace. None of the POWs will be allowed in the officers' club. Is that clear?"

I couldn't believe what I was hearing. We'd just walked out of a ghoulish prison in a Communist capital, and we couldn't get a beer at Clark?

"That, Colonel, is the most chickenshit thing I've ever heard in my life."

"Nevertheless," he said, "you're going to give your men that order."

I hated it. Man, I hated it. I called my guys together.

"Men," I said—I was going to get it over with and take my licks— "it's been my honor to have been your SRO and commander. You're wonderful soldiers and warriors, and I'm proud to have served alongside you. No one will ever know what we've been through. No one." I paused a moment. "But, men, these jerks are forcing me to issue one final order. We cannot, repeat, can*not* go to the officers' club. The bar is off limits."

They went nuts. I didn't blame them.

"What kind of crap is this?"

"Screw you, Colonel!"

They were howling mad. I let them vent. Hell, I joined them.

We were free at last.

7
Home Skies

*   *   *   *   *   *

In the end, the men took being barred from the officers' club at Clark in stride, and the truth is that base personnel treated us like kings. They knew how hungry we all were, and they laid out a royal feast: thick steaks and lobster and mountains of fresh fruit—just about anything we could have imagined. But after all those weeks and months of prison fare, the one thing every single one of us craved was ice cream. That was the common denominator. None of us could get enough of it. We hunkered down and ate bowl after bowl.

Of course, they arranged for everyone to call home. Each of us was assigned an escort. The escort officer sat each man down and explained how much money he'd earned while he'd been in prison and told him about some of the things that had happened in the world since he'd been away. Everything was planned down to the last detail. The day after we arrived at Clark, we were given physicals. The following day we were measured for uniforms and given haircuts and dental examinations. Then there was an intelligence debriefing. The commanders didn't rush anything. They knew we needed time to adjust. The new uniforms delivered to us were outfitted with the medals we'd all earned. It was really glorious.

Next, they loaded us onto a bus and drove us to the Clark base exchange, which they'd closed so we could have it all to ourselves for a few hours. We bought watches and wallets and stereos and all kinds of junk we thought we needed. About a week after our arrival, we all boarded airplanes for home. My flight landed first in Honolulu. Even

Free at last: arrival in Honolulu. Three o'clock in the morning, but look at the crowd that showed up to support the returning POWs! The outpouring of affection took all of us by surprise.

though we touched down at three in the morning, there were a thousand people at the airport to welcome us. American flags all over the place. People singing "God Bless America." I walked by one elderly lady who threw a lei over my head, and this lei had bunches of little airline liquor bottles tied to it. She winked at me, and all I could do was laugh and hug her.

Our next stop was San Francisco. I immediately boarded another plane for Kelly AFB in San Antonio. My first sergeant from Udorn, Gerald Roy, was there waiting. The security guards wouldn't let him come out to meet me. Whether I liked it or not, I was still SRO, and I still had to make a few remarks each time we landed. As I was making my little speech, I saw Roy being restrained by the guards. I pointed toward him and used the microphone they'd given me.

"Escort that man over here!"

So the guards escorted Sgt. Roy over, and we embraced. It was great to see him. As soon as he let go of me, he spun toward the guard who'd been hassling him.

"See, you son of a bitch? I told you I knew him!"

Next stop was Maxwell AFB in Alabama, and there to greet me were my parents and my wife and kids. We didn't know if we were laughing or crying. There were more medical examinations and another intelligence debriefing that took a couple of days to complete. They wanted to know everything—the entire experience.

Finally, I was allowed to return to my hometown, where there was another big reception at the base in Orlando. I couldn't get over the amount of attention we were receiving. It was something none of us had really been prepared for. Looking back on it, I suspect that the American public felt a little guilty about the way Vietnam veterans had been treated. The POWs may have gotten the benefit of some pent-up good will. We were invited to events at the White House and to big gatherings put on by people such as businessman Ross Perot and Governor Ronald Reagan in California. It was gratifying.

While I was in prison in Vietnam, until the Paris Peace Accords were signed in late January 1973, my family had had no idea what had happened to me. My status was MIA. I know it was as hard on all of them as

My parents welcome me back home. For most of my time in prison, my family had no idea if I was dead or alive.

it had been on me. Almost everybody eventually reached the conclusion that I'd been killed. The only exception was my mother. Throughout the ordeal, she never gave up believing I had been captured and was alive. Even though all the letters she wrote me were returned as undeliverable, she kept writing them. It was a matter of faith, and when I came back in one piece, it was only more proof for her that someone up there had been looking out for me. I certainly couldn't argue with that.

The Air Force informed me that I was entitled to a one-month vacation. Not only that, the higher ups asked me to pick my next assignment. They basically said, "Whatever you want to do, wherever you want to go—it's yours." It was an easy call for me. I'd never been to a senior military school—which was something I needed for my career—and here I was now a full colonel. I volunteered for the Air War College at Maxwell. Our country was still in turmoil from the after-effects of the war, and the Watergate affair was dominating the news, but, for me, it was mostly a year of fun. I'd had a great deal of time to think during my time in prison in Hanoi, and I'd made a solemn oath to myself that when I got out, I was going to take advantage of everything life offered me. I'd learned just how precious our time on Earth is and how lucky I was to have the opportunities I'd had. I'd also resolved that I was going to spend the rest of my life trying to be happy.

In June 1974, I became the vice wing commander of the 48th Tactical Fighter Wing, an F-4 fighter wing at Lakenheath Royal Air Force Base in England. I was there for about three years when the United States Air Force announced that it was bringing in the F-111. This news was not good because to me the F-111 is a bomber—not a fighter. I did not relish the idea of suddenly becoming a bomber pilot in midcareer. I requested a transfer. My goal was to be a fighter-wing commander, so I was assigned to the 12th Air Force Headquarters at Bergstrom AFB in Austin, Texas. It was basically a holding tank for old colonels without a real job. I worked for a three-star general there who promised me if I hung in, I'd get my fighter wing, so I bit the bullet and bided my time. But it was tough. I was a fighter pilot and didn't enjoy sitting around on my butt.

Then one day the general called me in.

"Joe," he said, "I'm getting transferred. They're giving me command of Pacific Air Forces. I want to wish you good luck."

"What do you mean 'good luck'?" I said. He probably heard a little panic in my voice.

"Well," he went on, "I'm really hoping you get that fighter wing someday, but that's going to be up to the new commander now."

"Sir," I said, "I don't know the new commander, and he doesn't know me. I've paid my dues, sir. Is there anything you can do for me?"

He looked at me and said, "Good luck, Joe."

And that was it. I walked out of his office and hustled down to personnel and retired on the spot. I guess it was a pretty dumb thing to do because I had no job, no real prospects, no career in waiting. I'd been counting on that fighter wing and hadn't made any contingency plans. I really felt let down.

The year was 1978, and I didn't have anywhere to go other than back to Orlando, so I went back and started the job hunt. After surveying the opportunities, I hired on at Martin-Marietta as an engineer on the Pershing Missile project. In many respects, it was a very good job. The salary was excellent. The place was accommodating, the people were nice, and it was challenging enough work, but it just wasn't very stimulating. I was used to working ninety to one hundred hours a week, and now I was in the office maybe forty hours a week. After flying a cutting-edge machine such as the F-4, it's hard to get excited by a desk and a stack of paper. Still, I loved being back in Florida, where I could hunt and fish. I built a house near a little lake and planted fruit trees in the yard. The truth was, though, I'd never stopped dreaming about an around-the-world balloon flight. In my mind, I was always working toward that.

That first year I'd gotten back from Vietnam, 1973, I'd called up my good friend Ed Yost in South Dakota and told him I wanted to fly a balloon solo around the world. The first order of business, I explained, was to prove I could cross the Atlantic Ocean in a balloon by myself. I knew I'd need a good aeronautical man to help with the project, and there wasn't a better balloon designer or more imaginative thinker than Ed Yost. I'd met him back in the Project Manhigh days when he was working for the General Mills balloon division. Later, while Ed was working at Raven Industries on a contract with the Office of Naval Research in 1960—just a couple of months after my flight in *Excelsior III*—he had invented, built, and flown the first modern hot-air balloon. His breakthrough design consisted of a nylon envelope, a propane burner, and a half-inch piece of plywood for a seat. On that maiden flight, he lifted off from a field in Bruning, Nebraska, and stayed aloft for twenty-five minutes. A few weeks later Ed tried again and this time stayed up for two hours and reached an altitude of 9,000 feet. In spite of a lack of much formal education, he was the closest thing to a mechanical genius I'd ever met. He could design anything, build anything, fix anything. He'd single-handedly launched the era of modern hot-air ballooning.

I knew I'd need a sponsor for what I had in mind. I sure didn't have the money to finance a transatlantic flight myself. I sent out a bunch of funding requests, both for the Atlantic flight and the eventual circumnavigation, and made a big presentation to the Disney people. Unfortunately, I couldn't convince anyone that there would be enough public-relations value connected with these kinds of pure adventure flights or assure them that they wouldn't be attaching their name to a potential disaster.

About a month after I'd called Ed in 1973, he got back in touch to say he'd found a potential sponsor for me. It was an advertising agency in New York, so we headed up there to pitch the idea. I gave them the whole dog-and-pony show, and the guy at the agency said, "Here's what we want you to do. One of our major clients is Lark Cigarettes, and we want to put the Lark logo on your balloon." That didn't sound too bad. But there was more. "And because the logo includes the Lark Cigarette Girl, we want you to fly the Lark girl with you across the ocean."

"Listen, sir," I told the guy, "this is going to be a pretty hazardous flight. People have been trying to do it for more than a hundred years. A bunch of them have died in the process. I wouldn't want to risk someone else's safety." The advertising men all seemed perfectly willing to risk their girl's life, and I could already see the headline:

KITTINGER CROSSES OCEAN ON A LARK

Besides, the whole thing for me was to make a *solo* flight. We told them thanks, but no thanks.

Three years later, in 1976, Ed called me and said *he* wanted to try the Atlantic crossing, and, of course, I agreed to help, which is how I became chief of operations for his attempt to be the first man across in a balloon. Actually, my role was to run the flight from the halfway point to the European mainland. Ed had already reached an agreement with Vera Winzen—she was Vera Simons at this point, having divorced Otto

Winzen and married David Simons following the Manhigh project—to manage the flight operations from Ed's launch point near Bangor, Maine, to the halfway point in the Atlantic. Because I was still vice wing commander at Lakenheath that year, I simply waited until I received word from the National Geographic Society, one of Ed's sponsors, that he'd launched. I took leave at that point and drove down to Heathrow Airport outside London, where I met the National Geographic representative. She had leased two rooms at Heathrow and had extra phones installed so that we could establish our command post.

It took us a day or so to set up operations. We were joined not much later by Ed's wife, Charmian, and an entrepreneur from Florida, Bob Snow, who had become involved with Ed's project. We all got ready, and when Ed reached the halfway point across the Atlantic, I called Vera back in the States to let her know I was taking over. I knew how headstrong Vera could be, so it didn't exactly shock me when she announced that she'd decided to retain control and handle the flight all the way across.

"Vera," I said, "listen, he's at the halfway point. We're ready here. Let me have it."

"No," she said. "I'm still in control."

Well, this was kind of crazy. I told Charmian that as far as I was concerned, it was her call. If she wanted Vera to keep control of the flight, she needed to let me know so I could go back to the base and resume my job. Charmian gave it some thought and finally told me she wanted to stay with the original plan and have me bring Ed the rest of the way. I asked her to inform Vera, which she did. It was a little more drama than we needed. Ed was counting on our working together, and I felt much better once I could settle in and focus on the business at hand.

It's good that we got it worked out when we did. It may have saved Ed's life. Just a few hours later, we received word that the weather pattern was not going to allow Ed to reach the mainland after all. The winds aloft were petering out, and if he stayed in the air too much longer, the balloon—Ed had named it the *Silver Fox*—would begin to curl back away from the continent. I immediately got on the phone with Air and Sea Rescue at Ramstein AFB in Germany. I knew what they needed to hear.

"This is Colonel Joe Kittinger," I told them. "I am currently on leave from the United States Air Force, and I represent a balloonist over the middle of the Atlantic Ocean. The balloonist's wife is here with me, and she is requesting assistance and asking for a rescue of her husband."

They wanted to know when I needed the rescue operation to take place. I gave them a time of ten the following morning. Next, I had London Approach Control contact an airliner and ask the pilot to relay a message to Ed. I said to tell him that I wanted him to put his balloon in the water precisely at 10:00 a.m. Ed's gondola was built to double as a Catamaran-type sailboat—as I said, Ed was an imaginative guy—so I knew he could bob around safely for a while. I wanted to get him down in the morning, though, so that we'd have all day to find him and get to him. The Atlantic's a big ocean, and rescue operations don't always run smoothly.

I called the Air Force in Germany and gave them an approximate location. They were going to fly the rescue operation out of Woodbridge, a Royal Air Force station in Suffolk that served as a base for the United States Air Force's 67th Air Rescue and Recovery Squadron. They told me they'd need to depart at 1:00 a.m., and I asked if they'd be willing to take some people along with them. I had a *National Geographic* photographer and Bill Graves, one of the magazine's executives, with me. It was 9:30 in the evening by this point, and I told Bob Snow and the *National Geographic* guys that if they wanted to make the trip, they'd need to be at Woodbridge and ready to go by midnight. It hadn't been easy, but I'd gotten permission for all of them to accompany the operation. After all that, they decided to stop for a bite to eat on their way up to the base and got there too late. They missed the flight.

The rescue plane, a Lockheed HC-130, took off on time, but the tracking system that should have allowed the crew to zero in on Ed's radio signal malfunctioned. They were out over the middle of the ocean with no way to get an accurate bead on Ed's position. They were still a couple of hundred miles away when Ed came down. He put the *Silver Fox* in the water right on the dot at 10:00 a.m., just as I knew he would. Systems would break down and people would show up late, but you could always count on Ed Yost.

The Air Force rescue crew finally raised Ed on the radio, but it's not as if a guy in the ocean can offer much in the way of landmarks to describe his position. Still, Ed looked up and saw that two jet contrails crossed right above his position and, using that information, the plane was able to find him. He was a real needle in a haystack out there, and we all were very relieved when we received confirmation that he'd been located.

The thing was, Ed was doing just fine down there in the water. He was about 200 miles due east of the island of Santa Maria in the Azores, and his gondola was riding the current just as Ed had designed it to. The Air Force was on the radio back to its base asking for permission to put two of their jumpers in the water, but I got on the line.

"Wait a minute. Stop."

There were about five people on the conference call.

"Is the balloon pilot in distress?" I asked.

They looked down at Ed, and he waved back at them, as casual as could be, I'm sure.

"Well, no," they said. "He's in the water, but he seems to be OK."

"Then do not drop the jumpers," I advised.

The plane radioed back. "The jumpers really want to jump."

I knew what was going on. The search-and-rescue crew practiced all the time, and they were almost desperate to get an actual rescue jump in. Plus, it would have been fun for these guys to show their stuff. I knew I would not be a very popular colonel with the jumpers, but there was no emergency at this point, and there was the very real chance that somebody could screw up and get hurt unnecessarily. I repeated my recommendation that they not jump, and it was confirmed by the squadron commander at Woodbridge—much to the crew's dismay.

The United States Coast Guard has a station on Long Island that tracks every ship in the world. These guys can see the registry of any ship, the speed, the skipper, the cargo, its current location, and its destination. So I got them on the line and had them give us the location of the ship nearest to Ed's position. It turned out that the German freighter *Elisabeth Bolton*, en route to Alexandria, Egypt, was just 40 miles away and heading right toward Ed. Because he was officially a vessel in distress, the ship was required by international maritime law to stop and pick him up.

And that's what happened. The *Elisabeth Bolton* hoisted Ed and his gondola aboard. Its crew made an attempt to snag the balloon, but the *Silver Fox* filled with water, broke away, and sank. Ed was in good spirits and none the worse for wear. He'd come closer than anyone ever had to making it all the way across the Atlantic.

The only real disappointed parties were the Air Force rescue guys and *National Geographic*, which had failed to get any photos of the final moments of the flight it had sponsored—even though a crew member of the C-130 did get a shot of Ed floating in the ocean. Someone at the magazine raised the ship on the shortwave and requested that Ed be dropped off in Gibraltar so that they wouldn't have to go all the way to Egypt to pick him up. The ship's captain explained that the unscheduled stop would cost in the neighborhood of ten thousand dollars, but the *National Geographic* management said fine, so the *Elisabeth Bolton* dropped Ed off in Gibraltar.

A couple of months later, when the magazine received a bill for ten thousand dollars, its managers wrote to the shipping company and announced that in the story about Ed's flight, they planned to include a prominent photo of the ship and to say some very complimentary things about the pickup operation. They said they hoped all of this good will would be accepted in lieu of the fee. The shipping company wrote back and said, in essence, "Thank you very much for the opportunity to receive exposure in *National Geographic*. We are very excited about the prospect. Also, please send us our ten thousand dollars."

Ed Yost being towed to shore in Gibraltar. Ed made the first hot-air balloon crossing of the English Channel in 1963. His attempt to cross the Atlantic Ocean in a gas balloon came up 700 miles short. (Courtesy: National Geographic Society.)

Ed's flight in the *Silver Fox* really opened some eyes. He'd stayed in the air more than one hundred hours and covered a distance of 2,740 miles. Even though he came up short of his goal, the world could see that this thing could be done. You'd have to be damn good, and you'd have to get damn lucky, but flying a balloon across the Atlantic was possible. As Ed told the press after his flight, "It is surely only a matter of time."

A couple of years later, in 1978, Ed called me to say that he might have a sponsor for me if I still wanted to try it. A guy in New York said he was willing to foot the bill on the condition that he accompany me on the flight. I really hated the idea of a passenger I didn't know or have any confidence in, but if that was the only way we could finance the thing, I was willing at least to listen.

At this same time, two experienced aeronauts from New Mexico were planning their own Atlantic crossing. Businessmen Ben Abruzzo and Maxie Anderson—who were later joined by a thirty-year-old airplane pilot named Larry Newman—had credibility, in large part through their association with Ed Yost, who had already built a balloon and gondola for them. When Ed started working with me, we estimated that we were about a month behind the New Mexico trio. So my New York sponsor, who'd been a little slow with the money to that point, called Abruzzo and issued a challenge: "We'll race you. We're both just about ready to go, so I'll put up ten thousand dollars, and we'll both cash in on the publicity. We'll launch at the same time, and whoever touches down in Europe first wins the prize."

Abruzzo's response to that challenge wasn't just "no." It was "Hell, no!" I couldn't really blame him. Ben was smart enough to know they had a lead, and he had no interest in sharing the limelight—even for ten grand. About that time, my New York sponsor just kind of disappeared. I couldn't find him, much less get him to write a check so that I could finish my preparations. So Abruzzo, Anderson, and Newman launched in their balloon, the *Double Eagle*, from Spragueville, Maine, on the evening of August 11, 1978, and landed triumphantly in Paris six days later. They went into the record books as the first to cross the Atlantic Ocean by balloon. I was a little disappointed I didn't get my chance, but I also didn't consider it over for me. After all, my desire from the beginning had been to make the flight solo—as Lindbergh had done in the *Spirit of St. Louis* the year before I was born.

I decided to keep planning and to keep looking for a sponsor. And, of course, my ultimate ambition was still the around-the-world-flight. That dream was still very much alive.

A few years before accepting the job at Martin-Marietta, I ran into Bob Snow again at Rosie O'Grady's, a gay-nineties theme restaurant that was part of the entertainment complex he owned in downtown Orlando called Church Street Station. Bob was a former Navy fighter pilot and a virtuoso Dixieland trumpet player. In 1967, he'd sold his Porsche to make the eleven-hundred-dollar down payment on his first restaurant/ bar operation in Pensacola. In 1972, he'd opened in Orlando. His whole operation was built around the concept of carefree good times, and he turned it into the fourth-largest tourist attraction in the state of Florida. Bob was a brilliant businessman and promoter, and he believed strongly in the value of aerial advertising: banner towing and sky writing. When he heard I'd left the Air Force, he got in touch with me and asked if I'd be interested in coming to work for him. He made a great pitch, and he had quite an operation. He owned a fleet of airplanes and balloons and did all kinds of publicity events. The problem was, he couldn't come close to matching my Martin-Marietta salary, so I'd turned him down.

"Well," he told me, "if you don't want to work for me, just come on out and fly my airplanes whenever you feel like it. Or fly the balloons. Consider my aircraft your aircraft."

Now how could I turn down an offer like that? Plus, Bob was an extraordinarily fun guy to be around. I started going out on weekends and flying his aircraft. I also started to do some gas ballooning with him. We entered a couple of races together. Bob could see I was having a ball, and every few months he'd ask again if there was any way he could talk me into accepting a job with his Flying Circus.

Finally, one day after I'd been at Martin-Marietta for about five years, it hit me. Life is short, and the only thing I really loved doing—it hadn't changed since that first flight at Goodfellow in the T-6 with Dan Elliott thirty years earlier—was to fly. That's what really mattered. So I handed in my resignation and called Bob Snow. Not much later I was running Rosie O'Grady's Flying Circus. I would fly paying passengers in a hot-air balloon in the early morning, then tow an advertising banner behind a Stearman or an Ag Cat. I was flying every day, and I'd never been happier. I wasn't making much money, but what I found out was that didn't really matter. We had four airplanes, three pilots, a seamstress, three mechanics, and our own hangar at Executive Airport. Bob and I worked well together, and we spent a lot of our off-hours cooking up new ways to have a good time.

One afternoon shortly after I hired on with Bob, he told me that he was going to teach me how to sky write. We went to the bar, ordered glasses of wine, and he started sketching the letters of the alphabet on cocktail napkins, explaining how a pilot forms the letters. It's trickier than it looks. Snow had been doing it for years, and he had a very specific routine for each letter. We sat there for about five hours, reviewing the patterns until I was sure I had all twenty-six letters memorized.

The next morning I took one of our airplanes up to 10,000 feet above Orlando—FAA air traffic controllers at the airport would give us our altitude—and began to write a giant ROSIE O'GRADY'S in the sky. The smoke that we used to form the letters was created by a Texaco product called "Corvis oil" that is injected into the exhaust. I was pretty excited about the whole thing. I started into my first letter and made a perfect **R**. Then I moved on to the next letter, but as I completed it, I realized I'd gotten ahead of myself. Instead of an **O**, I'd written an **S**. I wasn't quite sure what to do next. This was a situation we hadn't covered on any of the bar napkins. You couldn't erase a smoke letter, so I circled back and made a big slash right through the **RS**. Then I flew a couple of miles away and started over. This time I got it right:

ROSIE O'GRADY'S

After I landed, the phone in the hangar rang. I knew who was on the line before I picked it up.

"Listen, Kittinger," Snow said, "I can teach you how to sky write, but I can't teach you how to spell."

I wrote in the skies all over the United States for the next eighteen years—thousands of messages—and I can truthfully say that I never misspelled another word. Not that I ever flew a perfect sky-writing mission. There was always room for improvement. The hardest letter to form is the O, to get it perfectly round. Sometimes you're dealing with 50- to 60-mile-per-hour winds or turbulence that plays havoc with the routines. But I loved it all. It was another kind of flying, another set of challenges.

In the fall of 1978, I got a call from Dewey Reinhard, a balloonist in Colorado Springs, asking if I'd be interested in accompanying him on a gas balloon race. He explained that Dr. Tom Heinsheimer was in the process of reviving the classic Gordon Bennett Balloon Race after a forty-one-year hiatus. James Gordon Bennett, the flamboyant publisher of the *New York Herald*, had founded the competition in 1906 and held the race that year in Paris. It was a simple concept with simple rules. All the balloons took off from the same spot, and the balloon that landed the farthest away was declared the winner. The subsequent race would take place in the winning entry's home country. The American team of Frank Lahm and Henry Hersey won that first race with a twenty-two-hour flight that covered 647 kilometers. The race was held each year thereafter until 1939, when it was suspended due to the onset of World War II.

I immediately accepted Dewey's invitation, even though most of my gas balloon experience was with the modern plastic designs we'd used on the Air Force high-altitude flights in the late 1950s and early 1960s. Our aircraft would be an old-fashioned netted balloon, an envelope enclosed in a large net, the same configuration used by the original Gordon Bennett racers.

The first thing I did was call my friend Dawson "Klanky" Hargrove in Orlando. Klanky was a marvel with electronics, electrical systems, communications, and navigation systems. I asked Klanky to figure out what we'd need and to help us collect the equipment. In the spring of 1979, Klanky and I flew out to California in his aircraft, where we met Dewey, his wife, Jean, and his crew and began the process of assembling and weighing the gear. On May 26, we loaded everything into a van and drove over to the launch site, which was the parking lot of the *Queen Mary* in Long Beach. On the drive, Klanky asked Dewey and me what he probably thought was an innocent question.

"How many netted gas balloons have you guys inflated?"

A long, awkward silence followed. Not only had neither of us ever inflated a balloon system like this, but I'd never even set eyes on a netted balloon before this moment. But Dewey had gotten his balloon from none other than Ed Yost, so I had great confidence in it.

"Well," Klanky said, "I guess this should be pretty entertaining."

Eighteen balloons were entered in the race, and the pilots had come from all over the world. It turned out that Dewey and I weren't the only racers with Yost balloons. Ben Abruzzo and Maxie Anderson—just a year after their Atlantic crossing—were there with one of Ed's creations. My buddy and employer Bob Snow was set to fly with Ed himself. Lucky for us, Ed offered to help inflate the netted balloons for everyone. It was a spectacular scene as the balloons filled with gas and took shape in the shadow of the great ship. As each balloon lifted off, a band struck up the national anthem of its pilots: Switzerland, Belgium, Australia, Poland, Italy, Japan, the United Kingdom. And, of course, "The Star Spangled Banner"—three times.

Dewey and I lifted off at about 2:00 p.m. on May 27. Thousands of spectators were there to cheer each ascension. We flew right over downtown Los Angeles and drifted toward the Banning Pass. I took a moment to think about the occasion. The inaugural Gordon Bennett had taken place just three years after the Wright Brothers' first flight. With our netted balloon, it really did seem as if we were making a connection to the earlier days of aeronautics. The credit for it really had to go to Dr. Heinsheimer, who'd organized the whole event. He had given the international balloon community an invaluable gift.

In gas balloon racing, ballast is like fuel. You have to drop ballast (we used sand) to ascend, and as the sun sets and the gas contracts, the balloon descends. To maintain altitude, you have to drop more ballast. It usually takes about 10 percent of the gross weight of the balloon, gondola, and cargo to stop the descent. For example, if the entire system weighs 1,200 pounds, it would take 120 pounds of ballast to compensate for the nightly decrease in gas temperature. When the sun comes up the next morning, the balloon rises again. During the day, as clouds pass between the balloon and the sun, the system goes through a series of altitude losses and gains. The whole thing is about ballast management, and you need to conserve sufficient ballast to manage a reasonable and safe descent rate for landing. When your ballast gets low, and the sun is setting, it's prudent to try and get down. You don't want to be forced to land at night when you can't see dangerous obstacles such as power lines.

Dewey and I flew all day, all night, and into the afternoon of the next day. At 3:00 p.m., we decided we didn't have enough ballast to make it through another night and began to look for a landing site. The only problem was that surface winds were blowing at about 25 miles per hour—way too fast for a safe landing, but we really had no choice. We radioed our chase crew and began preparing for a rough ride. We had a good approach area in the high desert about 25 miles outside of Milford, Utah. We came down and bounced across the ground—hanging on as best we could—for about 300 yards before finally coming to rest. Dewey wrenched his back, and I had to hike out to a highway about two miles away and flag down a farmer, who gave us a ride to the hospital.

Abruzzo and Anderson won that race. They made it to Dove Creek, Colorado, a distance of 583 miles. Dewey and I took second with a flight of 415 miles. Third place went to Ed Yost and Bob Snow, meaning that all top three finishers had flown Yost balloons.

We all had also learned a great deal about how to fly a gas balloon race, and Bob Snow and I immediately began planning for the following year's competition. We entered as a team and launched the *Rosie O'Grady* from Fountain Valley, California, in the 1980 race with a hand from the comedian Flip Wilson—Bob knew how to stage a publicity event—and we were aloft for a total of twenty-seven hours. The problem was that the winds didn't cooperate that year, and all the balloons drifted northward. We were forced to put our balloon down north of San Francisco when the winds suddenly starting pushing us toward the Pacific Ocean. We made a smooth landing near Santa Rosa in the Napa Valley—a distance of 418 miles, which was only good enough for second place.

The *Rosie O'Grady*, Gordon Bennett version. Ed Yost's netted-balloon design recalled the glory days of American aeronautics. Here I'm ballasting during an ascent from Albuquerque in 1981 on a flight that terminated in Kansas twenty-three hours later.

The next year, 1981, Bob and I tried again. I wanted a first-place finish pretty badly by this point. We spent a fair amount of time talking about strategy and trying to make sure we had all of our bases covered. The launch site, once again, was Mile Square Park in Fountain Valley, and we lifted off with tremendous confidence. The winds were more cooperative that year, and we drifted northeast. We flew for forty hours and covered a distance of 624 miles. On our second night, we were really pushing it. We were so low on ballast that we threw our maps overboard to reduce weight. For the last eight hours, we drifted just a few feet above the desert floor. The night was illuminated by a full moon, and it was an eerie experience skimming the ground and hearing the howl of the coyotes. We had to put down at sunrise; otherwise, we would have begun to ascend and would have had no way to slow a descent later. We landed near the town of Myton, Utah. Once again, however, we came in second.

I didn't take the news well. I promised Bob that it would never happen again. If I entered another Gordon Bennett, I was going to win it. Period.

A few days later one of Bob's friends, a fellow he'd met in Zimbabwe on a hunting trip, sent him a letter. The guy had worn out his Cessna 180 flying all over Africa, and he needed a replacement. He wanted Bob to find him a good one and arrange to have it shipped to him. Bob came to me and asked if I knew where he could find a suitable airplane. We went out to a steakhouse to talk it over.

"Listen, Snow," I said. "I've got an idea. I'll find the plane, but instead of going to all the hassle of getting it shipped overseas, why don't we just fly the damn thing to him?"

"Fly it to Zimbabwe?" he asked.

"Sure," I said, still smarting from my third second-place Gordon Bennett finish. I needed something to wipe the taste out of my mouth. "There's not enough adventure in life. Let's have some fun."

Bob thought about it for less than a minute.

"That's a pretty good idea," he said. "Let's do it. Make it happen, Joe."

It took me a while, but I found a pretty good Cessna up in Seattle. It had only ninety hours of total flying time on it, and it had all the equipment we needed: an 80-gallon fuel tank, the whole package. I'd been down in California at a balloon event at the time, so I flew up to the little airport east of Seattle and met the owner. The airplane looked good, so we cut a deal. He signed the title over to me, and I wrote him a check. The place was thick with fog, and everybody was amazed that I intended to fly out of there. The now former owner called all of his buddies out to witness what he was sure was going to be a disaster. But I filed my flight plan, cranked up the engine, and took off. I climbed up through the overcast and flew down to Truckee, California, and from there headed east to Lakeland, Florida, where I planned some further modifications.

The first thing I did was take the seats out and install a second 80-gallon tank in the rear compartment. In the meantime, I started working on all the diplomatic clearances and overflight clearances. There was flight planning to work on and a long list of maps and let-down charts we'd need. It turned out that a hell of a lot of documents and paperwork was required to cross the ocean and then fly across Europe and Africa. I had to find a suitable life raft. I had to rent a high-frequency radio. I was a very busy guy, and this adventure was turning out to involve a great deal of desk work.

By the time we got the plane ready and had everything we were going to need, we were over the legal weight limit. Not only did we have 160 gallons of fuel, but all the charts and emergency equipment to boot. The airplane was literally packed tight top to bottom. There wasn't a spare inch of space inside that thing. The last piece of the puzzle was a ferry permit from the FAA that would allow us to go up to 25 percent over the gross weight limit. Once we had that, we were ready to roll.

In May 1981, we flew nonstop to Connecticut, where we refueled and spent the night. The next leg took us to Moncton Airport in New Brunswick, Canada. In those days, if you intended to fly a single-engine airplane across the Atlantic Ocean, you needed clearance from the Canadian government because the Canadians are responsible for search and rescue to the midpoint of the North Atlantic. The British pick up the responsibility for the rest of the journey. So we were required to demonstrate to the Canadian authorities that we had the right equipment and the proper training.

At Moncton, I had to take a written test. They inspected the Cessna. Then they gave us clearance to fly to Gander Airport in Newfoundland. We refueled again there and spent the night. The next morning we took off on the trickiest leg of the flight, across open ocean toward the coast of Europe. We got nearly to the halfway point when the alternator light came on. We were at the point of no return, and I had a decision to make. We had to have a radio to talk to people. More important, we had to have the battery to pump fuel from the extra tank. So I called an airplane overhead and announced that we were losing communication and were changing our destination to Sondrestrom, which was a municipal base in western Greenland, where the weather forecast looked OK and where there was a good instrument approach. I'd fortunately anticipated the potential for just such an emergency and had gotten advance clearance to land there. Otherwise, airport officials would have fined us eight hundred dollars.

We landed at Sondrestrom and found a mechanic who thought he could fix the problem. The days are long in Greenland at that time of year and, after the guy replaced the alternator, there was still plenty of daylight for me to run a test flight. I flew about half an hour, and the alternator light came on again. I landed, and the mechanic tried another alternator—the last one he had. That one didn't work either, so we were stuck in Sondrestrom. It was damned frustrating. Finally, the guy had an idea. He said he could use an automobile alternator.

"I know it'll work," he said. Snow looked at me. I looked at the mechanic.

"All right, let's try it."

This time I took the plane for a ninety-minute test flight, and it seemed to be working fine, so we fueled up and took off. With our weight, it took us forever to climb up above the 12,000-foot mountains to get out of there, but we were in good spirits because we were finally on our way. And then, an hour and a half out of Sondrestrom, the red light came on again. We couldn't believe it. Four alternators in a row!

Back to Sondrestrom. This time I took a different tack. I called the Air National Guard in New York. They had people who came out to Sondrestrom every year with a C-130 ferrying supplies to the DEW Line. (The Distant Early Warning Line was a chain of RADAR stations across the Arctic intended to detect incoming Soviet bombers during the Cold War.) I asked them if they would bring me an alternator and a relay and everything we might conceivably need to fix the Cessna. They said yes and got everything on a flight out the next morning. They dropped off the supplies, and we upgraded the airplane with all new parts.

The next day we flew nonstop across the North Atlantic to Keflavik Naval Air Station in Iceland and refueled. The next day we made Ireland. The day after that we landed in Rotterdam, where Bob and I had a mutual friend. Then it was on to Brussels and from Brussels to Rome. The longest leg of the entire flight was from Rome to Heraklion Airport in Crete: eleven hours nonstop. That's a fairly long day in a Cessna. From Crete, we flew to Khartoum, Sudan, which is pretty much the end of the world in terms of airplane supplies—or supplies of any sort. We were glad that everything on the airplane was working perfectly. From Khartoum we flew to Nairobi, and that was probably the most fascinating day of our trip because we flew at an altitude of 10 feet above the desert floor all the way. We literally had giraffes looking *down* at us as we went sailing by. This was what I'd envisioned that night at the steakhouse in Florida when we cooked up this crazy idea—not filling out paperwork and waiting for parts. This final leg made all the planning and work worthwhile. You haven't really seen Africa until you see it from a Cessna at 100 miles per hour 10 feet above the deck.

We spent the night in Nairobi and the following day made it to Salisbury, Zimbabwe—the capital city's name would become Harare a year later—where we delivered the plane to its new owner. We'd logged a total of ninety-five hours in transit. The guy seemed impressed that we'd brought it to him all the way from the northwest coast of the United States. He asked how the flight had gone.

"No sweat," I said. I didn't look over at Snow, but I'm pretty sure he was grinning.

Bob and I spent the next eight days in the bush with the airplane owner's safari company. I spent some of that time thinking about our journey and contemplating my ambition for an around-the-world balloon trip, the one I had worked out so painstakingly in my cell in Hanoi. I knew it was possible. What I didn't know was how realistic my dream was or how long it might take me to get all the elements in place to make it happen. In the meantime, however, there was the following year's balloon race to prepare for. I still hadn't gotten over my irritation at three consecutive second-place finishes.

Things didn't start out well for the 1982 race. In February, Bob Snow let me know that other commitments were going to make it impossible for him to participate in that year's Gordon Bennett, so not only did I need to find another sponsor, but I needed a new copilot. Soon. At a friend's suggestion, I wrote a letter to Charles Knapp, the CEO of the world's largest savings and loan, headquartered in Los Angeles. I proposed that Knapp make the flight with me; in return, I asked for ten thousand dollars to cover the Gordon Bennett entry fee, my transportation to and from Los Angeles—the race would again launch from Fountain Valley just to the south—and expenses for a driver and vehicle to transport the balloon and equipment to and from the race. A few days later I received a check for ten thousand dollars in the mail. Knapp was crazy about the idea. He'd never been in a balloon before, but he was an experienced airplane pilot with a taste for adventure and—more important to me at the time—with deep pockets.

I landed at LAX in May 1982, expecting to find my new copilot waiting for me. Instead, a beautiful blonde—Brooke Knapp, Charles's wife—rushed up, threw her arms around me, and gave me a big smack on the lips. Brooke was a pilot with her own Lear jet. A few years later she flew it around the world and set a number of records in the process. I met Charles that night at a swanky cocktail party he'd arranged to celebrate our upcoming flight. He was a very personable guy, and I got a good feeling about him right away.

The race commenced on May 5. We flew through the night, and when the sun came up the next morning, we were at 10,000 feet and on a course for Salt Lake City. Brooke had decided to chase us in her Lear, and that morning she began noting the positions of the other balloons in the race and radioing the information back to us. Ben Abruzzo apparently got on the Salt Lake City frequency and asked who the hell was in that jet.

Brooke radioed back: "Don't you wish you knew?" She was a character.

A little later she reported back that she'd heard a number of the balloonists making plans to land before nightfall. That was good news to us because we were confident we could stay up into the following day.

It was a spectacular flight. At one point that afternoon, I allowed the balloon to drop down to about 100 feet off the ground directly above a herd of Roosevelt elk. Not long after that I began some serious ballasting. We climbed back up to 13,000 feet and flew right over the tops of the Grand Tetons headed for Cody, Wyoming. At about that point, though,

204 CHAPTER SEVEN

the weather started to turn on us. The temperature had plunged, and it began to snow, but we were buoyed by reports that suggested our weather pattern would be taking us north toward Canada, which was good news because we'd dropped back down to about 8,000 feet and did not have enough ballast to get over the mountains looming just to the east.

It was dark by this time, and the storm was really howling. I kept checking our position with the local FAA radio station to verify our northward drift, but each time I checked, we were a little closer to Cody to our south. Before long it was pretty clear to me that we were going to have to put down. We were approaching the mountains, and the weather was getting positively nasty. The situation was not good at all, and it continued to deteriorate. We were surrounded by clouds and blowing snow and the black night. The radio station at Cody reported a 300-foot ceiling with 20-mile-per-hour winds. I started to wonder just what we'd gotten ourselves into.

I briefed Charles on the landing procedure. I warned him it might be a little dicey. We zipped up in our Arctic survival gear and crash helmets. I requested that the Cody FAA station notify the local police and the county sheriff to expect a balloon crash somewhere near Cody within the next thirty minutes. The operator made me repeat the message because he said he couldn't quite believe there was really a balloon aloft in that weather.

I switched on our beacon. As we broke through the clouds at 300 feet, I began to catch glimpses of the frozen ground. I was praying that we would miss any power lines in our path because I would never be able to see them until it was too late. I threw out the 200-foot drag rope and immediately saw a shower of sparks when the rope grazed a set of high-voltage lines. I yelled for Charles to hang on. We couldn't see the ground at this point, so there was no way to know exactly when the impact was coming.

We hit hard. There was no dragging across the ground. We came to a violent stop. I smacked into the side of the gondola and knew right away I was hurt. Our gear was all over the place. Charles was somehow able to crawl free of the whole mess. He'd lost his glasses in the crash, and his eyesight was terrible, but he said he could make out some lights in the distance. He thought it was probably a farmhouse. I told him to leave me with the balloon and to go for help.

He told me later that when he knocked on the door, the lady inside threatened to sic her dogs on him. His helmet was a football-style helmet, and it had gotten twisted around on his head during the landing so that it practically covered his face. He was peering through the ear hole and begging the woman to open her door.

"Ma'am, there's been a balloon crash on your property," he said. "There's an injured man out there, and we need immediate medical assistance. Please help us."

Finally, she opened her door and agreed to call an ambulance. Charles hurried back and kept me company in the blizzard.

At the hospital in Cody, the doctor took X-rays and diagnosed me with a dislocated shoulder and a broken arm. It was about what I'd figured. The doctor, who was not an orthopedic surgeon, gave me two options: they could drive me by ambulance to Billings, Montana—normally two hours away, but probably much longer in the snowstorm—or he could try to repair my shoulder himself.

"That's a tough call, Doc," I said. "Let me ask you something. If you were in my position, which would you choose?"

"I'm smarter than to get in a balloon in a snowstorm," he said. "I would never put myself in your position."

That's when Charles burst in to announce that we'd won the race. He'd gotten our crew on the phone, and they'd given him the news. He was almost as happy as I was. It was as if a weight had been lifted from me.

"Go ahead," I told the doctor. I was content now. "I'm in your hands."

I woke up an hour and a half later in post-op. Charles was waiting for me when I came out of the anesthetic. He told me we'd been aloft for a total of twenty-nine hours—sixteen of which had been at night—and that we had covered 894 miles. Some of the chase crew had made it to Cody by that time, and one of them had smuggled in a bottle of Jack Daniels. We all drank to our victory, but none of them could truly understand how sweet it was to me.

The next morning, after getting the word that the operation had been a success, I thanked the doctor and checked myself out of the hospital—against his orders. My crew picked me up and drove us out to inspect the crash site and get the balloon. Charles and I could see immediately that we'd hit a fence post; that's what had stopped us so suddenly, but we could also see what a lucky thing that had been. Just ahead and directly in our path was a string of power lines. The shoulder didn't hurt so bad after that.

In the fall of 1982, a couple of great things happened to me. The first was Sherry Reed. My marriage—which had been an unhappy one—had ended a few years earlier, and I'd finally found the perfect companion. I couldn't believe my luck to have met a smart, beautiful young woman who shared my spirit of adventure and love of the sky. She absolutely captivated me. Sherry was studying for her degree in journalism at the University of Central Florida and was working as an intern in the marketing department for Bob Snow's operation. She shared my passion for a great challenge, the desire to do things others say are impossible. Just being around Sherry made me optimistic that good things were ahead. And I was right.

The second great thing to happen to me was the Tropicana Aero Cup Race. Absolute-distance races such as the Gordon Bennett aren't the only format for a good balloon competition. I entered the Tropicana in November 1982, and it turned out to be a spectacular experience. The Tropicana was what balloon racers refer to as a judge-declared goal race, meaning that everybody launches from the same spot, and the balloon that puts down the closest to a predetermined point wins. Because this race was sponsored by Tropicana, the takeoff point was the golf course adjacent to the Tropicana Hotel and Casino in Las Vegas, and the judge-declared goal was the Tropicana Hotel and Casino in Atlantic City, New Jersey. In addition to the cup for the winner, the sponsors offered a one-hundred-thousand-dollar cash prize for any balloon that landed anywhere in the state of New Jersey. I doubt that Tropicana expected any of the balloons to get even close.

The rules of the race were a little unusual in that we were given a forty-eight-hour window for launch. We could go anytime between November 13 at 1:00 p.m. and November 15 at 1:00 p.m. The trick was analyzing the wind patterns aloft and figuring out the optimum time to launch. Bob Snow and I were scheduled to fly together, and we had contacted my old Air Force buddy from my Manhigh and Excelsior days, Duke Gildenberg. Nobody understood weather and balloons the way Duke did, and I knew he would be our secret weapon. The one hundred thousand dollars was quite an incentive, and I let both Bob and Duke know that I was damned serious about winning this thing.

I did a little research and found out that the distance record for the class of gas balloon we'd be flying was 1,729 miles set in 1947 by a Russian. The distance to Atlantic City was about 2,000 miles. That meant that if we even got close, we'd set an FAI distance record—another motivator for me. I did some thinking about what it would take to pull this thing off, and I came up with a plan. Then I got together with Bob for a strategy session to explain it.

"Snow," I told him, "I've got some good news and some bad news. The good news is that not only are we going to win the race, but we're going to set a distance record in the process."

Bob looked at me a little skeptically. He was waiting for the bad news.

"The bad news," I went on, "is that you won't be going. I've done the calculations, and in order to carry enough ballast, I'm going to have to do this thing solo."

I was a little nervous about Bob's reaction. The *Rosie O'Grady* was his balloon, and he would be putting up the money for the flight. But he never hesitated.

"I trust you, Joe," he said. "Go for it."

On the evening of November 12, I checked in with Duke, who was going to handle the weather forecasts from his home near Alamogordo. We were in touch by telephone. He told me that the winds on November 13, the first day we could launch, did not look favorable, but when Bob and I went out to the Tropicana the next morning, we saw seven of the balloons being inflated and preparing for takeoff. I could tell that Bob was concerned that some of the racers were getting the jump on the *Rosie O'Grady*. I told him to relax. The Tropicana wasn't a race so much as a strategic exercise. We were going to put our faith in Duke and wait it out.

A number of the balloons took off that first day, headed toward Tucson. That's exactly where Duke told me they'd go. All of that first batch of racers landed within twenty-four hours when the weather pattern stalled. The next day most of the remaining balloonists took off—including Ben Abruzzo, who clearly knew what he was doing. Seeing

Abruzzo go made Bob really nervous, but Duke said to wait, so we waited.

On the final day of our launch window, Duke continued to advise that we launch as late as possible. The few balloons that hadn't gone on November 14 took off early the next morning. But again we waited. Bob and I took our time inflating the balloon. We were ready by 12:30, but still we waited. Then, at 12:59, one minute before the deadline, with Bob biting his lip, the *Rosie O'Grady* was airborne. We took the precaution of having an official race observer alongside us to verify the time.

I always carried a 2-meter ham radio set with me on my gas balloon flights, and as I drifted eastward, I planned to contact local radio operators and have them call Duke in New Mexico to get his recommendations on optimum altitudes for the best wind patterns. As always, I had my ground crew chasing me, although on this flight the pickup truck couldn't keep up. Duke kept finding great wind, and I was really hauling. This was Sherry's first chance to participate in one of these balloon races, and she was grabbing commercial flights from city to city and trying to stay ahead of me. She'd call Duke, and he'd tell her where to go next.

Flying solo really put me to the test. I was busy all the time. On the second day, I had to drop my oxygen tanks as ballast at sunset in order to keep going. I raised Sherry on the radio that night as I flew over Chicago. She'd managed to get in the control tower at O'Hare. The weather was crystal clear as I drifted across the city. Man, what a beautiful sight that was as I passed over the lights of that huge metropolis and drifted out across the blackness of Lake Erie.

On the third day, with my ballast almost gone, I climbed up to 20,000 feet. I got a little groggy without oxygen, so I started doing everything very deliberately to try and avoid making a mistake. About noon, I entered snow clouds and was beginning to wonder how much longer I could last. I managed to get Duke on the phone through a local ham operator, and he informed me that I wasn't going to be able to make New Jersey because my winds were going to keep me too far to the north. I started thinking of the snowflakes as dollar bills that I wasn't going to be able to collect.

I didn't have enough ballast to make it through another night, so I began to valve the balloon and start my descent late that afternoon. I wasn't even sure I had enough ballast to make a safe landing.

Slowly, with night approaching, I came out of the overcast at an altitude of about 300 feet. I sailed along through the snowstorm, tracking over the frozen ground. At about 50 feet, I saw a farmer standing in his field just enjoying the beauty of the scene. He didn't see me. I had to yell down at him.

"Sir," I said, "can I land in your backyard?"

He looked up at me and didn't seem too very surprised.

"Please do," he said.

I made a perfect touch down in 5 feet of fresh-fallen snow. The farmer came rushing up to help.

"Sir," I said, "I believe I just set a long-distance record in a balloon, and I need to know what time it is and where I am."

He pulled his pocket watch out from under his coveralls.

"Well, sir," he said, "it'd be 5:01 in the afternoon, and you'd be at my pig farm in the state of New York."

I'd flown for seventy-two hours and traveled a distance of 2,033 miles, surpassing the existing distance record by more than 300 miles. I'd won the race, but I'd missed the New Jersey line and the one hundred thousand dollars.

The farmer's name was Bernard Kopjke. He drove me to a motel outside of Buffalo, where I was reunited with Sherry and my chase crew about six hours later.

When we woke up the next morning, Sherry went out and bought a dozen roses. I bought a case of champagne and a jeroboam—three liters—to boot. We drove back out to the pig farm to get the balloon. Bernard and some of his neighbors helped us get everything packed up and stowed in our vehicles. When we were done, we gathered in the barn. Sherry gave Bernard's wife the roses, and I presented him with the jeroboam of champagne. I'm not sure he'd ever seen a bottle that big.

"And now," I announced to the small crowd, "we'll all have a drink of champagne!"

"Hold on," Bernard said. I was worried for a moment that he didn't approve of drinking alcohol, but that wasn't it. He glared at his neighbors. "Not with my bottle you don't!"

I showed him the case and assured him that he wouldn't have to share his bottle. We toasted Bernard. We toasted the *Rosie O'Grady*, and I offered a toast to Duke Gildenberg.

A few days later I got a call from a representative of the Tropicana Hotel and Casino. They were organizing a victory celebration at their Atlantic City property—I guess they could afford it since they hadn't had to shell out the one hundred thousand dollars—and they wanted to make sure Sherry and I could attend. I told them we would come only if they would also extend an all-expenses-paid invitation to Bernard Kopjke and his wife. I didn't say why, just that Bernard was a pig farmer in upstate New York and I wanted him there. They agreed, but Bernard turned down the offer. He never left his pigs alone, he said.

It was a great party in Atlantic City—even without Bernard.

8
Destination: *Unknown*; Fuel on Board: *Zero*

✳   ✳   ✳   ✳   ✳   ✳

In the spring of 1984, a Canadian businessman named Gaetan Croteau contacted Ed Yost about his desire to sponsor a record-setting balloon flight. He was willing to spend up to $250,000. Ed told him, "I know just the guy for you," and in a matter of weeks I was at work once again on a transatlantic flight. But this time there were no ifs, ands, or buts. It was to be a *solo* flight. I made sure that was understood.

Ed fortunately still had the balloon and the gondola he'd built for me back in 1978. There were some modifications to be made, but we weren't too far from being ready to go. Once we had the money we needed in the bank, I called Bob Rice in Massachusetts. He was not only an ace meteorologist, but he knew aeronautics. A tremendous talent. He would be the most important member of my team. Next I got in touch with Klanky Hargrove in Orlando. I asked Klanky to put together the electronics and avionics. The rest of the support crew consisted of top-notch balloon people from across the country. In July, I gathered everyone in Caribou, Maine. I wanted to launch from U.S. soil, and this little village in northeastern Maine seemed to be the perfect spot.

My plan was a little unusual. I decided to take the whole team up there, let everybody get comfortable with the place and with each other, get everything ready to go—then put all the hardware in storage and send the team home while we waited for our weather window. I'd been on too many balloon projects where everybody shows up, raring to go, and then sits around waiting and waiting and waiting for good weather. With a large team, not only does that get expensive, it turns out to be a serious drain on morale. People get bored and frustrated. I didn't want to have my crew sitting around for thirty days twiddling their thumbs. So we did all the preparation. We got everything in order, went through all our checklists, and then crated the balloon and packed up the gondola and the equipment. We stored it at a little airport in Caribou. The whole business took about a week. Then we all went home and went about our business. I asked Bob Rice to keep a close watch on the weather patterns and to let me know when he thought we had a good opportunity. I advised everyone else to be on call.

It was a Sunday afternoon, September 8, when I finally heard from Rice.

"Joe," he said, "it looks good for Thursday or Friday."

I contacted everybody on the team and asked them all to meet me in Caribou on Tuesday. Ed Yost came from South Dakota. Dave Sipple, one of our engineers, came from Colorado. Bob Snow had come onboard as one of our sponsors, and Bob, Klanky, Sherry, and I flew up from Orlando. Once we ripped the cellophane off the equipment and charged up the batteries, we were pretty much ready to get on with it.

Rice continued to monitor the weather patterns and let us know that Friday was looking like the better choice. There was a hurricane barreling up the Eastern Seaboard, and he thought we'd be smart to wait. One thing I'd learned about ballooning: trust your weatherman. So Friday it was.

Because Canada is responsible for air and sea rescue in the western half of the northern Atlantic Ocean, it dispatched a team from Transport Canada to check out my equipment. The team inspected my survival gear and my emergency locator beacon. They needed to assure themselves that I knew what I was doing, and I didn't blame them. The only thing that was a little hard to understand was their insistence that I file a flight plan. I tried to explain how ballooning works. You don't have a lot of control over where the winds blow you. Your plans are only as good as your weather forecasts. But they were adamant, so I made a quick trip out to Loring AFB in Limestone, Maine, to file a flight plan with the International Civil Aviation Organization (the worldwide governing body for flight plans).

I don't think they'd ever seen a flight plan quite like mine.

POINT OF DEPARTURE: *Caribou, Maine*
DESTINATION: *Unknown*
ROUTE OF FLIGHT: *Unknown*
DURATION OF FLIGHT: *Unknown*
ALTITUDE: *Unknown*
FUEL ON BOARD: *Zero*

Having the paperwork seemed to make the Canadians happy.

As I saw it, my primary job at this point was to be rested. Lindbergh had struggled with fatigue. Even though his flight was only thirty-three hours, he'd already been up a long time and was already extremely tired before he took off. I was determined not to let that happen. I was going to be bright-eyed and bushy-tailed when my balloon left the ground. My flight was going to take days—not hours—and I needed all the head start I could get. Besides, I had a capable team on the ground—led by Ed Yost and Klanky—to keep everything on track and in order.

I went to bed early on Thursday night. I got up at ten on Friday morning and had a leisurely breakfast with Sherry. Bob Rice called and told me that everything looked good for a launch at eight that evening. Not much later, Yost and his balloon crew began to inflate the 101,480-cubic-foot balloon with helium. I took a shower, shaved—and took a nap. I was serious about this rest business.

At five that afternoon, I drove out to the launch site. The balloon was inflated, the gondola was outfitted and ready. Everything was totally organized, and everybody was relaxed. We watched the sun go down. About that time, I received a call from the owner of Weather Services Corporation in Boston, where Bob Rice was employed. I'd never talked to this fellow before.

"Colonel Kittinger," he said, "I need to inform you that we here at the weather service have great concern about the weather pattern you're intending to launch into."

This was not exactly what I wanted to hear. We had everything ready for launch, and this guy was calling me *now*?

"Who precisely is *we*?" I asked.

"I'm speaking on behalf of the management here at Weather Services," he said.

"Is Bob Rice part of the *we*?" I was more than a little annoyed.

"No," he admitted. "Bob isn't with us on this, but the management here recommends that you *do not launch*. We want to be on record with this."

"Listen," I said, "put Bob Rice on the phone."

They went and got Bob.

"Bob," I said, "what is all this bull?"

"Joe, I think we can do it. I stand by my forecast." Bob's voice was calm and firm. "There is some risk, but we've got a real good pattern developing out there. But, Joe, I have to tell you. If anything goes wrong, I'll probably get fired."

"I don't give a damn," I told him. "That's your problem, Bob. All I want to do is get across that ocean. Your job is to tell me when to go."

We'd already held long, detailed discussions about weather and the potential dangers in the weeks leading up to this moment. We'd talked about what would happen if I lost communications. There was no guarantee I was going to be able to make contact with Bob during the flight. He would remain in Boston, and I had elected not to put a communications crew in Europe. Satellite communication technology didn't yet exist, so we had planned the entire trip assuming we would have no contact at all. I knew where the weather systems were supposed to be, I knew my trajectory, I knew how the patterns were likely to change. We'd done our due diligence.

Ready for launch in Caribou. My team puts the finishing touches on another beautiful Yost balloon prior to my three-and-a-half-day transatlantic solo flight in 1983. My job was to be rested and ready to go. (Courtesy: National Geographic Society.)

I pondered my dilemma for a couple of minutes, while Bob and the weather service waited on the line, and the rest of my crew waited on the ground in Caribou. My guess was that the management in Boston wanted to cover their butts in case I killed myself. I'd never met any of them, but I knew Bob Rice. He was my guy, and he had cleared me for launch. So I made the decision. To hell with the rest of them.

"I'm going," I announced and hung up the phone. There was no turning back now.

In my effort to cover all my own bases, I had invited a Catholic priest and a Baptist minister to attend the launch. I'd tried to find a rabbi but hadn't been able to line one up in Caribou. If I'd known about a Buddhist in the area, he would have been invited. We assembled the team and the townspeople who'd come out to witness the event, and after a couple of prayers we all drank a champagne toast to a successful flight. I gave Sherry a big kiss, and I climbed into Ed's gondola. In honor of Bob Snow, we called it the *Rosie O'Grady*. The balloon looked great, and everyone was in high spirits.

At about 8:00 p.m., I waved and weighed off. Away I went into the black of night. It was really a magnificent moment for me. I'd been working for this for more than ten years. From the Hanoi Hilton to the coast of Maine.

As the wind picked me up and sent me eastward out over the ocean, I thought of the dense blackness of the universe I'd witnessed on *Excelsior III*. The night was almost that dark. Bob Rice had instructed me to rise up to somewhere between 4,000 and 5,000 feet and to remain there until sunrise. Altitude management was going to be critical throughout the flight. We'd calculated the ballast I'd need, and there was absolutely nothing extra. Every time the sun set on me, the balloon would lose about 10 percent of its lift as the gas cooled down. But there was a limit to how high I could ascend in an open gondola and remain functional. It was an extremely tight operational window.

About a minute before my lift off, somebody had handed me a box of Kentucky Fried Chicken, so once I reached 5,000 feet and leveled off, I decided to treat myself to a snack. Unfortunately, the chicken was already frozen solid. I knew right then that this Atlantic crossing wasn't going to be a luxury flight.

Sherry, Bob Snow, Bob's wife, and a few others were flying from Caribou down to Boston to join Bob Rice in the command post set up at Rice's office. Just as I was trying to devise a means of thawing out my chicken, Snow came on the radio.

"Listen to this, Kittinger," he said, and I heard a loud pop.

"Is that what I think it is?" I asked.

"Yep," he said. "We're drinking champagne, my friend."

A minute later Snow was back on.

"Listen to this," he said. This time it was a cracking sound, like something was breaking. "Lobster!" he announced. "French champagne and Maine lobster!"

It was cruel. I finally gave up on the iced chicken.

"Joe?" It was Bob Rice now. "I want you to ascend to 8,000 feet."

At first, I thought it was a joke, as if they wanted to find temperatures for me that were just a little colder. Our plan had me at my current altitude all night. I definitely didn't want to waste the ballast it would take to gain another 3,000 feet without a pretty good reason.

"Bob, are you sure about this?"

"Yes," he said. He was resolute. "I want you at 8,000. The hurricane's coming in at a slightly different angle, and I think this'll be safer."

"You're the boss," I said and began to ballast right away. I went to 8,000 feet and stayed there for the rest of a very cold, very dark night.

When dawn broke, I was drifting over wide open ocean, heading for Newfoundland, water as far as I could see. As the sun warmed the balloon, I gained another 2,000 feet, which put me at an altitude of just less than 2 miles. At about noon, I decided to have some lunch. To save weight, most of my meals were packed in freeze-dried pouches. I had a little gasoline cook stove to heat up water, to which I would then add the reconstituted food. I set up the stove in one corner of the gondola and got it going. The chicken was still hard as granite, and I was pretty hungry by this point. Then, suddenly, the stove caught fire and the flames quickly spread to the rear of the gondola. The thing must have developed a leak. I had a momentary thought of trying to fix it, but the reality of hanging over the ocean in a basket full of burning gasoline hit me. I heaved the stove overboard and put the rest of the fire out with the extinguisher I'd stowed with my gear.

Of course, there went my hot water. For the rest of the trip, I'd be limited to the five cans of spaghetti and meatballs I'd packed—or, to be more precise, the cans of *frozen* spaghetti and meatballs. I opened one of the cans. The meatballs might as well have been rocks, but I was able to mush up the spaghetti enough to chew it and get it down. I kept thinking about Bob Snow with his lobster and champagne.

In spite of the cold, I had plenty of warm clothes. At night, when the temperature dropped down below zero, I had a sleeping bag I could crawl into. My water bottles stayed frozen solid the whole way, and I had to stick them inside my clothes and warm them up with my body heat in order to get a drink. The process took a while, and it wasn't very comfortable. Consequently, it seemed as if I was thirsty all the time. But there was no shortage of power. I had a bunch of DieHard batteries, so I never had to worry about the radio.

I flew smack dab over Halifax later that afternoon. That would be the last land I'd see for quite a while, so I took a real good look. This was my final decision point. If I wanted to abort the attempt, I'd have to do it here. With the exception of the food issue, though, everything was working great. There was no hesitation. I was on my way.

Not much later, my gondola was rocked by a tremendous explosion. My first thought was that the balloon had blown up. I couldn't believe it. It was like a dynamite blast. I looked up and saw the duct at the bottom of the balloon vibrating violently. I started running through my emergency procedures in my head and wondering how far I'd drifted since seeing Halifax.

After a few moments, it hit me. The Concorde! I'd just been sonic-boomed by a supersonic transport. When you experience it on the ground, it's impressive. In a balloon over the open ocean, let me tell you, it carries a whole different kind of wallop. It scared the hell out of me. I would experience a few more of those booms in the coming days. They all got my attention, but nothing like that first one.

I stayed extremely busy flying the balloon. Of course, I was making this flight well before the availability of geographical positioning systems or the more sophisticated navigational aids we have now. I did have a LORAN set on board, but I could never get it to lock on for more than a few seconds. I also had a sextant, and I knew how to use it, but I had cloud cover all the way, and without a good sun shot, the sextant was useless. That left me with good old dead reckoning. I luckily could get a pretty accurate idea of my heading by watching the wind on the surface of the ocean. I knew it was going to be a bit of hit and miss, but I also knew that I was moving eastward in the direction of the European continent, which was a mighty big target.

As the sun set on me after that first full day, I dropped one of the 50-pound sacks of sand that constituted my ballast. I flew through the night. When the sun came up the next morning, the warming rays heated up the balloon and took me all the way up to 18,000 feet. By this point, I was using the breathing equipment I'd brought. I had a mask and two big bottles of oxygen. It would have been very tough without that oxygen. I also had a medical kit. One of the doctors who'd advised me during my planning had given me some pills to keep me awake, but I decided I could do the flight without them.

During the journey, I slept in ten-minute increments. I had an alarm clock that would run for ten minutes. We'd calculated that if the balloon developed a serious leak, I would likely descend at a rate of about 1,000 feet a minute. At an altitude of 15,000 feet, it would take me fifteen minutes to hit the water. Once I rose above 10,000 feet, if something happened while I was asleep, the alarm clock would wake me up in time for me to have a chance to take action, so that was my sleep cycle all the way across. I had an immersion suit in case of a disaster that forced me into the water. The gondola Ed Yost had given me was built—like the one he flew—to double as a boat, but with the heavy winds and 50-foot seas below me, I knew chances of survival were remote if I had to go in the water. It was already September, so I just accepted the fact that if I went down, hypothermia or the ocean itself would get me before any rescue effort could.

My second night—actually it was about three in the morning—I found myself getting a little bit bored. I hadn't managed to contact anyone on the radio since Halifax. I knew that all airliners monitor the emergency frequency 121.5, so I dialed it in and went on the air.

"If anybody's around, please give me a call."

Right away, I got a call from a transatlantic airliner, TWA 101. I told the pilot to go over to frequency 123.45, and we started to chat. I explained that I was trying to cross the ocean in a balloon. He asked me where I was.

"Well," I said, "I'm over the middle of the Atlantic Ocean. Where are you?"

"I'm about 300 miles out of Heathrow," he said, "and I'm going to be starting my letdown soon."

He asked my name, and I told him.

"You know," he said, "this is a pretty amazing coincidence. Your chase crew is onboard my airplane. We chatted briefly as they got on."

Four hundred planes flew back and forth across the Atlantic every day, and I just happened to contact the one carrying my team to Europe. The pilot offered to go back and bring Sherry and Bob Snow up into the cockpit. I was able to talk to both of them in the middle of the night. We talked for maybe fifteen minutes. They were cruising at 40,000 feet, and I was a speck somewhere in the darkness below. The conversation was a whole lot of fun for me and really gave me a shot of adrenaline that I needed at about that point.

By this time, I'd been in the air for two and a half days. The next afternoon at about five, I came over the Bay of Biscay with the western coast of Spain in the distance. I could see the ships below me, and for the first time since Halifax I knew right where I was. A friend of mine on the chase crew, George Riviere, had come over with Sherry and Bob. George had rented a King Air and was flying around looking for me. He had a British television company reporter and a cameraman onboard. Although it seems farfetched, they actually found me. They interviewed me on the air as I came across the coast of Spain.

Now I knew I'd done it. The first solo balloon flight to make it across the ocean. I wasn't ready to land yet, though. I was dead set on beating the distance record that Abruzzo, Anderson, and Newman had set in the *Double Eagle*. The distance is calculated on a Great Circle route. They'd flown 2,600 miles, and I knew that if I put down in Spain, I'd come up short. If I wanted the record, I had to keep flying. I still had ballast left. I couldn't see any sense in stopping. I decided to see how far I could go. In the back of my mind, I thought maybe I could make it to Moscow and put the *Rosie O'Grady* down in Red Square. That would turn a few heads.

I stayed up and flew on through the night. When the sun rose on day four of my journey, I could see Nice and the French Riviera below. I was out over the Mediterranean, maybe 40 miles from the coast. Bob Rice had already gotten word to me that a big high-pressure area over the North Pole had moved down and stalled, but when that high started to move again, the pattern I'd been flying in would deteriorate quickly. He told me to expect to begin hooking to the north, and that's exactly what was happening. That's when I knew I wasn't going to be able to go much farther. I'd gotten all the distance I was going to be able to get. By my calculations, though, I'd already surpassed the *Double Eagle*. I had the record. I was ready to come down.

The National Geographic Society had signed on as one of my sponsors, and its people were determined to get photographic coverage of my landing for the magazine. They'd missed Ed Yost's touchdown in the water, and they'd missed the *Double Eagle's* landing outside Paris because they hadn't gotten a helicopter, so this time they leased a chopper in Marseille and followed me the rest of the way. They knew Bob Snow had also helped sponsor the flight, so they graciously offered him a seat on the chopper for the final chase. Snow, even more graciously, offered the seat to Sherry. I know he really wanted to be there for the landing, but the guy was such a good friend and decent man he gave it up. I'll always be indebted to him for that.

The National Geographic people chased me through the afternoon and crossed the coast of Italy alongside me. As we approached Milan, I was only down to about 8,000 feet, and I figured I could stretch it out a little longer. I was thinking that I'd make it across the Adriatic and well into Yugoslavia—maybe farther. Then my winds started hooking strongly to the north. Looming ahead in that direction were 12,000-foot mountains. As if that weren't daunting enough, a big line of dark thunderstorms was developing right in my path. I had no ballast left. I was going to have to bring it down.

About this time, things started to happen fast. Sherry got me on the radio and asked how things were going.

"Honey," I said, "I'm real busy right now. Don't call me."

I wanted to talk to her, but I'd been aloft for almost four days, and I knew that I was not as mentally sharp as I wanted to be. I told myself that from that point on, I would question myself on every decision I made. When I decided on a course of action, I'd challenge it and rethink the problem. With the mountains coming up, the thunderstorms building, and my piloting an aircraft over which I had very little control, a dumb mistake could kill me.

I was out of ballast now, but I needed to get down as quickly as possible. I started tearing up my maps and throwing them overboard. I threw clothes out. Anything to make myself lighter. Now I was beginning to notice power lines everywhere I looked: tremendous 250-foot towers. Directly ahead of me was nothing but forest. I judged the thunderstorms to be about 10 miles distant. I'd never wanted to get a balloon down as badly as I did at that moment.

I was tracking at about 30 miles per hour across the ground, which is pretty damn fast for a balloon. I was maybe 1,000 feet from the power lines below. Finally, I cleared the last of the wires. Now I was over the trees, still racing along at a frightening clip. Landing in trees is typically not a good choice for a balloonist, but I was out of options. I let down my drag rope. I tensed for the impact. The instant I hit the trees I pulled the rip panel on the balloon. The next thing I knew, I was out of the gondola. I tumbled through the branches and landed on a rock. I knew immediately that I'd broken my right foot, but, more important, I was

Self-portrait over the Mediterranean. Approaching the France-Italy border, nearly out of ballast and exhausted, I'm still convinced I can make it across the Adriatic and into eastern Europe—maybe even all the way to Moscow. (Courtesy: National Geographic Society.)

down and I was alive. That was plenty good enough for me.

The chase helicopter landed about 150 meters down the hill in a little clearing. Within moments, here came Sherry, charging up the slope carrying two bottles of champagne that she'd brought all the way from the States. I gave her a big kiss. It was pure elation. The adrenaline had snapped me back, and I was whooping and hollering like you can't imagine. Sherry opened one of the bottles, and I poured it over my head. Then she opened the second one, and we sat down on the ground and drank that sucker.

Just beyond us in the forest was a team of seven Italian lumbermen. They'd been going about their business felling trees when I came crashing down through the canopy. First a balloon. Then a helicopter. Then a pretty woman carrying bottles of champagne. They didn't seem to know whether to be scared or to bust out laughing.

Right about that time, we heard my emergency locator beacon begin squawking. It had gotten knocked out of the gondola, and it took us a few minutes to find it and shut it off. At this point, my foot was really beginning to hurt. The adrenaline was wearing off, and I was suffering. Sherry rounded up the woodchoppers, and they picked me up and carried me down the hill to the helicopter.

I asked the pilot to take me to Nice. There were closer hospitals, but I knew they had satellites for TV back to the States in Nice, and I knew that my sponsors wanted all the publicity they could get, so we flew back to France. The funny thing was that after getting my foot put in a cast, I couldn't get any crutches. In France, apparently, you get crutches at a drugstore, and by this point it was nine in the evening, and the drugstores were closed, so I had to hop around hanging onto people. It definitely put a crimp in my style.

Landing site in the trees in Cairo Montenotte. Just moments after Sherry reached me with the champagne. Weary, with a broken foot, I'm still full of adrenaline and as elated as I've ever been following a flight. Curious Italian woodchoppers observe from the shadows. (Courtesy: Peter Turnley.)

We drove from the hospital to the satellite station that belonged to ABC. All of the networks had asked for an exclusive interview. We'd said no; we wanted everybody to be able to broadcast the story. At first, ABC balked at allowing NBC and CBS access to their satellite facilities, but when I threatened to cancel the whole thing, they relented. I ended up talking with both Tom Brokaw and Peter Jennings, and all the networks had coverage of the *Rosie O'Grady* that night.

Before I'd launched from Caribou, Bob Snow and I had made a bet: if I landed in the water, I had to buy dinner for the crew at Maxim's in Paris. If I touched down on land, Snow had to buy. It had been a motivating factor for me, I'll tell you. I knew that was going to be quite a bill. Bob joined us in Nice, and we decided we'd go back to Italy and have a little party with the woodchoppers the next night. The night after that we'd all go to Maxim's. On Bob's tab. Except for my foot, this whole thing was turning into quite a time.

The next afternoon my public-relations guy, Mark Kirkham, received a call from the U.S. ambassador to Italy, Maxwell Rabb. The ambassador informed us that the Italian government had decided to honor me formally for terminating my record-setting flight on Italian soil— or, more accurately, in Italian trees. They wanted us to be there the following night. Mark apologized and told them about our reservations at Maxim's.

"Let me start again," Ambassador Rabb said. "Kittinger landed in the nation of Italy. You are now in France. This looks like an insult to the Italians. You could cause us serious diplomatic problems if you turn down this honor. It would really help me and the United States for Kittinger to be here for the ceremony."

We talked about it and tried again to explain our dilemma.

"Listen," the ambassador said. "Would you like me to have the president of the United States call Kittinger to explain the situation?"

Kirkham was quick with a reply.

"Where do you want us to be, Mr. Ambassador?"

"Be at the Milan airport at ten," he said.

And that was it. I told Snow to call Maxim's. Our celebration dinner would have to wait.

That night we returned to Cairo Montenotte, where I'd landed, and had a big party with the locals. Kirkham had arrived there about four hours before the rest of us and had gathered all the woodchoppers together. We were expecting a camera crew, so he briefed them on an entire routine.

"When I hold up one finger, you say 'HIP HIP, HOORAY!'" Kirkham had these guys all practicing together. "When I hold up two fingers, you say 'WE LOVE YOU, JOE!' And when I hold up three fingers, you say 'GOD BLESS AMERICA!'"

They all drank some wine and then practiced some more. By the time Sherry and Bob Snow and I arrived, there were twenty-five television cameras. It was an event! Hundreds of people. I looked over and saw Kirkham flashing these hand signals to the woodchoppers, and every so often you'd hear "God Bless America! Hip Hip, Hooray!" We couldn't stop laughing at the absurdity of the whole thing. We drank wine with these guys all night.

Just before our departure early the next morning, one of the woodchoppers got on his knee and proposed marriage to Sherry. They all hated to see her go.

The next day an executive jet picked us up at the Milan airport and zipped us down to Rome in high style. We were met by a very gracious Ambassador Rabb, and Sherry and I stayed that night in the American embassy. We were treated to a lavish dinner and party and repeated the whole thing the following night. I began to wonder if they were ever going to let us go. On the third night, they took us to the palace to meet the president of the Italian Republic. His name was Alessandro Pertini, and he was quite a character. Eighty-seven years old when we met him, he was a Socialist and one of the most popular presidents in Italy's history. When he left office two years later, he was said to be the oldest president in the world. Then they surprised me by awarding me the Legion of Merit medal. They told me it was the highest honor a civilian can receive. There were dozens of paparazzi surrounding us and snapping pictures. I certainly couldn't have imagined anything like this when I'd ascended from Caribou with my frozen chicken.

Later, at dinner, President Pertini leaned toward me. He lowered his voice and nodded in Sherry's direction.

"Is this your wife, Kittinger?"

"No, sir," I said. "She's my girlfriend."

He looked at me for a long moment. Then he winked and nodded conspiratorially. He was a hilarious guy and a fantastic host.

After dinner, we said our good-byes and flew to Paris, where we were met by the American ambassador to France. Not to be outdone by his Italian counterpart, the ambassador had us whisked to the embassy in Paris and ensconced in the same bedroom Lindbergh had slept in the night after he flew the Atlantic. Sherry and I decided we could get used to this kind of treatment.

That night we finally had our blow-out celebration dinner at Maxim's. Rumor had it that Ho Chi Minh had once worked as a busboy there during his exile days in Paris in the 1920s. There were fifty people in our party by that point. Snow had invited a bunch of the television people to join us. We drank champagne until it ran out our ears, and we discovered that Maxim's has a tradition that none of the restaurant staff goes home until the last guest has left. We walked out of the place at half past three in the morning, and all the staff lined up to applaud us. I'm not sure if they were applauding the Atlantic crossing, the amount of money we'd dropped in their establishment, or just the fact that we were finally leaving.

The next day we returned to the United States. I had been scheduled for an appearance on *The David Letterman Show* in New York, but first Bob Snow and I were taken down to Washington for a meeting with President Reagan. I had flown an American flag from the balloon rigging all the way across the ocean, and I gave it to Mr. Reagan. He seemed to enjoy hearing about the adventure. About this same time, I got a call from an old friend—Claude Govan, whom I'd last seen training Italian pilots in Vicenza. Govan had retired and was living in New Jersey. He'd heard about the Atlantic flight and said he just wanted to congratulate me. We reminisced about our days in Germany, when second lieutenants were dropping like flies. It made me think about how much had happened in the years since. About how lucky I'd been. About the way Govan had been treated when he'd had to shoulder the blame for the death of Doak Walker. And about how much remained undone.

A day or two later we were finally back in Orlando and had a chance to reflect on the whole episode. I had made it 500 miles farther than Abruzzo, Anderson, and Newman. I was very happy about that. I knew it was a record that was likely to stand for a very long time. Bob Rice had put me into a great weather pattern, essentially on the lee edge of a hurricane. At times, I was traveling more than 70 miles an hour. My maximum altitude was 22,000 feet. The coldest temperature was 20 degrees below zero. I'd gotten three and a half hours sleep over the three and a half days of the flight—all in ten-minute increments.

Every member of my team had performed magnificently. Ed Yost's balloon never leaked. I'd had no difficulty with any of the systems. The only real glitch had been the stove; I should have spent more time testing it. But I had two primary goals for the flight: to set a distance record and to have fun. I had succeeded at both.

I wanted to take advantage of the momentum we'd created to try and line up a sponsor for the around-the-world flight. One of the reasons I'd been so aggressive about postflight publicity was that I wanted to get the attention of anybody who might be able to help me. I got in touch with Coca-Cola and Budweiser. I made my pitch to the corporate people. I'd proven I knew how to plan and run this kind of operation, and I was absolutely convinced I could make that flight. I never gave up trying to put the project together.

Fifteen years later my friend Steve Fossett came along and beat me to it. Steve took the last great ballooning prize. He just kept at it and kept at it until he did it. He was one tough customer and the kind of guy who literally did not take no for an answer. I admired his determination and resourcefulness.

All I could do was salute him.

Dr. Tom Heinsheimer agreed to cancel the 1983 Gordon Bennett race because a group in France wanted to use the name for their own event celebrating the bicentennial of manned balloon flight. Dr. Heinsheimer held his Gordon Bennett Balloon Race again in 1984, but by that time both the National Aeronautic Association and the Balloon Federation of America had joined the FAI in backing the competing group that had decided to challenge Tom's ownership of the Gordon Bennett name. The French group named their competition the Coupe Aéronautique Gordon Bennett. From that point forward, we have had dueling Gordon Bennett races. The problem with a balloon race in Europe is that political boundaries have made it an extremely problematic arena. The original rules said you take off and see how far you can go, but in the 1970s and 1980s that was a dangerous procedure on the Continent. Two American aeronauts were killed when they were forced to land prematurely to avoid penetrating East German territory. Two more American racers were shot down by a Belarus helicopter. These incidents forced the Coupe Aéronautique to establish awkward political and geographic constraints for the European race, constraints that many of us believe violated—and continue to violate—the spirit of Gordon Bennett's vision.

So Dr. Heinsheimer and our contingent of the balloon community have continued with what we consider the real Gordon Bennett Race, even though the FAI has consistently opposed it and we have been denied the international recognition we believe we deserved. (In 1990, the FAI would go so far as to declare that "any balloonist who participates in a non-FAI event with the words 'Gordon Bennett' in the title shall have his/her sporting license revoked for three years.") It's not a very inspiring story. Balloonists are adventurers by nature, and most of us can do without the legalities and politics. I decided to continue to compete in the U.S. Gordon Bennett Race.

Bob Snow and I entered the 1984 race together and won, flying from Palm Springs, California, to Hobart, Oklahoma, a distance of 1,001 miles—the longest Gordon Bennett flight ever. Before lifting off, we'd stowed two bottles of Opus One wine in our gondola. Opus One was the product of a joint venture by Robert Mondavi and Baron Phillipe de Rothschild to create the first American ultrapremium wine. A single case of the stuff had gone for twenty-four thousand dollars at an auction three years earlier. We thought an Opus One toast would be a marvelous way to celebrate the win we anticipated, but as we'd ended the final leg of the flight in winds that were much higher than we'd have preferred, I gave Bob the task of ballasting. After our ballast had been depleted, Bob was forced to start throwing our gear over. Clothes, food, water—everything he could get his hands on. He did a great job, and we managed to land in one piece.

When our chase crew, which included Sherry and Bob's wife, Linda, met us, I reached for a bottle of Opus One.

"Get the other one, Bob," I said.

I looked over and saw Bob pawing around on the bottom of the gondola and sifting through what remained of our gear. A long silence followed.

"Bob, you're not going to tell me you threw a bottle of Opus One over, are you?"

Snow looked at me. He didn't say a word. He didn't have to.

We may have set a world record that day for the most expensive ballast drop of all time, but I got over it pretty quickly. I'd now won two Gordon Bennetts in a row, and the original rules said that any balloonist who wins three consecutive races has the privilege of retiring the trophy. I'd had a chance to inspect it, and it was a beauty. Paul Conrad, the Pulitzer Prize–winning author and sculptor, had designed it.

I wanted that trophy for my own living room—or perhaps for the National Air and Space Museum.

I entered the 1985 Gordon Bennett with high hopes and higher expectations. The race that year was particularly significant for another reason, though. For the first time, Sherry was going to be in the gondola with me. She'd seen enough of this stuff to understand what it takes to tackle a challenge such as the Gordon Bennett. Balloon racing can be grueling, uncomfortable, and—at times—terrifying. It's not for everybody. In fact, Sherry's first gas balloon flight only months earlier had ended in disaster. We'd been guests at Malcolm Forbes's Chateau de Balleroy in France when the balloon she was in exploded 800 feet above the ground. Luckily, it was an old-fashioned net balloon, and the material inside the net had formed a sort of impromptu parachute, which kept the descent from becoming a total free fall. Sherry survived, but she came away with two broken legs. After that, she was understandably reluctant to fly with pilots she didn't know. I certainly never had any doubts about her ability to perform under pressure. While the balloon in France was falling from the sky and the other passengers were in a state of panic, Sherry calmly took out her camera and snapped a photo of the remnants of the balloon. Then she took the hands of the other two women passengers and led them in a prayer.

We launched from Palm Springs on May 9 and drifted slowly toward the northeast. We were in the air for almost seven hours when we found ourselves stalled over Twenty-nine Palms, California, a distance of only 20 miles. When the sun set that evening, we began to drift backwards— back toward Palm Springs. A light breeze kicked up around midnight and began taking us in the direction of Las Vegas. The only problem was that our new path threatened to take us into restricted airspace, an area called R-4806 to the northwest of Nellis AFB, the place I'd done my flight training for the Air Force thirty-six years earlier. Even though

Grapes of victory in Hobart, Oklahoma. Sherry (to my left), Bob and Linda Snow, and I celebrate our win in the 1984 Gordon Bennett with some precious California red.

we were at 13,000 feet and finally starting to cover some distance, I told Sherry that we were going to have to put the balloon down to avoid penetrating R-4806. I didn't want to become the first Gordon Bennett racer to be shot out of the sky over U.S. territory.

I pulled on the valve rope to start dumping our helium . . . but nothing happened. I tried again. I put all my weight on the rope, but the valve cover wouldn't budge. I had absolutely no control over my aircraft. We couldn't land, and I couldn't arrest our climb. We continued our drift toward R-4806.

We were out of oxygen, and even though we were still below 14,000 feet, I knew that when the sun rose and started heating the gas, we'd be up to 22,000 feet in no time. It would be a challenge just to retain consciousness. Much higher than that, and we'd be in life-threatening territory. I got on the radio and called Nellis. I described our predicament and declared an emergency. They ordered me to land before I entered protected airspace. For some reason, I couldn't quite convince the Nellis air-traffic people that I had no way to bring my craft down. Moments later we crossed into R-4806.

We sat down in the gondola and tried to stay still to reduce our oxygen requirements. Every few minutes I'd tug on the valve rope again, but to no avail. The sun was coming up at this point, and in short order we were at 22,500 feet. I kept trying the rope, just in case. Then, on one of my pulls, the valve cover slid loose, and we began to dump helium. The mechanism must have frozen during the night, and the warmth of the sun had finally thawed it out. We began to descend.

Nellis was back on the radio, ordering me to land immediately. I asked if they wanted me to put down inside R-4806 or to try and drift on past restricted airspace. They again ordered me to land immediately.

About ten minutes after we touched down, an Air Force helicopter landed nearby, and three armed security police came sprinting in our direction. They were not gracious hosts. They demanded our identification and asked why we had entered a prohibited area against orders. I tried to explain, but they were unsympathetic. While I was filling out some paperwork, one of the cops saw Sherry's camera and immediately confiscated the film. We answered what seemed to be hundreds of questions. Finally, they decided they were through with us and began walking back to the helicopter. Since Sherry and I were essentially stranded in the desert—our chase crew wouldn't be able to get anywhere near us—I asked if we could get a ride to Nellis.

"Negative," one of the security detail said. "You cannot ride in our chopper."

I yelled after them: "Sir, we have almost no water and no transportation!"

We stood there and watched the Air Force chopper take off and head back to the base. Luckily for us, back in Palm Springs, Tom Heinsheimer had been tracking all the balloons. He made calls to the appropriate authorities at Nellis and talked the Air Force into sending the chopper back. They ferried us to the edge of R-4806 and deposited us on a road just beyond Air Force property, where our chase crew eventually found us. It was quite an experience.

The whole thing had seemed like a disaster as it was happening, but the funny thing is that Sherry and I had covered a distance of 279 miles from Palm Springs in fifty-five hours—good enough for first place that year. Sherry became not only the first woman in history to be part of a winning Gordon Bennett team, but also the youngest winner ever. For me, it was a third consecutive win.

That beautiful trophy was finally mine.

9
Ballooning and Salooning

✳   ✳   ✳   ✳   ✳   ✳

Sherry flew another Gordon Bennett with me in 1988, and that one really put her devotion to adventure—and to me—to the test. The launch point for the race was once again the desert environs of Palm Springs. Our weather team's prediction for winds aloft suggested that we'd briefly dip down across the Mexican border and then pop back up into Texas. The first part of that forecast turned out to be spot-on. We swung down across Baja California and headed east; then the winds died, and we were becalmed: absolutely dead still at an altitude of 15,000 feet above the Sea of Cortez about halfway between Baja and the Mexican mainland. To make matters worse, the normally reliable *Rosie O'Grady* was leaking. We had life preservers in the gondola, but the ocean temperature was about 55 degrees Fahrenheit, and I knew we wouldn't live very long if we had to go into the water. The sun set with us still 50 miles from shore. The situation was serious. We were running out of ballast and continuing to lose altitude. I knew I had a decision point coming up, and I wanted to be well rested when it arrived.

"I'm really tired," I told Sherry. "I'm going to take a little nap. Just keep the balloon at our current altitude. Don't worry about ballast. Drop whatever you need to, but keep us right here."

I woke up about half an hour later. I took stock of our dilemma and decided I had no choice but to declare an emergency. I was able to contact a U.S. Drug Enforcement Agency (DEA) airplane that happened to be in the vicinity. I explained that I was in a balloon over the water, and that we were in trouble. I told them whom to contact back at our command post in Palm Springs and asked them to relay the message that it was looking as if we might have to bring the *Rosie O'Grady* down in the open ocean. In the back of my mind, though, I considered a water landing as absolutely the very last resort. In fact, I had come up with a contingency plan. Sherry and I would take the radio and climb up into the balloon's rigging, above the load ring, and I'd use my knife to cut away the gondola. I knew we'd shoot up pretty fast, probably up to somewhere around 22,000 or 23,000 feet. It would be cold and hard to breathe, but at least we'd be alive. The way I looked at it, the water meant death.

Then, we began to move. Very . . . very . . . slowly. But it was movement. And then we saw an island ahead. Just like in a movie. An island! And we were heading right for it. It was pretty small, but there was a full moon that night, and I could see clearly the spine of a mountain range with peaks that looked to be maybe 2,000 feet high. Beyond the ridgeline, the range dropped off steeply. The whole island was only about 5 miles across. There wasn't much space between the cliffs and the edge of the water. If I was going to get us down, I'd have to get it exactly right.

In the meantime, the DEA plane returned. The agents informed me they had a small boat onboard and that they could drop it on a parachute, but I was too busy to talk to them. I'd committed us to a landing, and it had to be perfect. If we came in too low, we'd crash in the mountains; too high and we'd overshoot and end up in the water. The instant we cleared the peaks, I started valving helium, trying to set up our approach. At an altitude of about 200 feet, I wasn't sure we could do it. I glanced down at the life preservers; there'd been no time to strap them on. We came in fast and touched down just short of the beach: dry and grateful. It may have been the best landing of my ballooning career.

It was four in the morning. I immediately got on the radio and told the DEA guys not to drop the boat. We were safe—at least for the time being. I sure didn't intend to paddle a little boat all the way to the mainland, so Sherry and I piled inside the gondola and went to sleep.

When day broke, I wanted to get right to the business of building a signal fire so the rescue mission we were expecting could locate us. While Sherry constructed a still to collect water—we couldn't see any potential water sources anywhere—I built a huge fire that we could light the moment we saw an aircraft in the vicinity. In the meantime, we started exploring our own private desert island. We found out later that the name of the place was Isla Angel de la Guarda (Guardian Angel Island). Sounds like a fairy tale, but it's true. The island is an uninhabited, undeveloped shard of the Midriff Island chain that Mexico has designated a national park. We also found out something we were just as glad we didn't know at the time. The island has one of the world's healthiest populations of rattlesnakes, including one species that occurs nowhere else. People come from all over to study the snakes.

All we had for sustenance was a gallon of water, a small can of peaches, and some peanuts. We listened for an airplane or helicopter engine all day. Finally, at about four that afternoon, we heard what we'd been waiting for. I got on the radio.

"Rosie Chase, this is Rosie Balloon."

I heard Mark Kirkham's voice answer: "Rosie Balloon, this is Rosie Chase."

I touched off my fire to give Mark a visual of our location, but the driftwood I'd piled up must have been hundreds of years old, so there was no smoke whatsoever—just an intense heat. Mark nevertheless managed to find us. He couldn't land, but he flew immediately to the mainland and hired a boat to come pick us up. A nice fellow came out that evening and ferried us back to civilization, where we had a great reunion in a little Mexican village. The cantina had one bottle of champagne, and we bought it. The owners could have charged us anything, and we would have paid it—gladly. Then, right in the middle of dinner, someone announced that the cantina would be shutting the generator off at nine. We finished our champagne in the dark. It tasted just as good. That's when Mark announced that Sherry and I had touched down farthest from the landing spot of anyone in the race that year. I'd won my fourth Gordon Bennett, and Sherry and I had won our second as a team. What really sticks in my mind about that flight, though, was Sherry's composure amid the drama. She kept her calm and focused on what we had to do to survive. You can't ask anything more from your copilot. From then on, she's been with me every step of the way.

The Gordon Bennett racing was always done with gas balloons, but that wasn't the only way to get off the ground without an engine. I'd made my maiden hot-air balloon flight with Ed Yost way back in October 1964, following my first tour of duty in Vietnam, and I soloed on my second flight two days later. Since then I've made more than six hundred flights in hot-air systems. Of all the methods I've tried, it may be the very finest way to travel.

Not long after our near disaster over the Sea of Cortez, Sherry, Bob Snow, and I headed to Australia to help celebrate that nation's bicentennial and to participate in a big hot-air balloon rally there. Eighty-seven balloonists from around the world gathered in Perth on the West Coast. The plan was to traverse all 3,000-plus miles of the continent.

It wasn't really a race so much as an aeronautical caravan. We had teams in motor homes—850 members strong—chasing us through the desert all the way to Sydney. By the time we arrived there, we had collectively decided two things: that hot-air balloons are the only way to tour Australia and that Aussies get the prize for the population most determined to have a good time.

In 1989, the last Gordon Bennett race in this country—at least the last race in the series organized by Dr. Heinsheimer—was a fairly short one for me and Sherry. We flew from Palm Springs to Little America in Wyoming and were in the air for only twenty-two hours. We still took second place and had one of the great thrills of our lives when we crossed the Grand Canyon—from the South Rim to the North Rim, and just skimming the North Rim at sunset. I defy anyone to show me a more spectacular aerial route anywhere in the world.

Guardian Angel Island. Sherry and I retrieving the *Rosie O'Grady* after our near disaster over the Sea of Cortez. We're smiling because we'd won our second Gordon Bennett race as a team.

Not only was 1989 the last of these races for us, but it was also the last flight in the *Rosie O'Grady* balloon we'd flown so successfully for so long. It had competed in a total of twenty-one races, flown more than five hundred hours, and set several FAI distance and duration records. It was sad for me when I packed and crated up that gorgeous balloon for the final time. It now resides in the Anderson-Abruzzo International Balloon Museum in Albuquerque.

In July that year, a group of American balloon enthusiasts that included me and Sherry, Bob Snow and his wife, Linda, Dr. Tom Heinsheimer, a television production team, and the entire *Rosie O'Grady* crew flew to Europe for an international hot-air balloon event in Lithuania. We all met up in Augsberg, Germany, and headed east in another of our great caravans. Our little army rolled through Prague and Warsaw on a trip of more than 1,000 miles, arriving in Vilnius on July 23. Russian military personnel were in attendance at the opening ceremonies in a big out-door stadium—this was before the breakup of the Soviet Union—and for some reason the commander did not want any of the balloonists to have a view of the municipal airport at any time during their flights. A restriction forbid any balloon to rise higher than 200 feet. In most parts of the world, we're required to maintain a minimum altitude of 1,000 feet when flying over populated areas, so this restriction was welcome as far as we were concerned. There's nothing more exhilarating than sailing along at rooftop level.

The weather was perfect for the next six days, and we flew every one of them. Sherry bought a two-gallon jug of jawbreakers and bubblegum and tossed candy out to the kids wherever we landed. I absolutely loved Lithuania. Not only was the countryside completely unspoiled, but once we were outside the cities, there were almost no power lines or other obstructions with which to contend. It was the closest thing to worry-free flying I've ever experienced. Each evening we returned to our hotel in Vilnius and discussed the day's adventures over shots of Russian vodka.

On July 29, Sherry and I hopped into one of the vans towing our trailer with the hot-air balloon and headed for Moscow. We had no permission from Interpol or anyone else, but we'd always wanted to visit Russia, so we decided to risk it. We had no difficulty on the roads. We pulled right into Moscow and checked into the French-built Cosmos

Hotel. Bob Snow and the rest of the gang joined us the following day. We inflated our balloon in Gorky Park and took up some Russian officials on tethered flights. Bob Snow and his buddies got their instruments out and struck up their Dixieland band. They played "When the Saints Go Marching In" and "Midnight in Moscow" and "God Bless America." Then we started flying some of the kids who began to gather around. In the space of two hours, we gave tethered balloon rides to around one hundred kids. I kept expecting the KGB to show up and shut our little circus down—or worse.

The only problem we had during our extemporaneous stay in Moscow was that somebody broke into our van and stole the registration. The thief also made off with the license plates. I had the investigating officer write out a letter on Moscow police stationery stating that our papers had been stolen. On the way back to Augsberg, I had to show that letter at every border we crossed, but it always did the trick.

In 1991, Bob Snow opened a casino-hotel complex called Main Street Station on the edge of downtown Las Vegas, and Sherry and I went out there to help him get the business going. We did banner towing, sky writing, hot-air balloon flights—the whole bit. Bob had a great concept, and the place was phenomenal. Unfortunately, the operation was plagued by construction cost overruns and went belly up not long after the grand opening. While we where there, though, Sherry and I decided to get married. We took our vows in Bob's saloon and borrowed his Beech Staggerwing for a quick trip up to Lake Tahoe for a honeymoon. We felt terrible for Bob, who had put his heart and soul into the short-lived casino venture, but it was a very happy time for the two of us. We knew how lucky we were to have found each other, and we looked forward to a continuation of our life of adventure and good times.

Our next hot-air ballooning escapade came three years later in 1992. Mike Kendrick, who ran the balloon operation for Richard Branson's Virgin Airlines, invited Sherry and me to attend a big aeronautical gathering to celebrate the birthday of Jordan's King Hussein. The event was at Wadi Rum, a spectacular valley carved into the sandstone and granite of southwestern Jordan. It's where *Lawrence of Arabia* was filmed, and, let me tell you, the place is much wilder and more spectacular when seen in person.

Lifting the Iron Curtain. Preparing for a tethered ascent over Gorky Park in 1989 with a full load of Russian kids, the strains of Bob Snow's Dixieland band serenading the Soviet capital in the background.

We landed in Amman that November and drove by bus 150 miles across the desert to the site at Wadi Rum. We were issued tents for our accommodations, and each night we were entertained by a troop of musicians from a nearby village. I flew a hot-air balloon shaped and painted like a Virgin Airways 747. We made a series of hot-air flights over the next five days, and on the next-to-last day we assembled all the balloons in front of the suite of tents erected for King Hussein. The king arrived by royal helicopter (which he personally flew) with Queen Noor and their followers. Military formations, including the king's special camel brigade, paraded past the reviewing stand. The plans called for us to inflate the balloons and ascend for the king's pleasure, but gritty 25-mile-per-hour winds kept us firmly on the ground. Then, at the exact moment the military ceremonies ended, the winds died.

It was as if the king's supreme powers had generated a great calm across the desert. We inflated and lifted off in a grand final salute.

The next phase of my life in the skies came seemingly out of nowhere. Like ballooning, it harkened back to earlier days when flying was still a novelty and a true adventure.

In the United States in the years following World War I, there were lots of Jenny airplanes around, and a man could buy one for a very reasonable price. Enterprising pilots bought them and flew from town to town selling rides to the public. It was the Golden Age of Aviation. An airplane ride in those days—these planes were open-cockpit aircraft that allowed you to taste the wind—was a real kick, and some of these pilots made a pretty good living. The standard marketing gimmick was to come in low right over a little village, buzz the town to get the locals' attention, drop a handful of leaflets advertising rides for sale, then land in a nearby farmer's field and set up business. The pilot usually worked out a deal with the farmer to spend the night in his barn, and the public came to call these pilots "barnstormers." This life always sounded pretty good to me: you had the opportunity to see the country, you brought joy to people wherever you went, and—weather permitting—you got to fly every day.

I had my first taste of barnstorming in 1994. My friends Steve and Suzanne Oliver owned a beautiful forest-green 1929 D-25 New Standard biplane. It was originally designed for the Gates Flying Circus, a barnstorming tour that featured daredevils, stunt jumpers, and one-dollar joy rides. The plane could carry up to five passengers in the front cockpit, with the pilot in the rear. It was the ideal barnstorming aircraft because of the spacious seating area, the unobstructed view from the front, and a configuration that made loading and unloading passengers a breeze. It had a dependable, easy-to-maintain engine—a 200-horsepower Wright J-6-7, the same one Lindbergh had flown across the ocean.

The Olivers casually asked me and Sherry if we'd like to try some barnstorming in the New Standard, and we decided to give it a shot. We went out to the airport at Lakeland, Florida, and sold a few rides at the spring Sun 'N' Fun event, an air show held there every year. I flew my passengers around the traffic pattern. The ride lasted just ten minutes, but I could see right away what a charge people got out of it. Toward the end of that first day, a ten-year-old boy came up to me after his flight, his eyes as big as half-dollars, and said, "Mister, that was the best ten minutes of my *whole life!*"

That was all it took. I was hooked. I was a barnstormer, and Sherry was my roustabout. We nicknamed the airplane "Stanley," and it became our home away from home. We barnstormed at airports across the

United States. That first year we made appearances at air shows from Vero Beach, Florida, to Tillamook, Oregon. Sherry rode in Stanley's front cockpit with all of our bags and spare parts. There was barely enough room for our gear, but she never complained. Sherry was the reason that I could pursue the whole barnstorming fantasy; without a roustabout to collect the money and load the passengers into and out of the aircraft, the barnstorming business wouldn't work. I was just damn fortunate to have a wife who enjoyed flying as much as I did and would put up with the constant packing and unpacking required as we moved from town to town. In this venture, as in most things in my life, luck was my companion.

We could hardly wait for the spring of 1995 to roll around so we could commence our second season of barnstorming. We were pros now, and we had the whole operation down to a science. In one eight-day period, we flew 955 passengers in a total of 43 hours and made 240 landings. I had a blast—I always had a blast if I was flying—and Sherry

Barnstorming with Stanley. I never grew tired of flying this vintage biplane or of seeing the smiles Stanley and I put on the faces of the thousands of people who went up with us.

worked like crazy selling tickets and taking care of the passengers. We barnstormed at an aeronautical gathering at Decatur, Alabama, and from there we went to Bartlesville, Oklahoma, for the annual biplane gathering. Then it was onto to Fayetteville, Arkansas. Our next stop was the Tenth Annual Roscoe Turner Hot Air Balloon Race in Corinth, Mississippi, in August. This town was holy ground for barnstormers, and that's where we struck barnstormer's gold.

Roscoe Turner, an aviation pioneer, had been born and raised in Alcorn County near Corinth. Turner had served as a spherical balloon pilot during World War I and spent the postwar years barnstorming the nation with his pet lion Gilmore. He became a celebrity, appearing in the classic Howard Hughes film *Hell's Angels* and hobnobbing with movie stars. Congress awarded him the Distinguished Flying Cross in 1952. In celebration of his one hundredth birthday—even though Roscoe himself was long gone—Milton Sandy Jr., a local business leader, organized a grand aeronautical festival in his honor. Sherry and I were invited to provide some modern-day barnstorming.

A few weeks before we arrived in Corinth, Milton asked if we'd be willing to help him get the word out about the festival. He wanted us to buzz the local schools and, just like Roscoe had done in the old days, drop leaflets that the kids could collect. It was a great idea, but I wasn't sure how the FAA would react to this plan. The agency doesn't generally approve of pilots throwing things out of low-flying aircraft, especially over population centers. I put in a request for a permit anyway.

The day before the festival, an FAA observer arrived in Corinth and informed me that I'd have to put on a demonstration of accuracy before he'd grant me the permit. He wanted to see how close I could come to hitting a target with these leaflets. I'd never tried anything like it before, but I decided to give it a shot. I did a check on wind conditions, ran a couple of simple calculations, and I had Sherry stand in an open field alongside the runway. I took Stanley up and made a pass at 500 feet, got the position I wanted, and tossed a leaflet over the side. I honestly had no earthly idea where it was going to end up.

The FAA observer was right there watching—a bit skeptically, I'm sure. The paper drifted down, blew a little this way and a little that. Sherry raised her right hand and, without moving a step, caught the damn thing just as if we'd practiced it a thousand times! It was mostly bald luck, but I never let on. The FAA guy was suitably impressed. The next day we buzzed Corinth with the mayor and a local actor dressed as Roscoe Turner, and we dropped leaflets into schoolyards all over town—we didn't miss once. The kids were let out into the playgrounds just as we came by, and it was so much fun to see the leaflets go fluttering down and to watch those excited kids scatter to grab them.

While we were in Corinth, we got up early one morning and pushed Stanley out of a hangar at the local airport. I was doing my preflight inspection when a man in overalls and suspenders sidled up. He had three little kids in tow, all in worn overalls and two of them barefoot.

"Come on up and take a look," I said, motioning them over. I helped the kids climb up into the cockpit. The man kind of hung back. "Would y'all like a ride in this airplane?"

"Mister," he said, "I can't afford shoes for them kids. I shore can't afford no airplane ride."

I looked at the kids, and they looked back at me.

"Climb in," I told the man. "We're all going for a ride. No charge."

We went for a long, leisurely aerial tour of greater Corinth. They pointed out their house and the school the kids attended. I had so much fun I didn't want to land. Just seeing what that flight did for those folks really had an impact on both me and Sherry. From that day forward, wherever we took Stanley, we always picked out somebody in the crowd—a family if we could find one—who looked as if they couldn't afford a ride. Sherry would approach them.

"See that pilot over there?" she'd say. "Well, he says he wants to give you a free airplane ride." They'd look my way, and I'd wave. Sherry would walk them over. She always made them feel special, and we never had anybody turn us down. We did it in every town we barnstormed. It was our salute to the wonderful communities that always treated us so generously.

The real jackpot that had been waiting for us in Corinth was Milton Sandy himself. I could see right away that this guy was a born public-relations genius. He had the imagination, the energy, and the southern charisma to make sure people all over the region knew all about Roscoe Turner and the doings in Corinth that weekend. The festival was a huge success, so Sherry and I started talking to Milton about our barnstorming venture. Because of FAA restrictions, we could no longer buzz the towns to announce our arrival and create excitement the way the barnstormers did back in the 1930s, so we needed some modern means of marketing. If we wanted to make enough money to cover our fuel, lodging, airplane-maintenance costs, and saloon tabs, we needed some publicity—which is how Milton Sandy became our own private public-relations agent.

Milton put out press notices to the newspapers, TV stations, and radio stations in the locations where we were scheduled to appear. For the next seven years, as we barnstormed rural America, the local media was always bombarded with press releases and telephone calls about the Kittingers and their vintage biplane. If you were on our circuit, you couldn't miss knowing that we were coming to your town. Milton also coordinated our travel plans and provided logistical support. I doubt we could have afforded to keep the enterprise going had it not been for Milton's generous help.

We flew more than ten thousand passengers in the open-cockpit airplane and put a smile on everyone's face. Toward the end of our barnstorming period, we began to specialize in taking invalids in wheelchairs up for rides. The front cockpit was big enough that with the help of a strong man Sherry could lift the chairs right up into the airplane. I'm not sure the FAA would have approved of our procedures, but we took lots of folks up who otherwise wouldn't have gotten the chance. We helped celebrate the early days of flight, and we made a ton of friends. I hope we rekindled some of the seat-of-the-pants spirit of adventure and daring that had ebbed from the public's conception of airmen and airplanes.

In the summer of 1997, I received one of the greatest honors of my life when I was inducted into the National Aviation Hall of Fame. I invited all my family and a bunch of my friends to Dayton for the occasion. It was a very big deal to me, so I wanted to gather everybody I cared about and turn it into a celebration. Sherry came up with the idea of having all of us wear a red bandana in the pockets of our tuxedos or tucked into the collars of the women's gowns. She handed the bandanas out to Team Kittinger, and as we were all walking down the steps, Bob Snow looked up and observed, "Here comes the Redneck Squadron!"

The name stuck. From then on, we were the Redneck Squadron. We've inducted new members each year since—we have more than a hundred by now—and whenever we gather, we make sure to wear our red bandanas.

The Aviation Hall of Fame induction was especially meaningful to me because of the particular dignitary who agreed to deliver the formal introduction at the ceremony: Dr. John Paul Stapp. "It remains for me to reveal Colonel Kittinger's most astounding accomplishment," Stapp told the assembled guests. "He is still here! He is the living proof that it is better to be everlasting than to be merely famous."

To have the privilege of standing on the stage with that man—he was eighty-six at the time, I was sixty-nine—struck me as nothing less than astonishing. Both of us had dedicated our lives to activities that, as Dr. Stapp liked to observe, "are not conducive to longevity." Yet there we were: alive, laughing, and ready for more.

With Dr. John Paul Stapp at the National Aviation Hall of Fame in 1997. It would be difficult to overestimate Stapp's behind-the-scenes contributions to the American manned space program—or to my career.

With my family at the National Air and Space Museum in 2008. I received the museum's Lifetime Achievement in Aviation Award. *From left*: my son Dr. Joe W. Kittinger III and his wife, Sandra, me, Sherry, my grandson Mitchell Kittinger, and my son Mark Kittinger.

Epilogue

I was born in the age of the barnstormers and lived to fly supersonic fighter jets. I have flown on four continents, across both the Atlantic and Pacific oceans, and have logged more than 16,800 hours in 93 different aircraft. I flew 483 combat missions, made 102 parachute jumps, and ejected twice from disabled jets. My ambition has been as singular as it has been transparent. From the instant of that first takeoff in Phil Orr's Piper Cub at Lake Tibet Butler when I was sixteen, all I've ever really wanted to do is fly—which, in my mind, is to be part of something altogether glorious.

The common denominator among the men I admire—Neil Armstrong and Charles Lindbergh and Scott Crossfield and John Paul Stapp—is that all of them wanted to make a contribution. They were looking not just for a challenge, to put their own mark on the world, but for a challenge that amounted to something—the Big Mission—and maybe, while they were at it, for something that pushed the envelope just enough to get the blood pumping.

For a man to be have the privilege of spending his life doing the thing he loves, he must be extraordinarily lucky—and I consider myself the luckiest man in the sky. I was in the right place at the right time, and I was fortunate to have received the guidance in my early years that allowed me to pursue my long-shot dreams. That's the luckiest break of all. Those formative years are everything: parents, companions, education, experiences. That's when you acquire the discipline. If you don't have it by the time you're twenty, it's probably already too late.

What the daredevil lacks is precisely the discipline and patience it takes to work through the methodical approach to a challenge. You can't skip steps. If there's any secret to this business, that's it. There are no shortcuts. Some guys want the glory: they want to hop from point A to point Z. Armstrong and Crossfield were very methodical individuals. They knew what the procedures were, they had their checklists, and they had the mental and physical discipline to follow them. All of us emerged from the crucible of the test-pilot business. We were taught to study a problem from every conceivable angle before tackling it.

Discipline and preparation are essential to meeting a challenge, but by themselves they're still not enough. You must also have the ability to function effectively as a member of a team. You can't do these things by yourself. It's not possible. You need dedicated people willing to sacrifice for a common goal. Everything I accomplished was thanks to a great team. You must be selective, though. You have to surround yourself with the right individuals. Not everybody can be on the team.

The greatest man I've ever been associated with was Dr. Stapp. He was the "right stuff" personified. He was a tremendous leader who never needed to throw his weight around. He was effective and courageous, but he was also a gentle man. After he left the Aero Med Lab at Wright Field, the Air Force kind of put him out to pasture. Many people, specifically doctors and generals, were jealous of Stapp —jealous of his intellect and maybe also of his spirit. He was not a politician—he was a visionary.

He is credited with creating Stapp's Law. It states: "The universal aptitude for ineptitude makes any human accomplishment an incredible miracle."

I've always believed in miracles.

The lowest point in my long life of adventure was my eleven-month stay in the Hanoi Hilton in North Vietnam. It was certainly not one of the Hilton chain's finer properties. There was no air conditioning, the rooms were unsanitary, the food was awful, the waiters were surly, and the wine list was an absolute joke. I think most of the other residents there would agree with my assessment. On a scale of one to five: no stars.

Those of us unfortunate enough to book an extended stay there survived because of the training we'd received from the U.S. armed forces. Thoughts of our families and our country kept us going when things were darkest. We were steeled by the example of the longer-term prisoners who'd endured the indignities of Hoa Lo for years before we checked in. I relied on all these things and on my faith in God to get me through. I came away from the experience with a determination to appreciate the good fortune with which my life has been blessed and to celebrate every single day of the rest of the grand adventure.

The year this book is being published marks the fiftieth anniversary of my ascent and jump from *Excelsior III*. It's hard to believe that so much time has passed. It's amazing to me that people still remember or care about what we did back in 1960, but something about it seems to capture the imagination. I guess it's because people fear falling from high places. There's a universal human terror involved that seems to fascinate us.

I believe that I will have the privilege of seeing my record broken. Someday the right combination of will, brains, talent, money—and luck—will coalesce; someone will make the long, lonely leap from beyond 102,800 feet and live to tell about it. I hope they do. Challenge and progress are the ways of the world.

I've lived all over the globe, and I've seen a great deal of amazing country. I've caught every kind of fish you can imagine. I've hunted Cape buffalo and shot elephant. But the most exciting hunting I've ever done has been right here on the St. Johns River where I grew up. My river. In the summer of my eightieth year, I headed out with my good friend Dave Liniger, co-founder of RE/MAX—a passionate pilot, aeronaut, and fellow adventurer—in search of a trophy alligator. The gators in central Florida are flourishing these days thanks to wise wildlife management and federal protection of the species. In fact, the gators have become so numerous that each year the state issues several thousand hunting permits to control the population.

Dave and I motored by air boat up the St. Johns in the dead of night. In September, the water is high, and the river becomes a swamp. It spreads across the lowland like a lake and covers everything but the trees. We shone our lights across the surface of the black water, searching for gator eyes. To judge a gator's size, the rule of thumb is: one foot of length for every inch between the eyes.

When I spotted our monster, I estimated the eyes to be a good foot apart and knew we had our work cut out for us. We were hunting with a crossbow attached to heavy-duty line. All you could see in the darkness were the eyes glowing like embers. We crept up on the gator. Your angle of attack has to be true or the tip of the arrow glances off the rugged hide. Dave made a perfect shot, right into the sweet spot on the back of his neck. We had him!

It's quite a ride, being tied to a mad alligator in the blackness of the swamp. It took us a good twenty minutes to tire him out and get him up to the boat, then another ten to land him. We taped the jaws shut, but we still had to slit the spinal cord to avoid having our legs snapped by that great mace of a tail. We stretched him out and measured him right at 12 feet. This magnificent specimen would weigh in at more than 700 pounds. It took another couple of hours for the adrenaline to wear off.

I was back where I'd started, and it was almost as if I had never left.

Lamb Savage's Fish Camp is long gone, of course, bypassed and all but forgotten by the mad rush of the modern world, destroyed by gravity and neglect, but the St. Johns is the same as ever—perhaps diminished some by overuse, but still moving at its own pace and still seductive to me. I can head out to Paw Paw Island, climb up onto the scrubby high ground by the same big sour-orange tree I sat under as a boy, and time

stops dead. I can just make out, in the near distance, my father chugging up in the *John Henry*, see my mother waving at me from onboard, and smell the fried chicken sizzling in the pan. Before I know it, I'm baiting a hook for another cast at the opposite bank, where I'd seen a big, fat bass lying in wait.

I can almost hear the jukebox. A midnight lullaby. I think it's old Bob Wills singing "San Antonio Rose."

Dave Liniger and I with our 12-foot gator. I turned eighty the year we captured this monster on the St. Johns River.

Awards and Honors

✴   ✴   ✴   ✴   ✴   ✴

Most of our greatest soldiers and pioneers labor in obscurity. The world never learns their names or hears of their achievements. I've been extraordinarily fortunate in my career to have received far more than my fair share of recognition. Yet for every honor I've ever been given, I've stood as a representative for a team of individuals who made it possible. They are my heroes, every one of them.

Military Decorations

Silver Star with Oak Leaf Cluster
Legion of Merit with Oak Leaf Cluster
Distinguished Flying Cross (Project Manhigh)
Distinguished Flying Cross (Project Excelsior)
Distinguished Flying Cross with four Oak Leaf Clusters (Vietnam)
Bronze Star with "V" device and two Oak Leaf Clusters
Meritorious Service Medal
Air Medal with twenty-three Oak Leaf Clusters
Purple Heart with Oak Leaf Cluster
Presidential Unit Citation
Air Force Outstanding Unit Award
Army of Occupation Medal
National Defense Service Medal
Vietnam Service Medal with seven Service Stars
Republic of Vietnam Cross of Gallantry with Palm
Republic of Vietnam Campaign Medal
Prisoner-of-War Medal

Civilian Decorations

Harmon International Trophy (Aeronaut)
Aeronaut Leo Stevens Parachute Medal
John Jeffries Award, Institute of Aerospace Sciences
Aerospace Primus, Air Research and Development Command
Hall of Fame, United States Air Force Special Operations
Fédération Aéronautique Internationale Montgolfier Diplome
Paul Harris Fellow, Rotary International
Distinguished Achievement Award, Order of Daedalians
Fellow, Society of Experimental Test Pilots
Elder Statesman of Aviation Award, National Aeronautics Association
Barnstormer of the Year, International Society of Aviation
  Barnstorming Historians
National Aviation Hall of Fame
International Forest of Friendship–Atchison
Wright Brothers Memorial Hall of Fame
Air Force Space and Missile Pioneers Award
Parachute Industry Association
Legion of Merit (Italy)
Santos Dumont Medal, French Aero Club
Le Grande Medaille, City of Paris
Revoredo Trophy, International Flight Research Corporation
Joe W. Kittinger Medal of Achievement, Board of County Commissioners,
  Orange County, Florida
Heroic Achievement Award, City of Orlando
John Young Award, Orlando Chamber of Commerce
Distinguished Achievement Award, for American former POWs
Achievement Award, Wingfoot Lighter Than Air Society
W. Randolph Lovelace Award, Society of NASA Flight Surgeons
Godfrey L. Cabot Award, Aero Club of New England
Prix de L'Aventure Sportive, French Sporting Adventure Trophy
Award, Chateau de Balleroy
National Air and Space Museum Trophy
  (Lifetime Achievement in Aviation Award)
John Young History Maker Award
Florida Aviation Hall of Fame

Acknowledgments

I gratefully acknowledge the following individuals who have inspired and helped me during my flight path through life: my mother and father, Heinie Aderholt, Neil Armstrong, Ken Arnold, Francis "Beau" Beaupre, Gottlieb Blenk, Jones E. Bolt, Jim Brown, Dr. John and Barbara Burson, Martin Caidin, Jerry Carlisle, Mike and Victoria Carns, Carlos Christian, Dr. Richard Chubb, John Craparo, Tom Crouch, Dan Elliott, Dr. Marv Feldstein, Lou and Margie Fischer, Tracy Forrest, Duke Gildenberg, Bob Gilliland, Terry Grove, Dick Hansen, Klanky Hargrove, Dr. Tom Heinsheimer, Mark Kirkham, Carl Langford, Sherri Lester, John Levinson, Dave and Gail Liniger, Bob Lodge, Bob Lott, Hap Lutz, Ray Madson, Lyle Mann, Billy Mills, Burke Morgan, officials of the National Geographic Society, Gene O'Baker, Robin Olds, Steve and Suzanne Oliver, Pat and Barbara Phillips, George Post, Tiny Reich, Dewey Reinhard, Bob Rice, Gerald Roy, Milton Sandy, Dave Sipple, Bob Snow, Dr. John Paul Stapp, Dale Sweet, Sean D. Tucker, and Ed Yost.

And, of course, many thanks to my very patient and talented coauthor Craig Ryan and to Clark Whitehorn and all the folks at the University of New Mexico Press.

Special thanks to my sons and grandchildren: Joe and Sandra, Jack and Daniella, Cyrus and Brooke, Ben and Katie, and Mark and Mitchell.

—Joe Kittinger (Orlando, Florida)

I am grateful to the following people for their help with the manuscript: Patrick Hampton, Jon Lee, Kathy Narramore, and Eugene Ryan. Thanks to Tom Crouch at the National Air and Space Museum for his support over the years, to Quinn Botthof for his vision and willingness to help, to Michael Lennick for his marvelous documentaries, to Annie Barva for her editorial acumen, and to Milton Sandy and the International Society of Aviation Barnstorming Historians for their dedication to the cause. It has been a privilege to work with Joe Kittinger on this project, and I thank him for the opportunity to help tell his remarkable story. A very special thanks to Sherry Kittinger for all her hard work and good cheer throughout the process.

—Craig Ryan (Portland, Oregon)

Index

PAGE NUMBERS IN ITALICS REFER TO PHOTOGRAPHS.

Abruzzo, Ben, 193, 197–98, 203, 207–8, 219, 225, 235
Aero Med Lab. *See* Aerospace Medical Laboratory
Aerospace Medical Laboratory, 39–40, 42, 45, 47, 54, 63, 70–71, 74, 79, 101, 246.
AIM-7 Sparrow Missile, 141–42
Air Commandos, 105–6, 117, 121, 123, 131, 158
Air Force Cambridge Research Laboratory, 102, 104
Aldrin, Buzz, 171
Anderson, Maxie, 193, 197–98, 219, 225, 235
Anderson, Orville, 65
Andreyev, Yevgeny, 97
Anthis, Rollen Henry "Buck," 110, 120
Apollo, Project, 69, 102
Armed Forces Institute of Pathology, 53, 54
Arnold, Ken, 73, 79, 85, 91, 251
A-26, 124–26, *127*, 158

balloon construction (plastic), 61–62
barnstorming, 238–42, *239*

Baron, Oakley, 40, 45–46
Bat-21 Bravo, 143–44. *See also* Gene Hambleton
Beaupre, Francis "Beau," 73, 75, *76*, 77, 79, 83, 85, 92, 251
Bergstrom AFB, 186
Bien Hoa, South Vietnam, *108*
B-52, 170–71
B-47, 71
BMSP (Beaupre Multi-Stage Parachute), 75, *76*, 81–84, 91–92, 94, 97
B-26, 22–23, 39, 106–7, *108*, 109–12, 114–17, 120, 123, *132*

C-47 Skytrain, 30, 39, 51–53, 61, 75, 107, 117
Chubb, Richard, 94, *95*, 251
Clark, Ramsey, 174
Clark Air Base, 180–81, 183
Coupe d'Aéronautique de Gordon Bennett, 226–27

David Clark Company, 79
Davis Monthan AFB, 131
DC-3, 51
DeBellevue, Charles, 135–36

deceleration studies, 42–45
Denton, Jeremiah, 171, 173
Diem, Ngo Dinh, 115–16, 121, 123
Dolgov, Peter, 97
Double Eagle, 193, 219–20
Draper, C. S., 102

Eglin AFB, 71, 116, 122
Eisenhower, Dwight D., 24, 98, 99
England AFB, 124, 158
Excelsior, Project, xiii–xv, 72–101, 155–56, 247, 249
Excelsior I, 78–83
Excelsior II, 84
Excelsior III, 85–97, *86, 87, 92*, 247
Excelsior IV, 98

FAI. *See* Fédération Aéronautique Internationale
Fédération Aéronautique Internationale, 96–97, 207, 226–27, 235
F-84E Thunderjet, 24–25, *25*
F-84G, 35–39, *38*
Feldstein, Marvin, 88, 90, 251
F-4 Phantom, 127–28, 131–33, *132*, 135, 138, 140–41, 143–44, 147–50, 159, *175*, 186–87
F-47 Thunderbolt, 19, 22, 30–31
555th Tactical Fighter Squadron, 131–32, 135–36, 138, 140, 142–43, 145–46, 151, 157, 160.
526th Tactical Fighter Squadron, 18
Flynn, John Peter, 160, 165–66, 171, 173–74, 176
Fonda, Jane, 168, 170, 174–75
F-100 Super Sabre, 39, 41, 69
F-111, 186
Forbes, Malcolm, 228
Fossett, Steve, 226
432nd Tactical Fighter Wing, 135, 138, 158
48th Tactical Fighter Wing, 186
Fulgham, Dan, 54–58

Gabriel, Charles, 140, 146
Gildenberg, Bernard "Duke," 62–63, 78, 87–88, 206–9, 251
Glenn, John, 102–4
Goldwater, Barry, 117
Goodfellow AFB, 15–16, 194
Gordon Bennett race, origins, 196; 1979 race, 196–98; 1980 race, 198; 1981 race, 199; 1982 race, 203–6; 1984 race, 227–28, *229*; 1985 race, 228–30; 1988 race, 231–33, *234*; 1989 race, 234
Govan, Claude, 19–22, 31–32, 225
Grissom, Gus, 69

Hambleton, Gene. *See* Bat-21 Bravo
Hanoi Hilton. *See* Hoa Lo Prison
Hargrove, Dawson "Klanky," 196, 211, 213, 251
Harkins, Paul, 110, 121
Harmon Trophy, 98, *99*, 250
Harnavee, Chaicharn, 160, 166
Heinsheimer, Tom, 196–97, 226–27, 230, 234–35, 251
Hersey, Henry, 196
High Dive, Project, 71–74, 76, 78, 82, 101
Hoa Lo Prison: general description of, 153; Joe Kittinger incarcerated in, 150–79, *175*; Joe Kittinger's reflections on, 246–47
Ho Chi Minh Trail, 125–26, *127*
Holloman AFB, 39–45, *43, 47*, 54–55, 57, 67, 69, 71–72, 78, 95, 102–4, 146, 149
hot-air ballooning, 187–88, *192*, 233–37
Hurlburt Field, 106

Italian Air Force, 30–32

Johnson, Kenneth, 151
Johnson, Lyndon B., 123
Jordan, Joe, *99*

Kennedy, John F., 106, 116, 123
Kiker, John, 135–36
Kirkham, Mark, 223–24, 233, 251
Kittinger, Joe W.: balloon racing, 194, 196–99, 202–10, 226–35; barnstorming, 238–42; childhood and teenage years, 1–10; in Europe, 18–38, 128–31, 186; high-altitude balloon projects, xiii–xv, 45–54, 59–104, 247; marriage to Sherry Reed, 236; as POW, 150–81, *175*, 246–47; transatlantic balloon flight, 211–26, *214*, *221*, *222*; in Southeast Asia, 107–28, 131–81
Kittinger, Sherry (Reed), 206, 208–10, 212–13, 215, 219–22, *222*, 224–25, 227–36, *229*, *234*, 238–42, 244, *244*, 252
Knapp, Brooke, 203
Knapp, Charles, 203–5

Lahm, Frank, 196
Lakenheath, RAF, 186, 189
Las Vegas AFB, 16–17. *See also* Nellis AFB
Lavelle, Jack, 138–40
LeMay, Curtis, 106
Lindbergh, Charles, 193, 213, 225, 238, 245
Liniger, Dave, 247, 248, *248*
Locher, Roger, 146
Lodge, Bob, 146, 251
Lovelace, W. Randolph, 74–75, 250

Madsen, Ray, 72
Manhigh, Project, 45–54, 59–69
Manhigh I, 62–67, *64*
Manhigh II, 67
Manhigh III, 67–68
Mann, Lyle, 131, 251
Markey, Winston, 102
Maxwell AFB, 185, 186
McClure, Clifton "Demi," 67–68
McNamara, Robert, 117–18, 120–23
MC-3 partial-pressure suit, *50*, 79, 96

Mercury, Project, 45, 68, 99–102, *100*, 104
MiG, 20, 135–42, 145–48, 156, 173, *175*
Mogul, Project, 58
Moore, Joe, 110–11
Morgan, Burke, 158, 251

Nakhon Phanom (NKP), 124, 126–28
National Geographic Magazine, 92, 98, 190–92
National Geographic Society, 84, 189, 220, 251
Naval Air Station (El Centro, Cal.), 46, *46*
Nellis AFB, 228–30. *See also* Las Vegas AFB
Newman, Larry, 193, 219, 225
Nielson, George, 101
Nixon, Richard M., 170
NKP. *See* Nakhon Phanom

Perot, Ross, 185
Pertini, Alessandro, 224–25
P-51 Mustang, 15–16, *17*, 18, 39
Piantanida, Nicholas, 97
Plantation, The, 174–77
Polfer, Ron, 170, 178
Post, George, 73, 77, 96, 98–99, 251
P-47. *See* F-47 Thunderbolt

Rabb, Maxwell, 223–24
Reagan, Ronald W., 185, 225
Reich, William "Tiny," 147–50, 154, 161, 251
Reinhard, Dewey, 196–98, 251
Rhein Main Air Base, 19–21
Rice, Bob, 211–16, 219, 225, 251
Rosie O'Grady, 198, *198*, 207–9, *214*, 215, 219, 223, 231–33, *234*, 235, *237*
Rosie O'Grady's, 194–95
Roswell incidents, 55–59
Roy, Gerald, 134–37, 184–85, 251
Ryan, John D., 139–40

Saltonstall, Leverett, 117
Sandy, Milton, Jr., 240–42, 251–52
Schirra, Walter, 102
Schriever, Bernard, 77–78, 83, 85, 88, 99, *99*, 105
Seek, Brian, 162–64
7th Air Force, 107, 110, 115, 138
Silver Fox, 189–91, 193
Simons, David, 45, 47–48, *50*, 51, 61–62, 65–68, 189
Simons, Vera, 47, 62–63, 65, 188–89. *See also* Las Vegas AFB
67th Air Rescue and Recovery Squadron, 190
Smith, Bud, 134
Smith, Margaret Chase, 117
Smithsonian Astrophysical Observatory, 101–2
Smithsonian Institution, 99–100
Snow, Bob, 189–90, 194–95, 197–99, 202, 206–8, 212, 215–16, 219–20, 223–25, 227, *229*, 234–36, *237*, 242, 251
Stapp, John Paul, 40–48, *43*, 54, 57–58, 62, 66–70, 72–75, 77–78, 83–85, 88–89, 91, 98, 100–101, 103–5, 146, 149, 243, *243*, 245–46, 251
Stargazer, Project, 101–5, *103*
Stars and Stripes, 156–57
Stennis, John, 117–19, 121–23
Stevens, Albert, 65
Stockdale, James, 171
Symington, Stewart, 117

Talley, Bill, 169
Tan Son Nhut Air Base, 111, 115
10th Special Forces (U.S. Army), 128–31

Triple Nickel. *See* 555th Tactical Fighter Squadron
Tropicana Aero Cup Race, 206–10
T-33 Shooting Star, 23–24, 40–42, 95
T-28, 105–7, 117
Turner, Roscoe, 240–41
12th Air Force, 186

Udorn Royal Thai AFB, 131, 133, 135–37, 139, 142–44, *142*, 146, 151, 184

Viet Nam Air Force, 109, 115–16
VNAF. *See* Viet Nam Air Force
Von Beckh, Harald, 40

Walker AFB, 56
Walker, Doak, 19, 21–22, 225
Weaver, Bill, 97–98
Wenzel, Kurt, 84, 91, *92*
Westmoreland, William, 110–11
Wheelus Air Base, 22, 25, 27, 29–30
White, Bill, 102, *103*
White, Edward, 69
White Sands (Proving Ground, Missile Range), 39, 78, 85
Williams, Jim, 160, 165
Winzen Research, 47, 52, 62, 67, 102
Winzen, Vera. *See* Vera Simons
Winzen, Otto, 47, 188–89

Yost, Paul "Ed," 187–93, *192*, 196–98, *198*, 211–13, *214*, 218, 220, 226, 233, 251

zero-gravity studies, 40–42
Zwayer, Jim, 97